INDUSTRIAL ORGANIZATION

INDUSTRIAL ORGANIZATION

R.P. Rai

CENTRUM PRESS
NEW DELHI-110002 (INDIA)

CENTRUM PRESS
H.O.: 4360/4, Ansari Road, Daryaganj,
New Delhi-110002 (India)
Tel: 23278000, 23261597, 23255577, 23286875
B.O.: No. 1015, Ist Main Road, BSK IIIrd Stage,
IIIrd Phase, IIIrd Block, Bangalore-560085 (INDIA)
Tel: 080-41723429
Email: centrumpress@gmail.com
Visit us at: www.centrumpress.com

Industrial Organization

First Edition, 2010

ISBN 978-93-80540-46-7

PRINTED IN INDIA

Printed at Balaji Offset, Delhi.

Contents

Contents

Preface

Industrial organization is a field of economics that studies the strategic behaviour of firms, the structure of markets and their interactions. The study of industrial organization adds to the perfectly competitive model real-world frictions such as limited information, transaction cost, cost of adjusting prices, government actions, and barriers to entry by new firms into a market. It then considers how firms are organized and how they compete. Perhaps a most appropriate term is the "Economics of Imperfect Competition". The development of industrial organization as a separate field owed much to Edward Chamberlin, Edward S. Mason and Joe S. Bain. There are two major approaches to the study of industrial organization: the first approach is primarily descriptive and provides an overview of industrial organization. The second, price theory, uses microeconomic models to explain firm behaviour and market structure.

According to the structure-conduct-performance approach, an industry's performance (the success of an industry in producing benefits for the consumer) depends on the conduct of its firms, which then depends on the structure (factors that determine the competitiveness of the market). The structure of the industry then depends on basic conditions, such as technology and demand for a product. For example: in an industry with technology that the average cost of production falls as output increases, the industry tends to have one firm, or possibly a small number of firms.

A basic textbook for students of economics and management, the book is also an important resource for advanced graduate students in international business and development economics. Teachers and researchers in the area of international economics will find in the book a useful teaching and research tool for a comprehensive analysis of a fairly complex phenomenon.

— *R.P. Rai*

1

Introduction

Industrial organization is a field of economics that studies the strategic behaviour of firms, the structure of markets and their interactions. The study of industrial organization adds to the perfectly competitive model real-world frictions such as limited information, transaction cost, of adjusting prices, government actions, and barriers to entry by new firms into a market. It then considers how firms are organized and how they compete. Perhaps a most appropriate term is the "Economics of Imperfect Competition". The development of industrial organization as a separate field owed much to Edward Chamberlin, Edward S. Mason and Joe S. Bain.

There are two major approaches to the study of industrial organization: the first approach is primarily descriptive and provides an overview of industrial organization. The second, price theory, uses microeconomic models to explain firm behaviour and market structure.

Structure, Conduct, Performance

According to the structure-conduct-performance approach, an industry's performance (the success of an industry in producing benefits for the consumer) depends on the conduct of its firms, which then depends on the structure (factors that determine the competitiveness of the market). The structure of the industry then depends on basic conditions, such as technology and demand for a product. For example: in an industry with technology that the average cost of production falls as output increases, the industry tends to have one firm, or possibly a small number of firms.

Components that make up the structure, conduct, and performance model for industrial organization.

- Basic Conditions: Consumer Demand, Production, Elasticity of Demand, Technology, Substitutes, Raw Materials, Seasonality, Unionization, Rate of Growth, Product durability, Location, Lumpiness of orders, Scale of economies, Method of purchase, Scope economies
- Structure: Number of Buyers and Sellers, Barriers to entry of new firms, product differentiation, Vertical integration, Diversification
- Conduct: Advertising, Research and Development, Pricing behaviour, Plant Investment, Legal Tactics, Product choice, Collusion, Merger and Contracts
- Performance: Price, Production Efficiency, Allocative Efficiency, Equity, Product Quality, Technical Progress, Profits
- Government Policy: Regulation, Antitrust, Barriers to Entry, Taxes and Subsidies, Investment Incentives, Employment Incentives, Macroeconomic Policies

Market Structures

The common market structures studied in this field are the following:

- Perfect competition
- Monopolistic competition
- Oligopoly
- Oligopsony
- Monopoly
- Monopsony.

Areas of Study

Industrial organization investigates the outcomes of these market structures in environments with

- Price discrimination
- Product differentiation
- Durable goods
- Experience goods
- Secondary markets or second-hand markets, which can affect the behaviour of firms in primary markets.
- Collusion

- Signaling, such as warranties and advertising.
- Mergers and acquisitions
- Entry and Exit.

A competitive market structure has the performance outcome of lower costs and lower prices, (Shepherd, W: 1997:4).

The subject has a theoretical side and a practical side. According to one text book: "On one plane the field is abstract, a set of analytical concepts about competition and monopoly. On a second plane the topic is about real markets, teeming with the excitement and drama of struggles among real firms" (Shepherd, W.; 1985; 1).

The extensive use of game theory in industrial economics has led to the export of this tool to other branches of microeconomics, such as behavioural economics and corporate finance. Industrial organization has also had significant practical impacts on antitrust law and competition policy.

Input-Output Model

In economics, an input-output model uses a matrix representation of a nation's (or a region's) economy to predict the effect of changes in one industry on others and by consumers, government, and foreign suppliers on the economy. Wassily Leontief (1905-1999) is credited with the development of this analysis.

Francois Quesnay developed a cruder version of this technique called Tableau economique. Leontief won the Nobei Memorial Prize in Economic Sciences for his development of this model. And, in essence, Léon Walras's work *Elements of Pure Economics* on general equilibrium theory is both a forerunner and generalization of Leontief's seminal concept.

Leontief's contribution was that he was able to simplify Walras's piece so that it could be implemented empirically. The International Input-Output Association is dedicated to advance knowledge in the field input-output study, which includes "improvements in basic data, theoretical insights and modelling, and applications, both traditional and novel, of input-output techniques."

Input-output depicts inter-industry relations of an economy. It shows how the output of one industry is an input to each other industry. Leontief put forward the display of this information in the form of a matrix. A given input is typically enumerated in the column of an industry and its outputs are enumerated in its corresponding row. This format, therefore, shows how dependent each industry is on all others in the economy both as customer of their outputs and as supplier of their inputs.

Each column of the input-output matrix reports the monetary value of an industry's inputs and each row represents the value of an industry's outputs. Suppose there are three industries. Column 1 reports the value of inputs to Industry 1 from Industries 1, 2, and 3. Columns 2 and 3 do the same for those industries. Row 1 reports the value of outputs from Industry 1 to Industries 1, 2, and 3. Rows 2 and 3 do the same for the other industries.

While most uses of the input-output analysis focuses on the matrix set of inter-industry exchanges, the actual focus of the analysis from the perspective of most national statistical agencies, which produce the tables, is the benchmarking of gross domestic product. Input-output tables therefore are an instrumental part of national accounts. As suggested above, the core input-output table reports only intermediate goods and services that are exchanged among industries. But an array of row vectors, typically aligned below this matrix, record non-industrial inputs by industry like payments for labour; indirect business taxes; dividends, interest, and rents; capital consumption allowances (depreciation); other property-type income (like profits); and purchases from foreign suppliers (imports).

At a national level, although excluding the imports, when summed this is called "gross product originating" or "gross domestic product by industry." Another array of column vectors is called "final demand" or "gross product consumed."

This displays columns of spending by households, governments, changes in industry stocks, and industries on investment, as well as net exports. In any case, by employing the results of an economic census which asks for the sales, payrolls, and material/equipment/service input of each establishment, statistical agencies back into estimates of industry-level profits and investments using the input-output matrix as a sort of double-accounting framework.

The mathematics of input-output economics is straightforward, but the data requirements are enormous because the expenditures and revenues of each branch of economic activity has to be represented. As a result, not all countries collect the required data and data quality varies, even though a set of standards for the data's collection has been set out by the United Nations through its System of National Accounts (SNA): the replacement for the current 1993 SNA standard is pending. Because the data collection and preparation process for the input-output accounts is necessarily labour and computer intensive, input-output tables are often published long after the year data was collected—typically as much as 5-7 years after.

Moreover, the economic "snapshot" the benchmark version of the tables provide of the economy's cross-section are taken only once every few years, at best. Although many developed countries estimate input-output accounts annually and with much greater recency.

Usefulness

In addition to studying the structure of national economies, input-output economics has been used to study regional economies within a nation, and as a tool for national and regional economic planning. Indeed a main use of input-output analysis is for measuring the economic impacts of events as well as public investments or programs as shown by IMPLAN and RIMS-II.

But it is also used to identify economically related industry clusters and also so-called "key" or "target" industries—industries that are most likely to enhance the internal coherence of a specified economy. By linking industrial output to satellite accounts articulating energy use, effluent production, space needs, and so on, input-output analysts have extended the approaches application to a wide variety of uses.

Key Ideas

Leontief's text remains one of the best expositions of input-output analysis. Nonetheless, two books—a rather fundamental one by William Miernyk and another by Ronald E. Miller and Peter D. Blair—probably have greater international currency. The latter is presently being rewritten and re-released, this time by Cambridge University Press.

Consider the production of the ith sector. We may isolate (1) the quantity of that production that goes to final demand, c_i, (2) to total output, x_i, and (3) flows x_{ij} from that industry to other industries. We may write a transactions tableau

Table: Transactions in a Three Sector Economy

Economic Activities	Inputs to Agriculture	Inputs to Manufacturing	Inputs to Transport	Final Demand	Total Output
Agriculture	5	15	2	68	90
Manufacturing	10	20	10	40	80
Transportation	10	15	5	0	30
Labour	25	30	5	0	60

or

$$x_{11} + x_{12} + x_{13} + c_1 = x_1$$
$$x_{21} + x_{22} + x_{23} + c_2 = x_2$$
$$x_{31} + x_{32} + x_{33} + c_3 = x_3$$
$$x_{41} + x_{42} + x_{43} + c_4 = x_4$$

Note that in the example given we have no input flows from the industries to 'Labour'. We know very little about production functions because all we have are numbers representing transactions in a particular instance (single points on the production functions):

$$x_1 = f(x_{11}, x_{12}, x_{13}, x_{14})$$
$$x_2 = g(x_{21}, x_{22}, x_{23}, x_{24})$$
$$\vdots = \vdots$$

The neoclassical production function is an explicit function

$$Q = f(K,L),$$

where Q = Quantity, K = Capital, L = Labour, and the partial derivatives () are the demand schedules for input factors.

Leontief, the innovator of input-output analysis, uses a special production function which depends *linearly* on the total output variables x_i. Using Leontief coefficients a_{ij}, we may manipulate our transactions information into what is known as an input-output table:

$$x_{11} = a_{11}x_1$$
$$x_{12} = a_{12}x_2$$
$$x_{13} = a_{13}x_3$$
$$x_{14} = a_{14}x_4$$
$$\vdots = \vdots$$

or

$$x_{ij} = a_{ij}x_j$$

Now

$$\begin{aligned}
a_{11}x_1 + a_{12}x_2 + a_{13}x_3 + a_{14}x_4 + c_1 &= x_1 \\
\vdots &= \vdots \\
a_{41}x_1 + a_{42}x_2 + a_{43}x_3 + a_{44}x_4 + c_4 &= x_4
\end{aligned}$$

gives

$$\begin{aligned}
x_1 - a_{11}x_1 - a_{12}x_2 - a_{13}x_3 - a_{14}x_4 &= c_1 \\
\vdots &= \vdots \\
x_4 - a_{41}x_1 - a_{42}x_2 - a_{43}x_3 - a_{44}x_4 &= c_4
\end{aligned}$$

Rewriting finally yields

$$\begin{aligned}
(1 - a_{11})x_1 - a_{12}x_2 - a_{13}x_3 - a_{14}x_4 &= c_1 \\
\vdots &= \vdots \\
-a_{41}x_1 - a_{42}x_2 - a_{43}x_3 + (1 - a_{44})x_4 &= c_4
\end{aligned}$$

Introducing matrix notation, we can see how a solution may be obtained. Let :

$$x = \begin{pmatrix} x_1 \\ \vdots \\ x_4 \end{pmatrix}; \qquad c = \begin{pmatrix} c_1 \\ \vdots \\ c_4 \end{pmatrix};$$

$$I = \begin{pmatrix} 1 & 0 & 0 & 0 \\ 0 & 1 & 0 & 0 \\ 0 & 0 & 1 & 0 \\ 0 & 0 & 0 & 1 \end{pmatrix}; \qquad A = \begin{pmatrix} a_{11} & \cdots & a_{14} \\ \vdots & \ddots & \vdots \\ a_{41} & \cdots & a_{44} \end{pmatrix};$$

denote the total output vector, the final demand vector, the unit matrix and the input-output matrix, respectively. Then:

$$\begin{aligned}
Ax + c &= x \\
(I - A)x &= c \\
x &= (I - A)^{-1}c
\end{aligned}$$

provided (I " A) is invertible.

There are many interesting aspects of the Leontief system, and there is an extensive literature. There is the Hawkins-Simon Condition on producibility.

There has been interest in disaggregation to clustered inter-industry flows, and the study of constellations of industries.

A great deal of empirical work has been done to identify coefficients, and data have been published for the national economy as well as for regions. This has been a healthy, exciting area for work by economists because the Leontief system can be extended to a model of general equilibrium; it offers a method of decomposing work done at a macro level.

Transportation is implicit in the notion of inter-industry flows. It is explicitly recognized when transportation is identified as an industry – how much is purchased from transportation in order to produce.

But this is not very satisfactory because transportation requirements differ, depending on industry locations and capacity constraints on regional production. Also, the receiver of goods generally pays freight cost, and often transportation data are lost because transportation costs are treated as part of the cost of the goods.

Walter Isard and his student, Leon Moses, were quick to see the spatial economy and transportation implications of input-output, and began work in this area in the 1990s. developing a concept of interregional input-output.

Take a one region versus the world case. We wish to know something about interregional commodity flows, so introduce a column into the table headed "exports" and we introduce an "import" row.

Table: Adding Export And Import Transactions

Economic Activities	1	2	…	…	Z	Exports	Final Demand	Total Outputs
1								
2								
…								
…								
Z								
Imports								

A more satisfactory way to proceed would be to tie regions together at the industry level. That is, we could identify both intra-region inter-industry transactions and inter-region inter-industry transactions. The problem here is that the table grows quickly.

Input-output is conceptually simple. Its extension to a model of equilibrium in the national economy is also relatively simple and attractive but requires great skill and high-quality data. One who wishes to do work with input-output systems must deal skillfully with industry classification, data estimation, and inverting very large, ill-conditioned matrices. Moreover, changes in relative prices are not readily handled by this modelling approach alone. Of course, input-output accounts are part and parcel to a more flexible form of modelling, Computable general equilibrium models.

Two additional difficulties are of interest in transportation work. There is the question of substituting one input for another, and there is the question about the stability of coefficients as production increases or decreases. These are intertwined questions. They have to do with the nature of regional production functions.

Forecasting and/or Analysis Using Input-Output

Table: Interregional Transactions

Table: Interregional Transactions

Economic Activities	Ag	North Mfg	... ...	Ag	East Mfg	... ...	Ag	West Mfg	... ...	Exports	Total Outputs
North Mfg											
...											
...											
Ag											
East Mfg											
...											
...											
Ag											
West Mfg											
...											
...											

Table: Input-Output Model for Hypothetical Economy Total requirements from regional industries per dollar of output delivered to final demand

Purchasing Industry	*Agriculture*	*Transport*	*Manufacturer*	*Services*
Selling Industry				
Agriculture	1.14	0.22	0.13	0.12
Transportation	0.19	1.10	0.16	0.07
Manufacturing	0.16	0.16	1.16	0.06
Services	0.08	0.05	0.08	1.09
Total	1.57	1.53	1.53	1.34

Input-output Analysis Versus Consistency Analysis

Despite the clear ability of the input-output model to depict and analyse the dependence of one industry or sector on another, Leontief and others never managed to introduce the full spectrum of dependency relations in a market economy. In 2003, Mohammad Gani, a pupil of Leontief, introduced Consistency Analysis in his book 'Foundations of Economic Science', which formally looks exactly like the input-output table but explores the dependency relations in terms of payments and intermediation relations. Consistency analysis explores the consistency of plans of buyers and sellers by decomposing the input-output table into four matrices, each for a different kind of means of payment. It integrates micro and macroeconomics in one model and deals with money in an ideology-free manner. It deals with the flow of funds via the movement of goods. In a technical sense, input-output analysis can be seen as a special case of consistency analysis without money and without entrepreneurship and transaction cost.

Economic base Analysis

Economic base analysis was developed by Robert Murray Haig in his work on the Regional Plan of New York in 1928. Briefly, activities in an area divide into two categories – basic and non-basic. Basic industries are those exporting from the region; non-basic (or service) industries support basic industries. Because of data problems, it is not practical to study industry output and trade flows to and from a region. As an alternative, basic and non-basic concepts are operationalized using employment data. The basic industries of the region are identified by comparing employment in the region to national norms. If the national norm for employment in, e.g. Egyptian woodwind manufacturing is five percent and the region's employment is eight percent, then three percent of the region's woodwind employment is basic. Once basic employment is identified, the outlook for basic employment is investigated sector by sector and projections made sector by sector. In turn, this permits the projection of total employment in the region. Typically the basic/non-basic employment ratio is about 1:1. Extending by manipulation of data and comparisons, conjectures may be made about population and income. This is a rough, serviceable procedure and it continues in use today. It has the advantage of being readily operationalized, fiddled with, and understandable. The formula for computing location quotients can be written as:

$$LQ = \frac{e_i / e}{E_i / E}$$

Where:

e_i = Local employment in industry i

e = Total local employment

E_i = Reference area employment in industry i

E = Total reference area employment

It is assumed that the base year is identical in all of the above variables.

Location Quotient for Selected Industries in Minnesota (2000)

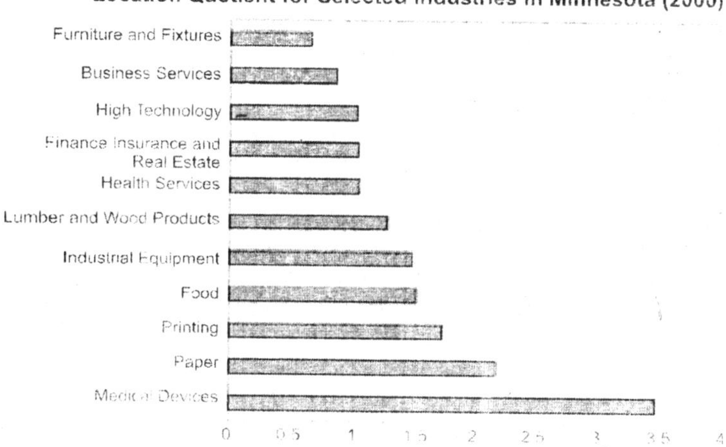

The figure showing location quotients uses data from *Compare Minnesota: Profiles of Minnesota's Economy and Population, 2002-2003*. It uses the term location quotient, a number derived by comparing percent employment in a place (Minnesota) with percent employment nationwide. Minnesota has about the same percentage of high technology employment as does the nation. It has more medical devices employment than the national average (due to companies such as Medtronic).

Economic base ideas are easy to understand as are measures made of employment. For instance, it's common knowledge that the economy of Seattle, Washington is tied to aircraft manufacturing, Detroit, Michigan to automobiles, and Silicon Valley to high tech manufacturing. When the newspapers discuss the closing of military bases, they will say some thing like: "5,000 jobs at the base will be lost. That's going to hit the economy hard because it means a loss of 10,000 jobs in the community.".

To forecast, what's mainly done is to compare the region with the nation and national trends. If the economic base of a region is in industries that are declining nationwide, then we have a problem. If our economic base is concentrated in sectors that are growing, then we are in good shape.

Methodologically, economic base analysis views the region as if it were a small nation and uses notions of relative and comparative advantage from international trade theory (Charles Tiebout 1963). In a sense the activity is macroeconomics "written small" (and it has not been of much interest to urban economists in recent years because it does not get at within-city relationships.) The analysis usually takes US growth patterns as a given. The fates of regions are determined by trends in the national economy.

Critique of the Economic base Concept

The economic base concept emerged in the 1920s, when economics focused on different industrial strengths and economic techniques were not as nuanced. The exporting (basic) activities were manufacturing and trade activities and they could be readily identified in the data series. One could think of changes in those activities as causing growth or decline.

Today, export activities purchase many services, and the comparative advantage of an area may well lie in the services it produces. Peter Drucker (1986) imagines a world dominated by trade in ideas and designs. There is little merchandise trade because technology permits small-scale manufacturing. Such a world would change our ideas of what's basic.

The concept is that of a trading region. But in practice economic base concepts are often applied to areas that fit the concept. The Minnesota study, cited before, compared the Minnesota to the US. One can speak of the economic base of Saint Paul, Minneapolis, or Duluth, but to go on and compare such areas using economic base techniques isn't very meaningful.

Forecasting is a precursor to actions, and there is no explicit way to get from the economic base to the kinds of actions most communities are interested in. That is, the economic base study doesn't say what to do. Leaders say they want desirable economic activities, such as high tech ones. Indeed, we have seen studies of the transport needs of high tech industries, studies done prior to investments to attract such industries (for example in Pennsylvania). Again, the economic base study doesn't say what to do.

Even if we could make what-to-do linkages, the calculus of "desirable" is not simple. We suppose that high pay, little environmental insult, upward mobility for workers, and stability or growth are among the attributes desired of new activities. The table below gives information on the pay attribute. Clearly, that attribute has to be traded off against other attributes.

Table: Average weekly earnings of production or non-supervisory workers on private non-farm payrolls by major industry, in current dollars

Industry	*Average weekly earnings (April 2003)*
Mining:	774.58
Construction:	721.58
Manufacturing:	629.43
Transportation and public utilities:	670.32
Wholesale trade:	627.13
Retail trade:	296.80
Finance, insurance, and real estate:	611.90
Services:	507.43
Total private:	511.39

The NBER Industrial Organization Program

The NBER's Program on Industrial Organization (IO) celebrates its fifteenth anniversary this year. Researchers in the IO program explore a wide range of topics within the field. Rather than attempting to skim the full scope of program activity, this report highlights work in three broad areas: regulation and antitrust policy; pricing behaviour by firms; and auctions markets. Discussion of the substantial body of research on technology and technical change is deferred to reports of the Productivity Program and the NBER Project on Industrial Technology and Productivity. Those interested in learning more about the IO program may visit the NBER website for links to the full set of Industrial Organization Working Papers: here

Regulatory and Antitrust Policy

When markets deviate from competitive ideals, assessing the desirability of government intervention requires a careful assessment of the costs of market failures relative to the benefits of imperfect regulation. The recognition that even imperfect markets may be preferable to regulated outcomes accompanied a dramatic transformation in the nature and extent of government intervention across a broad range of markets over the past thirty years. Many industries long subject to price and entry regulation in the United States — among them airlines, trucking, railroads, and banking — were deregulated. Telecommunications and electric utilities have been vertically disintegrated and structurally competitive segments were opened to market-based outcomes. Privatization of state-owned enterprises outside the United States has substantially increased reliance on market outcomes in many sectors, although regulators in some cases have replaced government managers in providing oversight. Where government intervention ha s been maintained, various forms of incentive-based regulation increasingly have replaced state ownership or traditional cost-of-service rate determination.

IO program members are among the leading scholars of antitrust and regulatory policy, and many have been directly involved in the design or implementation of reforms through their government service, advice to regulatory agencies, or consulting to affected firms. In the face of continuing policy debates over regulatory reform, highlighted more than a decade ago by Paul Joskow and Roger Noll in the NBER's 1994

American Economic Policy in the 1980s, the NBER recently sponsored a research project designed to leverage this expertise. Project participants were asked to identify key issues in economic regulation, assess the impact of regulatory reforms across a variety of industries, and evaluate significant contemporary concerns about these reforms. Two dozen scholars assembled for a September 2005 conference in Cambridge to discuss the results of this project, to be assembled in an NBER volume on "Economic Regulation and Its Reform: What Have We Learned?" This project complements a substantial body of primary research by NBER associates on regulatory and antitrust policy. A selection of research from the conference and from NBER working papers is described below.

Economic Regulation and Its Reform

Electricity Restructuring: Competition and Incentive Regulation

NBER researchers continue in the vanguard of research, market design, and implementation of electricity restructuring. Much of the empirical work to date has focused on restructured generation markets, in which prices generally are determined through a competitive bidding process. Frank Wolak describes the evolutionary nature of the restructuring process, emphasizing the tension between an imperfectly competitive market and an imperfect regulatory process in providing incentives for least-cost supply at various stages of the production process. In one of the first empirical analyses of restructuring supply-side benefits (11001), the potential for these incentives to reduce costs is highlighted: Kira Fabrizio, Catherine Wolfram, and I show that restructuring is associated with increased productivity, documenting generating-plant efficiency gains in the use of labour and materials input from replacing a regulated monopoly with market competition. As Wolak points out, though, the technical characteristics of electricity supply and demand suggest that market power may be of particular concern, limiting the benefits of restructuring. Joskow (8442) discusses the role of market power and other contributors to the 2000-1 California electricity crisis; Ali Hortacsu and Steven Puller (11123) measure efficiency losses from strategic bidding in the Texas ERCOT market; and Dae-Wook Kim and Chris Knittel (10895) compare direct measures of markups to those inferred from oligopoly models of market power in

California generation markets. Wolak also describes market design and regulatory policies that limit the ability of suppliers to exercise unilateral market power — such as forward contracting, horizontal divestitures, demand-side participation, and local market power mitigation — and uses examples from worldwide wholesale electricity markets to illustrate the importance of effectively addressing each aspect of the market design process to ensure the maximum benefits of electricity restructuring.

While early empirical electricity research focused predominantly on generation markets, researchers increasingly have turned their attention to retail markets and demand-side policy. Peter Reiss and Matthew White (8687, 9986) use data from San Diego households to measure consumer responsiveness to changing electricity prices and conservation programs enacted during the California electricity crisis. They argue that consumers may be more responsive to price fluctuations than previously thought. Severin Borenstein and Stephen Holland (9922) suggest that substantial efficiency gains could be obtained from shifting even modest shares of relatively price-insensitive customers from fixed retail electricity prices to those that reflect time-varying wholesale electricity prices. Borenstein (11594) provides insight into continued res istance to real-time pricing, highlighting substantial distributional effects of real-time prices across heterogeneous industrial and commercial customers that may make it difficult to gain political support without some system to compensation losers.

For services such as transmission and distribution, which typically remain subject to regulation even in restructured markets, innovations have shifted the focus from cost-based price setting toward incentive mechanisms. Joskow provides a comprehensive review of the theory and complexities involved in applying incentive-based regulation. He then discusses applications of incentive mechanisms to the regulation of prices and service quality for "unbundled" electricity transmission and distribution networks. Further, he assesses the evidence on the performance of incentive regulation for electric distribution and transmission networks and describes challenges for future policy and research.

Among those challenges are determining the role of competition in electricity retailing and transmission. Joskow and Jean Tirole (9534) analyse the likely performance of competitive merchant transmission markets, and conclude that this model is likely to yield substantial investment inefficiencies. While their prognosis for retail electricity competition is more optimistic (10473), they note a variety of challenges and efficiency limitations of competitive outcomes. In their work on "Reliability and Competitive Electricity Markets" (10472), they analyse the complexity involved in integrating economists' approach to market design with engineering system design for reliability across the entire electricity network. Finally, they highlight the implications for system investment, operation, and reliability of interactions among competitive markets, operational constraints, and regulatory and administrative practices.

Telecommunications

The telecommunications sector similarly has undergone a dramatic transformation over the past quarter century. Although telecommunications regulators adopted various incentive-based policies early, "forward-looking" cost-based regulation still plays a prominent role in setting prices for unbundled network elements (UNEs) that must be leased by local telephone companies to their competitors. As noted by Robert Pindyck (10287, 11225), the typical pricing formulas used to set UNE lease rates induce substantial investment and entry inefficiencies by failing to account properly for the substantial sunk costs of telecomm investments. Jerry Hausman and Gregory Sidak compare the outcomes of regulatory approaches in the United States, the United Kingdom, and New Zealand. They conclude that in both the United States and the United Kingdom, unbundling may have caused an increase in competition if one measures competition by market share of entrants, at the cost of adverse investment effects by both incumbents and new entrants. In the last section of their paper, they argue that emerging facilities-based competition should allow the end of telecomm price regulation and the regulatory burden that it creates for both consumers and the economy. If the nature of local exchange competition during the 1990s is a guide to the future, then Shane Greenstein and Michael Mazzeo's (9761) research suggests that we may see increasing product differentiation as a result of local competition.

Cable Television

Greg Crawford's analysis of the cable television industry highlights the impact of economic regulation on product quality and innovation. Regulation in this industry has varied greatly over time, as federal legislation has deregulated, re-regulated, and deregulated consumer cable prices. More recently, penetration by Digital Broadcast Satellites raises questions about the need for regulation to constrain cable prices. Crawford analyzes the interplay of price regulation and firm quality choices, with attention to the implications of satellite competition for performance in cable television markets. His work highlights ongoing concern over horizontal concentration and vertical integration in the programming market, and bundling by both cable systems and programmers, the latter being the subject of current policy debate at the Federal Communications Commission.

Airline Deregulation

In general, the empirical evidence on deregulation of structurally competitive industries suggests considerable gains from removal of price and entry regulation, although the transition from regulated to competitive markets may be longer and more costly than academics or policymakers originally envisioned. Borenstein and I describe the significant consumer benefits from reduced fares and increased flight frequencies and from nonstop service subsequent to airline deregulation, while acknowledging the industry's considerable financial volatility. We argue that market power concerns have diminished as growth by low-cost carriers now challenges legacy airlines in virtually all parts of the country. Recent research by Goolsbee and Chad Syverson suggests that even the threat of entry by carriers such as Southwest may reduce incumbent prices (11072). This surge in competition, combined with adverse demand shocks, high fuel prices, and high labour costs, has contributed to current financial distress among many legacy airlines, though. Financial distress and accompanying bankruptcies have been costly for shareholders, high-wage workers, and the Pension Benefit Guaranty Corporation, although many costs and dislocations may be transitional. For example, Borenstein and Rose (9636) show that schedule disruptions associated with airline bankruptcies are largely transitory; where they are more permanent, they appear to be modest relative to background fluctuations in flights and destinations served, and to be isolated to medium-sized airports. Overall airline investment and consumer benefits continue to be substantial. The greater long-run challenge may be the performance of government-controlled airports, air traffic control, and security infrastructure, which have not in general kept pace with the growth and changes in the industry.

Pharmaceutical Regulation

Pharmaceutical regulation has long generated concern over its effect on innovation incentives and product launch delays. Patricia Danzon and Eric Keuffel tackle these and other issues in their analysis of pharmaceutical safety, price, and marketing regulations on a variety of industry performance measures. They note that regulatory reforms such as the adoption of user fees, fast track, and priority review may have reduced review-induced delays, especially for priority drugs. For example, Ernst Berndt et al. (10822) finds that implementation of performance goals and user fees for FDA drug applications substantially reduced approval lags — by an average of roughly six months. They estimate a net savings of more than 125,000 life-years from these reforms.

Discouragement of innovation also can be a significant hidden cost of price regulation. Price controls present in many countries may reduce the price of existing pharmaceuticals, but also appear to discourage the development and diffusion of innovative new treatments. In their work on Medicaid prescription drug purchasing, Mark Duggan and Fiona Scott Morton (10930) highlight another indirect effect of price regulation: government rules that base Medicaid purchase price on the average price of that drug across private-sector purchasers increase equilibrium drug prices for non-Medicaid purchasers, and increase a firm's incentives to introduce new versions of a drug at higher prices.

Financial Services

Randall Kroszner and Phillip Strahan analyse the evolution of banking regulation of prices (interest rates), entry, capital, and investment decisions from the 1990s. to the last part of the twentieth century. They note that while industry adaptations to constraints partially reduced the costs of regulatory distortions, banking efficiency improved following the removal of most price and entry controls, generating substantial real benefits for the economy as a whole. Patrick Bolton et al. (10571) show that opening the banking sector to price and product-offering competition also may improve information provision and consumer-product matching, given the superior information that financial services sellers may have about product suitability for buyers of those services.

Eric Zitzewitz analyzes the implications of such asymmetric information for the regulation of non-banking financial services firms.

He argues that agency conflicts created by information asymmetries and consumer behavioural biases may impede market efficiency. For example, asset management and financial advisor firms may have incentives to discriminate according to customer sophistication or search ability, offering low-price, high-quality products to sophisticated clients and high-price, low-quality products to the less sophisticated. Ali Hortacsu and Syverson (9728) provide some evidence of this phenomenon in research on product differentiation and search costs in the mutual fund industry. Zitzewitz too discusses the implications of these factors for regulatory and antitrust policy in this sector, with particular attention to recent interventions by the New York Attorney General and the SEC.

Antitrust Policy

In regulated industries, firms may be subject to overlapping jurisdiction by both regulators and antitrust authorities. Dennis Carlton and Randal Picker analyse the tension that this produces, describing the historical origin of antitrust and regulation policy and the ongoing struggles to define the appropriate mechanism and substantive scope for regulating competition. They note that debates over the role of antitrust and regulation continue with particular prominence in today's network industries, whether telecommunications, transportation, or electricity. Moreover, core issues such as interconnection and mandatory access have increased in salience as reform-induced restructuring has led to vertical disintegration of firms and increased competition with incumbents in many industry segments, while the Supreme Court's decision in *Trinko* leaves open substantial questions about how these relationships will be governed.

For most sectors of the economy, interactions among firms are governed by court interpretations of antitrust policy rather than by economic regulatory agency decisions. NBER researchers have explored a variety of aspects of antitrust policy, from theoretical and empirical analyses of merger policy to consideration of vertical restraints. The appropriate role and application of antitrust policy in innovative sectors has attracted particular attention, both as a matter of principle and in the context of high-profile cases such as U.S. v. Microsoft. In these sectors, the tension between encouraging competition through entry and maintaining profit incentives for dynamic growth and efficiency is particularly acute. Ilya Segal and Michael Whinston (11525) focus on this tension in research that analyzes a number of specific policies, highlighting those that benefit both entry and innovation. Carlton and Robert Gertner (8976) argue that dynamic efficiency requires coordination of antitrust policy with intellectual property laws in an attempt to resolve tensions created by the tendency for network industries to evolve toward closed systems. Michael Katz and Howard Shelanski (10710) argue that traditional merger analysis, based on static welfare analyses, may miss important dynamic efficiency implications of mergers in highly innovative sectors. Carlton (11645) emphasizes the importance of dynamic barrier-to-entry analysis as one component of this.

Pricing Behaviour in Oligopoly Markets

The behaviour of firms in oligopoly markets is one of the mainstays of IO research. NBER researchers have made considerable progress in better understanding firms' pricing decisions, particularly with reference to price dispersion. Although competitive models tend to assume that consumers are perfectly informed about each firm's single price, many markets deviate substantially from this description. The ability to price discriminate — charging different prices for a product either across firms or to different customers of the same firm — may enable firms to extract greater consumer value from a transaction or to expand the set of customers they serve. This phenomenon appears ubiquitous in the economy.

Consumer search costs may be an important source of sustained price variability in a market. For example, cash prices for a given prescription drug vary widely across pharmacies within a particular geographic market. The magnitude of price dispersion is correlated with attributes that appear related to the costs and benefits of consumer search, for example, greater price variation for drugs prescribed for one-time use to treat an acute condition, relative to those prescribed for ongoing purchase as maintenance therapies. Alan Sorensen (8548) uses information on retail price dispersion and prescription attributes to analyse the distribution of consumer search costs for these products. His estimated model of consumer pharmacy choice suggests that search intensities in this market are relatively low — implying that, on average, only 5 to 10 percent of prescriptions are comparison-price shopped.

One way to increase search intensity is to lower its cost. Internet retailing often has been cited as intensely price competitive in large part because of easy consumer search for low-price vendors. Joel Waldfogel and Lu Chen (9942) argue that this reduces the price advantage of brand-name retailers. They find that consumer exposure to price comparison sites such as DealTime.com reduces Amazon purchase shares for those consumers, and that reductions are roughly twice as large for sites that include retailer reliability information (which may substitute for retailer brand reputation) in addition to item price. Goolsbee and Judith Chevalier (9085) develop a method of estimating price elasticities for online booksellers using publicly available data on Amazon and Barnes & Noble.com, and conclude that consumers are quite sensitive to prices, particularly at Barnes & Noble.com. Glenn Ellison and Sara Fisher Ellis on (10570) show that Internet retailers respond strategically to the increased pricing pressure imposed by these price comparison sites, though. Their analysis of the online computer components market demonstrates that retailers engage in a variety of practices to mitigate the extreme price-sensitivity that price comparison sites may induce, allowing firms to mark-up prices at least enough to cover fixed as well as marginal costs for efficient retailers. Glenn Ellison (9721) provides a theoretical model of one such practice, "add-on pricing" — for example, advertising low prices for one good in the expectation of selling additional (or higher quality) products to consumers at a high price at the point of sale. His work shows that this practice can sustain softer price competition as a competitive equilibrium.

A rich body of research by Florian Zettelmeyer, Fiona Scott Morton, and Jorge Silva-Risso uses data on individual consumer automobile purchases to explore the interaction of retail auto pricing, consumer information, and Internet information and referral services. These researchers first document significant reductions in average automobile purchase price associated with using an Internet referral service (8667), on the order of 2.2 percent after controlling for selection effects in who uses the service. They then show that Internet referrals disproportionately benefit minority buyers, offsetting the average 2 percent price disadvantage these groups incur because of their personal costs of search or negotiation for purchases made through traditional dealer channels (8668). In research that matches consumer survey and transactions data to explore the mechanism underlying these price effects, these researchers conclud e that increased transparency of dealer invoice costs combine with greater negotiating clout of the online referral service to reduce a customer's price by an average of

1.5 percent (11515). Consumer information appears to be particularly important in extracting value from auto price negotiations. For example, Megan Busse, Zettelmeyer, and Silva-Risso find that purchasers obtain 80 percent of the value of auto manufacturer promotions in the form of heavily promoted customer rebates, but only 35 percent of the value of promotions that are paid as dealer discounts (10887). This research agenda has provided unparalleled insights into pricing determinants in a significant consumer market, and generated important new findings for the role of the Internet in changing outcomes in conventional retail channels.

Auction Markets

While Internet retailing in general has attracted considerable attention and interest, the icon of Internet selling may well be eBay. Its popularity as a mechanism for matching buyers and sellers has spawned a rich economics literature as well as numerous competitors; much of this is described in Patrick Bajari and Ali Hortacsu's survey of Internet auctions research (10076). The seeming ubiquity of auctions, for goods ranging from fine art to Beanie Babies, and in settings that range from government procurement to pollution permits, has prompted several NBER researchers to model the benefits of auctions over alternative market transaction mechanisms. Alexandre Ziegler and Edward Lazear (9795) analyse the choice between retail store-based and auction markets. They describe the relative benefits of each, and characterize the conditions that lead to more efficient market organization through retail stores relative to auctions. Eduardo Engel, Ronald Fischer, and Alexander Galetovic (8869) analyse Demsetzian auctions for exclusive rights in settings that range from procurement to royalty contracts, and conclude that "competition for the field" through ex ante auctions welfare dominates duopoly competition whenever marginal revenue is decreasing in quantities sold. Bajari, Robert McMillan, and Steve Tadelis (9757) highlight limitations of auctions relative to negotiations in procurement settings, particularly those dominated by incomplete information. With Stephanie Houghton, Bajari and Tadelis estimate adaptation and renegotiation costs to procurement contracts awarded by auction mechanisms (12051).

As Susan Athey and Philip Haile point out (12126, p. 1), "auctions have provided a fruitful area for combining economic theory with econometric analysis ... to understand behaviour and inform policy."

Athey and Haile describe methodological innovations, many by NBER researchers, which have facilitated estimation of more realistic models and provided significant insights into auction market operation and performance. A significant thrust of this work has been to allow the data more freedom to drive results by relaxing parametric and functional form assumptions. For example, Haile, Han Hong, and Matthew Shum (10105) develop nonparametric tests of one of the key valuation questions in auctions: are bidders' valuations generated by independent private values for the good, in which case bidders need not be concerned about the "winner's curse," or by common values, in which case bidders must optimally shade their bids knowing that winning means they had an excessively optimistic estimate of the good's true value. They apply this test to different types of U.S. Forest Service timber auctions, and find support for its ability to distinguish between settings in which common values are likely to be more or less significant.

Another approach to allaying concerns about constraints imposed by structural model estimates of auctions looks to experimental data. In this spirit, Bajari and Hortacsu (9889) use experimental data to calibrate the quality of structural estimation based on four alternative theoretical models of bidder behaviour. Andreas Lange, John List, and Michael Price (10639) develop an innovative combination of field data and lab experimental data to evaluate the impact of secondary resale markets for timber on bidding behaviour in timber auctions.

Improving the models and methods available to analyse auction markets can yield important economic insights into these markets, and can aid participants in developing appropriate bidding strategies. But an important policy goal is also to understand the performance of these markets. Mireia Jofre-Bonet and Martin Pesendorfer (8626) develop a method of estimating a dynamic model of behaviour in repeated highway construction procurement auctions with firm-level capacity constraints, and then quantify efficiency losses that result in this setting. In many repeated auctions settings, the potential for collusion among bidders may also be a significant concern. Ken Hendricks, Rob Porter, and Guofu Tan (9836) develop a theory of collusion in affiliated private value and common value auction environments, and use their model to test for bidding rings in federal offshore oil and gas lease auctions. They show that the winner's curse in common value settings works against bid rigging for marginal tracts. Bajari and Fox (11671) analyse potential collusion in FCC spectrum auctions; Orley Ashenfelter and Kathryn Graddy (10795) provide a case study of price-fixing in auctions using the Sotheby's/Christie's art auctions case, drawing out the lessons for auctions and competition policy from details of this case.

Conclusion

This report of necessity focuses on a fraction of the IO research conducted by NBER scholars, although I hope it provides an indication of the breadth and depth of contributions made in this area. Interested readers are encouraged to peruse the NBER website to access the entire body of scholarly work in this area.

Industrial Organization and the Law in The First Decade of Zimbabwe's Independence

Nineteen Eighty-Nine was the year in which the Zimbabwean government, in its economic policies, voluntarily turned away from its earlier profession of socialism and embarked on a policy of trade liberalization. In the longer term, therefore, the first decade of Zimbabwe's independence may prove to be anomalous — an ephemeral hiccup in its essentially 'capitalist history. From another perspective, however, the impact of labour policies during this period may prove to have more lasting effects than even the government dreamed of. The altered legal framework during the first decade of Independence has given both labour and capital practice in forms of confrontation and manipulation that are unlikely to be forgotten in a hurry by either side of this production relationship.

The politicization of work and the workplace in Zimbabwe may not easily be eradicated, even by the massive unemployment currently being experienced by youthful school-leavers, which is likely to continue irrespective of what economic policies are adopted in the future. The replacement of racial discrimination during the colonial era by the problems of class differentiation among Blacks after Independence has clearly had an important (and thus far negative) impact on production output in many enterprises. These and many other experiences of Zimbabwe's temporary flirtation with socialism can be expected to influence both her immediate adjustment to 'liberal' economic policies, which will tilt the balance once again in favour of capital and its management, and any equilibrium which may be established in the longer term.

It is important, therefore, that we understand in some detail exactly what did happen during the 1980s in Zimbabwe's industrial sector, rather than run the risk that, as political ideologies, together with what counts as legitimate history, change, these experiences will be expunged from our collective memory as being history incompatible with contemporary reality in the future. It is important to record in accessible, published form the shop-floor findings of industrial sociology during the 1980s, so that they will be available to future generations of researchers and teachers in this field.

The Enterprises Studied

Although all of the workshop participants' research interests were defined individually, their choices have, fortunately, enabled this collection to cover most of the major forms of enterprise ownership in Zimbabwe. State-owned companies are represented by 'Parastatal', a single enterprise studied successively by both Shadur and Mutizwa-Mangiza. Within the private sector, the local subsidiaries of different transnationals were investigated by Maphosa and Gaidzanwa. 'Zimcor', discussed by Cheater, straddled this divide, with a majority state shareholding and participation by both transnationals and local companies, while 'Zimtex' is an example of a wholly local company quoted on the Zimbabwe Stock Exchange, with some individual shareholders resident overseas. Our examples therefore cover a wide range of ownership variation, with the exception of the handful of recently formed cooperatives. These companies, with a minimum of 500 employees, also represent the large-firm sector of the Zimbabwean economy. They have all been made anonymous.

Given the diverse nature of the enterprises studied, the congruence of the research findings by the different authors is striking, attesting to the significance of structural processes in widely differing contexts. Their interpretations of their data, however, sometimes differ. In particular, readers may be struck by the divergent interpretations offered by Shadur and Mutizwa-Mangiza of what was happening in the management of the same enterprise. Perhaps their differences confirm Karl Mannheim's (1936) assertion that there is no 'God's-eye view' of social reality, merely a series of different perspectives, even among scientific observers who, like the social actors observed, may be differently-placed in respect of their gender, nationality and other social attributes. In this respect, though, one might note the shared interpretations of the Zimbabwean industrial scene by the four Zimbabwean contributors, irrespective of their differences of race and gender. It is, therefore, especially useful to have this shared insiders' perspective leavened by that of Shadur as an outsider.

Research Themes

The articles collected here deal with a number of substantial themes, on some of which we do not have as much hard data as we would like. For others, however, more detailed information has already been published: the bibliography on industrial sociology in Zimbabwe at the end of this collection is, we hope, comprehensive and will allow interested readers to pursue specific issues in more detail should they so wish.

Among the many issues raised in these articles, some recur in many different contexts, indicating their structural importance in the system of industrial relations in Zimbabwe. These recurrently important themes include: the changing legal framework of labour relations; the limited extent of de *facto* workers' participation in the different enterprises and the causes of these limitations; the inverse relationship between democratization and bureaucratization in the workplace, which is related to differential education; the importance of the informal structure of social relations in the workplace; the links of urban workers to the countryside; the growing impact of class differentials among Zimbabwean Blacks and their impact on production relations; the impact of its non-productive welfare functions (housing, etc.) on production relations within an enterprise; the impact of race on production relations; the role and problems of supervisors on the shop-floor; and the politicization not only of production relations but also of the relationships of workers' dependants to employing companies and of the role of the 'workers' representative'.

It may be helpful to consider, in the necessary comparative detail, at least some of these themes as they are reflected in the different articles, and to provide additional background information which the papers often assume in their own arguments.

The Legal Framework of Labour Relations

Classically, newly established socialist states have begun their transformation with new laws governing land tenure and marriage. Zimbabwe, however, gave early attention to legalizing the state control of remuneration (in the Minimum Wages Act, No. 4 of 1980) and of the relations between employer and employee (in the Employment Act, No. 13 of 1980). Contrary to popular belief, however, as reflected, for example, in Sachikonye (1990, 3-4), the Minimum Wages Act did not establish for the first time the principle of a minimum wage: for certain categories of industrial worker that principle was established by the Industrial Conciliation Act (No. 21 of 1945, section 27(1)) and the Native Labour Boards Act (No. 26 of 1947, section 21(2)) and made non-racial by the Industrial Conciliation Act (No. 29 of 1959), while its generalization to agricultural workers dates from 1979 (S. I. 917 of 1979).

The Minimum Wages and Employment Acts were 'holding operations', establishing a measure of central control while the state prepared a more coherent legal framework to restructure the triangular interface between industrial capital, labour and itself. This exercise took longer than expected: the Labour Relations Act (No. 16 of 1985) was promulgated at the very end of 1985, after extensive criticism of early draft bills by both labour and capital, and became effective at the beginning of 1986. The Labour Relations Act incorporated the core provisions of both of the earlier Acts.

There is considerable misunderstanding of the intentions of both the Industrial Conciliation and Labour Relations Acts, perhaps because both are sufficiently long (89 and 80 pages, respectively) to deter all but the most determined reader. A detailed comparison of their provisions, however, is necessary to cut through misinformed popular and state discourses on the subject of labour relations in Independent Zimbabwe. Even before such a comparison, though, one needs to note the background context — to both pieces of legislation — of the development of a new state (dating from 1890) and the strengthening of its powers. The original Industrial Conciliation Act (No. 10 of 1934) was the first attempt by this new state to exert any measure of control over a fledgling, but growing, industrial base. Earlier statutes attempting to control labour, such as the Masters and Servants Act (No. 5 of 1901) did not apply to skilled workers. The Industrial Conciliation Act exempted certain categories of employee from its provisions: those working in agriculture, domestic service, the civil service, education (including universities) and those working free for charities.

The Labour Relations Act extended considerably the theoretical reach of the state into employment, exempting only those whose conditions of employment are provided for in the Constitution of Zimbabwe.

Before comparing the content of the Industrial Conciliation and Labour Relations Acts, one should first note their different intentions. It is clear that the Industrial Conciliation Act assumed conflict between capital and labour (or at least between employers and employees) to be endemic, requiring a system of bureaucratized adjudication to resolve such disputes. Laying down the rules for entering into and adjudicating such conflicts was considered to be the responsibility of the state, but the ensuing negotiations and their outcome were the responsibility of the conflicting parties. To this end, the Act established two two-tier adjudication hierarchies, one concerned with matters of registration and membership of trade unions and employers' associations (an industrial court to which decisions of industrial boards could be appealed), and the other concerned with the resolution of industrial conflict through bureaucratic procedures (industrial tribunal(s) plus industrial councils/ conciliation boards, both of the latter composed of both employers and employees). The Act thus brought under the bureaucratic control of the state the recognition of both trade unions and employers' organizations as part of the system of regulating industrial conflict and its resolution. Finally, it dealt with ancillary matters, including the status of unregistered trade unions and employers' organizations, procedures of mediation and arbitration, the control of savings and other funds owned by trade unions and employers' associations, and matters of publication. The objectives of the Industrial Conciliation Act were thus very limited and based on the pattern of labour relations which had emerged in the United Kingdom, Europe and North America before the Second World War.

With two important exceptions, the colonial state regarded matters of employment and dispute resolution connected with employment as strictly private affairs. These exceptions included the state's outlawing after 1959, firstly, of the differentiation or discrimination of work or work conditions on the basis of 'race, colour or religion', and, secondly, of victimization of employees giving information to the state's industrial-conciliation machinery against their employers (section 136). For the rest, the Act specifically stated that 'This Act shall not bind the State' (section 3) and severely restricted the capacity of the Minister of Labour to intervene in industrial matters. The colonial bureaucratization of labour relations involved state control exercised through civil servants, not politicians.

The role of the Minister of Labour and Social Welfare, as it then was, under this legislation was restricted to: statutorily receiving a copy of all agreements negotiated by industrial councils or conciliation boards (section 86); declaring — at the request of the industrial council or conciliation board concerned — and publishing such agreements to be binding on all parties in a particular area or sector of industry, taking into account also the interests of consumers and 'the public as a whole' (sections 113, 114, 116); having the right to make a final determination to refuse to make an agreement binding if he considered it to be contrary to the interests of consumers or the general public, but being subject to the adjudication of the industrial tribunal if he refused to make an agreement binding on any other grounds (with the later provision that the State President could, by notice in the *Government Gazette,* declare the Minister's decision to be final: section 117(4)); being able to prevent the referral, by an industrial council or conciliation board, of a dispute to an industrial tribunal for adjudication if such action would likely result in changes to an industrial agreement during its agreed duration (section 100(1)); being able to take over and operate, in the event of industrial action which prevented its normal operations, any enterprise delivering essential services (defined as the supply of light, power, water, sanitation works, fire extinction and the mining of coal (section 142)); and consulting employers on matters affecting the interests of employers or employees (section 150(3)). In addition, only the Minister could authorize, in writing, anyone to hold office simultaneously in more than one (registered or unregistered) trade union, employers' organization, or both (sections 47(1), 67(1)).

The Minister did not constitute the final state authority in any essentially judicial matters. He could not be appealed to over recognition or registration or the operation of workers' or employers' organizations, or the termination of membership in unions or employers' bodies. He appointed members of the Industrial Court (of record) and the chairmen of industrial tribunals (which could also act as courts of inquiry), but had no statutory right to become involved in the outcome of decisions on conflict resolution made by either of these appeal divisions of the adjudication hierarchies. The essentially apolitical nature of the Industrial Conciliation Act was also reflected in its insistence that no registered or unregistered trade union or employers' organization might affiliate itself to any political party or organization, use any of its funds to further any individual or collective political interests, allow its property or facilities to be used for any political purposes, or receive financial or other assistance from political organizations of any kind (sections 49, 66). Such pretensions to apolitical labour relations parallel the separation of legislative, executive and judicial powers. Both are concerned to develop a legal-rational bureaucracy, Max Weber's (1947) acme of efficient organization, especially in industrialized societies.

But in some views, of course, both apolitical labour relations and the separation of powers are dismissed as mystifications of capital's interests.

These views argue that labour relations are, by definition, political, concerned with the power relations linking capital to labour. Any legislation that does not favour labour, therefore, by definition favours capital, and all ostensibly apolitical legislation falls into this category. Such views were espoused by Zanu(PF) (cf. ZANU[PF], 1980) and the new Zimbabwean government after Independence. Hence it is not at all surprising that the fundamental assumptions as well as the content of the Labour Relations Act are very different from those of the Industrial Conciliation Act. The Labour Relations Act explicitly takes the part of labour in the capital-labour relationship, as can be demonstrated by classifying its objectives into four divisions. Firstly, this Act declares and defines 'the fundamental rights of employees [and] unfair labour practices', and regulates 'conditions of employment and other related matters'. Specifically, worker organizations are given the right to recommend industrial action (including strike action: section 29(4)(g), and the Act indemnifies individual workers as well as workers' committees and registered (but not unregistered) trade unions against civil liability for lawful collective industrial action), while employers are not given the right to lock-outs or other collective action (sections 120-123, 29(5)). In its second category of objectives, the Labour Relations Act moves on to provide for state control over the economy in ways antithetical to the assumptions of the colonial system that employment is a private matter: 'to regulate and control collective job action [and] employment agencies; to provide for the control of wages and salaries [and] the appointment of workers' committees'. A third set of objectives of this Act includes taking over, renaming and expanding the institutional base of colonial labour relations, providing for 'the formation, registration, certification and functions of trade unions, employers' organizations, employment councils and employment boards; the establishment and functions of the Labour Relations Board and the Labour Relations Tribunal'. Finally, the Labour Relations Act reveals a Utopian view of what the future might hold, in seeking 'to provide for the prevention of trade disputes, and unfair labour practices' — a united future, without preventable conflict.

In this ideological perspective, then, the law can dissolve the inherent class antagonism between capital and labour and create industrial harmony.

It is, moreover, the duty of the state and its political functionaries to oversee the dissolution of this class antagonism. Apolitical systems must be politicized. One result of this politicization, however, appears to be the conversion of a legal-rational bureaucracy into a patrimonial bureaucracy, as controlling politicians have appropriated the state apparatus in order to achieve these goals. The Industrial Conciliation Amendment Act (No. 23 of 1981, section 5(6)) outlawed discrimination on the basis of 'tribe, etc.' as well as race, and the Labour Relations Act equally prohibits discrimination in employment 'on the grounds of race, tribe, place of origin, political opinion, colour, creed or sex' (section 5(1)) But Zimbabweans have cause to believe that their state sector now operates on the particularistic principles of tribalism, nepotism and ministerial directives on appointments. It is no longer a universalistic system, if it ever was.

It is instructive to note the sheer extent to which labour relations were politicized in the Labour Relations Act by noting what functions were vested in the Minister as final authority in contrast to the colonial situation outlined above — and I should note that this list is incomplete! The Minister currently: defines unfair labour practices (section 10); grants permission to delay or withhold wage payments (section 13(2)); allows welfare and fringe benefits to be diminished (section 16(2)(b)); makes 'regulations providing for the development, improvement, protection, regulation and control of employment and conditions of employment', which regulations 'prevail over the provisions of any other statutory instrument or of any agreement or arrangement whatsoever' (section 17(1) and (2)), including, it would appear from this wording, the law of contract.

Specifically in terms of sections 17(3), 19, 20 and 22, the Minister may regulate, among many others, minimum and maximum wages, bonuses, increments, allowances, benefits, social security, retirement and superannuation benefits, wage deductions, hours of work (including overtime), rest and meal breaks, the provision of food, leave of all kinds, holiday entitlements, the establishment of and contributions to pension schemes, medical and other insurances, the settlement of disputes, the recruitment of all types of labour, whether Zimbabwean or foreign, and the reinstatement of workers suspended or dismissed without his permission.

The Minister also exercises direct and indirect control over employment councils, employers, trade unions and workers' committees. Firstly, the Labour Relations Act sets up a deliberate monopoly system in its requirement that 'there should be no more than one certified trade union or employers' organization for each undertaking or industry' (section 45(l)(d)). Secondly, 'if the Minister has reasonable cause to believe that the property or funds of any trade union, employers' organization or federation are being misappropriated or misapplied', or that their affairs 'are being conducted in a manner that is detrimental to the interests of its members as a whole', the Minister may appoint an investigation into the organization's affairs, and may accept or reject any recommendations to withdraw its recognition by the state and for it to cease operating (section 136). For some odd reason, more control (both financial (section 61) and political) is exercised by the Minister over trade unions than over employers' organizations. 'Where the national interest so demands', the Minister may not only 'cause to be supervised... elections to any office or post in a registered or certified trade union or employers' organization' (section 55(1)).

He may also, for reasons of 'national interest', prohibit any candidate from conducting an election campaign for such office (section 55(2)(d)).

The Minister may direct employers, workers and their respective organizations to negotiate or renegotiate a collective-bargaining agreement (section 25), and that parts of such a collective-bargaining agreement (notably concerning wages) be implemented before they are ratified by the negotiating parties as required in the Act (section 83). He may also refuse to allow the registration by the state of such agreements until amended (section 84). Moreover, the Minister may: 'make such regulations as he considers necessary for the control of workers' committees' (section 26(1)); specify maximum trade union, employers' organization and employment council dues (sections 28(2), 57, 58, 64(d)), levies to support the Labour Relations Board and Tribunal (section 139), and the mode of payment of such dues (section 60); direct payment of union dues 'into a trust fund and not to the trade union concerned' (section 60(3)(b)); approve or revoke the authority of a trade union to act on behalf of non-union members, as an 'agent union' (sections 31, 32, 56); and institute accreditation enquiries into the registration of any trade union or employers' organization (sections 39, 41). The-consent of the Minister is necessary for any employer to 'threaten, recommend or engage in a lock-out' or to take punitive action in respect of continued employment, wages or benefits as a result of a lock-out (section 121), even though, as I have already indicated, employers do not in fact have the right to such collective action in the first place! Perhaps section 121 is merely making doubly sure... Such industrial action may in any case be terminated or delayed for up to 90 days by a 'show-cause order' or 'disposal order' issued by the Minister (sections 122, 123). Any party aggrieved by the issuance of, or refusal to issue, such an order may appeal directly to the Labour Relations Tribunal (section 126(1)), but such an appeal does not affect in any way the implementation of such an order, although the Minister may, during the period in which an appeal is considered, 'give such directions to, or impose such restrictions on, any of the parties as he considers fair and reasonable, taking into account the respective rights of the parties and the public interest' (section 126(2)).

Employment boards, governing conditions of employment, are appointed by and report to the Minister (sections 70-73, 77), who is required 'as far as is practicable under the circumstances' (section 72(2)), to ensure 'equality of representation' of the interests of employers and employees. He must 'pay due regard to' (but not necessarily appoint!) any persons nominated by any interested party to such an employment board (section 71), and may vary its investigative authority (to another board, or to a trade union) if he considers that the interests of the employees concerned 'would be more properly served' by such a transfer (section 78).

The Minister also appoints, and may suspend or dismiss, all members of the Labour Relations Board (sections 88, 91), which is the board of appeal against determinations made by the state's regional hearing officers. In turn, appeals against the Board's determinations are heard by the Labour Relations Tribunal, members of which are appointed, suspended and dismissed by the State President (sections 99-104). From the Tribunal, appeals must be made directly to the Supreme Court of Zimbabwe. At the first level of appeal in this hierarchy, there is explicit scope for political determination: 'The Minister may give to the Board directions of a general or specific nature, and the Board shall comply with such directions' (section 93(4)). Interestingly, an appeal may be made to the Board only with the consent either of the regional hearing officer, or of a member of the Board itself (section 113): thus the right of appeal is not automatic but instead is controlled by interested gate-keepers who are part of the determination system. Moreover, although the Board and Tribunal alike may co-opt non-voting experts to assist their deliberations (sections 93(5), 105(5)), political appointees, not experts, decide. For example, if an aggrieved party alleges unfair labour practices, the Minister may order either a labour relations officer of the state or the Labour Relations Board to investigate such allegations (section 114).

The comparison of new and old appeal structures shows quite clearly the different principles on which the Industrial Conciliation and Labour Relations Acts were constructed. Laying out the comparisons in tabular form allows us to see how much authority in respect of industrialconflict resolution has been removed from the disputing actors themselves and vested in politicians controlling the state apparatus. The authority of such politicians now extends to the lower reaches of the expanded bureaucratic hierarchy controlling both capital and labour.

As might be expected in such a structure, the Labour Relations Act provides for direct links between civil servants (notably the labour relations officers and hearing officers) and the Minister. Such civil servants must inform the Minister 'forthwith' when they order compulsory arbitration of a dispute (section 117(1)), but it is then the Minister's responsibility to refer the matter to the Labour Relations Tribunal or to appoint (at the request of the disputing parties) an independent mediator (section 117(2)). Thus a senior politician is required to communicate between state functionaries and the political appointees to higher-level decision-making organs. Whereas colonial civil servants, not politicians, had decision-making authority over industrial relations issues, in Independent Zimbabwe civil servants merely implement at the lowest level of the system political decisions taken elsewhere in the expanded and fully politicized state system. Of course, one must distinguish among different types of politicization. Zimbabwe's ruling party has been quite happy to politicize the state apparatus with its own ideology and personnel. But given its orientation to the perspectives of labour, the Labour Relations Act shows one startling similarity to its predecessor: section 35(c) prohibits the use of association funds, whether by trade unions or employers' associations, for 'electioneering' or any other unspecified 'political purposes'. Moreover, sections 39 and 40 allow for 'any interested party' (including the one concerned) to request the Registrar of Labour Relations to vary, suspend or rescind the registration or certification of any trade union or employers' organization and to supply his reasons for so doing. Legitimate reasons for such action are not defined in the Act, allowing the Registrar very wide latitude. Once an employers' organization or union loses its recognition by the state, given the accreditation provisions of the Act (sections 41-44), it could be extremely difficult to restore such recognition. It would seem, from these provisions, that an organization could lose such recognition on 'political' grounds — an irrefutable allegation that it had, indeed, used funds for some 'political' purpose.

Another aspect of politicization also merits specific attention. As I have noted earlier, one of the assumptions underlying the Labour Relations Act is that a directive state can eliminate the class conflict between capital and labour. Yet whereas the Industrial Conciliation Act had required the Minister to permit an individual to hold office in both a union and an employers' organization, the Labour Relations Act (section 45(l)(b)) requires the Registrar of Labour Relations to 'ensure compliance' with the requirements that 'a trade union shall not represent employers or managerial employees' (the latter defined as enjoying a 'confidential relationship' with an employer concerning the rights and interests of other employees), and that an employers' organization shall represent only managerial employees. There is a fundamental contradiction in a position that, on the one hand, defines the class lines ever more stringently and, on the other, avers the possibility of harmonious relations between capital and labour, for such a position explicitly prevents the development of cross-cutting ties which blur definitional boundaries through the development of mutual rather than opposing interests.

Under such circumstances, it would be naive to expect in the future that workers and managers will immediately forget the techniques they have learned over the past decade to exert political influence within this politicized system. To put it differently, can the system be depoliticized?

Certainly at this point there is no indication that government intends to depoliticize the constitution or operation of its own institutions. In its attempt to cut down the bureaucratic delays that have frustrated retrenchment since 1985, the independent state has used its 'traditional' operating principles in formulating the Labour Relations (Retrenchment) Regulations (S. 1.404 of 1990), which provide for the Minister to appoint seven members (three civil servants, two employers' representatives and two workers' representatives) to the new Retrenchment Committee. This committee must decide on applications referred to it within two weeks and make recommendations to the Minister, which he may accept or reject. If the Retrenchment Committee fails to make such recommendations, the Minister will decide anyway! Both Minister and Committee are bound by two basic principles: that retrenchment should be avoided and that its consequences should be mitigated (section 7). It is true that various researchers (Cheater, 1986; Gaidzanwa. this volume) have reported dissatisfaction among workers with the practical implementation of these worker-oriented legal provisions, and that both politicians and civil servants (especially those supposed to implement the Labour Relations Act) have tended to develop class interests consonant with, rather than opposed to, those of capital. Nonetheless, the political rhetoric of national unity requires that government be seen to be on the side of the workers (and peasants). It is thus unlikely that the law will alter its form of discourse and highly probable that an even larger gap will develop in the era of trade liberalization between the law and its practical implementation. In government as in industry, informal social relations and connections are therefore likely to become increasingly important.

Formal Bureaucratic and Informal Production Relations

Larger enterprises in the Zimbabwean economy are becoming increasingly bureaucratic in their mode of operation, whether these bureaucratic procedures and relationships grow out of managerial conflict at the shopfloor level or are imposed from above (for example, in standardized practices devolved from head office in the case of subsidiaries of transnational corporations). Perhaps the most obvious index of such bureaucratization is the current popularity of the Paterson Method of job classification, which emphasizes the decision-making content of jobs in grading them as unskilled, semi-skilled or skilled and has many local variants in Zimbabwean enterprises. As Shadur (1989, 235) notes: 'There are grounds for concluding that the Paterson Method has been adopted on a major scale in Zimbabwe as a result of the weak labour movement which has not had the expertise and strength to resist this method', but personnel departments all over Zimbabwe have over the past decade been involved in job-regrading on this basis. However, Gaidzanwa indicates that standardized practices at 'Gold Mine' were very difficult to enforce, and Cheater deals with the responses of both workers and management to increasing bureaucratization more generally. Both papers, together with that of Mutizwa-Mangiza, describe some of the specific difficulties of supervisors in a situation of ongoing bureaucratization.

Supervisors have structural difficulties in all systems, of course, especially when they have been promoted from the shop-floor, and most of these difficulties centre on the differing informal social relationships between workmates and between unequals. These difficulties may be further complicated when, as Maphosa indicates, the supervisor's promotion has resulted from his initial election to workers' representative and/or to party political office. But there are particular difficulties for supervisors in negotiating informally with their subordinates about regular as well as overtime work when these subordinates have access to other productive resources. Gaidzanwa notes, for example, that locals from the communal land surrounding Gold Mine, having their agricultural interests tended by their wives, were less tractable than 'foreigners' working at the mine to supervisory 'discipline' at work. Yet even while they regarded their mine wages as supplementary to their total productive resources, the local workers were also particularly threatened by any failure of this wage source, given the inadequacy of agriculture as a sole source of income under local environmental conditions. Local workers, therefore, had to confront at closer range the trade-offs available to them from (migratory or commuter) wage employment and agriculture in ways that, perhaps, workers without such options may have envied.

As what Maphosa calls 'bureaucratic logic' tightens its grip on the organization of production, and the 'chain of command' lengthens inexorably (best exemplified in Parastatal), so informal social relations become more, not less, important to ordinary workers. As Maphosa and Mutizwa-Mangiza point out, even those workers elected to represent others on the workers' committees do not have the necessary education or skills to manipulate the bureaucratic order: they must, therefore, manipulate people in order to get what they want. This falling-back by workers on personal relationships in the work-place exacerbates the politicization of ostensibly bureaucratic relations, diverting them into patrimonial forms and contradicting the original intention of state policy-makers to quash especially racial discrimination by legal-rational means.

Race and Class

The Industrial Conciliation Act was and is widely and wrongly thought to have disadvantaged workers mainly on the basis of race. In fact, as I indicated earlier, this Act explicitly outlawed differentiation or discrimination, including in industrial agreements, on the basis of 'race, tribe, colour or creed' in respect of work, though it did permit such discrimination on the basis of age, sex, experience, length of employment and type of premises (sections 36(2), 78(2)). The Act did not permit the Industrial Registrar to register any trade union or employers' organization formed 'for the purpose of furthering the interests of its members on a basis of race, colour or religion' (section 40(1)(e) and required him to enquire publicly, for 'reasonable cause', into unions and organizations believed to be functioning so as to further the interests of their members on the basis of 'race, colour or religion' and to cancel the registration of offending bodies 'unless cause [was] shown to the contrary' (section 57(1)(h)). The onus was thus on such organizations to prove to the state that they were not operating in a racist manner.

But the real problem in colonial Rhodesia was not legalized, structural racism of the kind characteristic of South Africa: it was *de Facto*, practical discrimination in everyday life, and that problem has by no means yet been resolved, eleven years after Independence. In the early 1980s, such practical discrimination was responsible for considerable industrial unrest in individual enterprises. Some of the papers here address this issue in the context of removing the colonial overlap between race and class. Maphosa broadly indicates the background problems inherited from colonialism. Shadur deals with these continuing problems after Independence. Cheater shows how government policy rapidly Africanized enterprise management, while exacerbating the class divide between workers and executive management. In yet more detail, Gaidzanwa shows how the response of Black managerial staff to perceived racism in promotions at Gold Mine was politicized in various ways: by calling in the local Member of Parliament and mobilizing workers' wives in a public demonstration.

Democratization and The Politicization of Production Relations

Politicization may be a strategy of last resort, used by managers and workers alike. Gaidzanwa, for example, notes that in contexts not involving accusations of racism, the ZANU(PF) Women's League at Gold Mine was mobilized to demonstrate against managerial employees with whom workers were dissatisfied. Maphosa observes that such politicization, especially by members of workers' committees, was particularly likely to occur in mining enterprises operating in relatively isolated areas. In an earlier publication, Cheater (1986, 93) described the Zimtex supervisors' 'takeover' of the local Zanu(PF) apparatus in order to reduce their post-Independence supervisory problems at work, which had been caused by after-hours political action against them in the workers' village.

These examples of the politicization of work relations, whether by supervisors, managers or workers, are perhaps related to the high but unfulfilled expectations of workplace democratization found by Maphosa immediately after Independence. These expectations far exceeded the level of democratization that the state (never mind management) was prepared to allow, as both Maphosa and Mutizwa-Mangiza detail in their articles. It could be argued that the workers were deliberately misled on the subject of worker participation by political rhetoric (for example, in the Zanu(PF) Election Manifestos of 1980 and 1985 (see ZANU[PF], 1980 and 1985)), and that their subsequent politicization of work relations represents a backlash against their continuing subordination, now to bureaucratic rather than racial control. Such bureaucratic control is especially clear in the case of the parastatal enterprises, with their extraordinarily long chains of command culminating in the Cabinet as final decision-making manager, and in the Labour Relations Act itself. The question for the structurally-adjusted future must then become: how will previously politicized workplaces be controlled, and by whom?

2

Market Structure

Introduction

In economics, market structure (also known as market form) describes the state of a market with respect to competition.

Basic Market Structures

- Perfect competition, in which the market consists of a very large number of firms producing a homogeneous product.
- Monopolistic competition, also called competitive market, where there are a large number of independent firms which have a very small proportion of the market share.
- Oligopoly, in which a market is dominated by a small number of firms which own more than 40% of the market share.
- Oligopsony, a market dominated by many sellers and a few buyers.
- Monopoly, where there is only one provider of a product or service.
- Natural monopoly, a monopoly in which economies of scale cause efficiency to increase continuously with the size of the firm. A firm is a natural monopoly if it is able to serve the entire market demand at a lower cost than any combination of two or more smaller, more specialized firms.
- Monopsony, when there is only one buyer in a market.

The imperfectly competitive structure is quite identical to the realistic market conditions where some monopolistic competitors, monopolists, oligopolists, and duopolists exist and dominate the market conditions.

The elements of Market Structure include the number and size distribution of firms, entry conditions, and the extent of differentiation.

These somewhat abstract concerns tend to determine some but not all details of a specific concrete market system where buyers and sellers actually meet and commit to trade. Competition is useful because it reveals actual customer demand and induces the seller (operator) to provide service quality levels and price levels that buyers (customers) want, typically subject to the seller's financial need to cover its costs. In other words, competition can align the seller's interests with the buyer's interests and can cause the seller to reveal his true costs and other private information. In the absence of perfect competition, three basic approaches can be adopted to deal with problems related to the control of market power and an asymmetry between the government and the operator with respect to objectives and information: (a) subjecting the operator to competitive pressures, (b) gathering information on the operator and the market, and (c) applying incentive regulation.

Quick Reference to Basic Market Structures

Market Structure	***Seller Entry Barriers***	***Seller Number***	***Buyer Entry Barriers***	***Buyer Number***
Perfect Competition	No	Many	No	Many
Monopolistic competition	No	Many	No	Many
Oligopoly	Yes	Few	No	Many
Oligopsony	No	Many	Yes	Few
Monopoly	Yes	One	No	Many
Monopsony	No	Many	Yes	One

The correct sequence of the market structure from most to least competitive is perfect competition, imperfect competition,oligopoly, and pure monopoly.

The main criteria by which one can distinguish between different market structures are: the number and size of producers and consumers in the market, the type of goods and services being traded, and the degree to which information can flow freely.

Perfect Competition

In neoclassical economics and microeconomics, perfect competition describes a market in which there are many small firms, all producing homogeneous goods. In the short term, such markets are productively inefficient as output will not occur where marginal cost is equal to average cost, but allocatively efficient, as output under perfect competition will always occur where marginal cost is equal to marginal revenue, and therefore where marginal cost equals average revenue. However, in the long term, such markets are both allocatively and productively efficient. In general a perfectly competitive market is characterized by the fact that no single firm has influence over the price of the product it sells. Because the conditions for perfect competition are very strict, there are few perfectly competitive markets.

A perfectly competitive market may have several distinguishing characteristics, including:

- Infinite Buyers/Infinite Sellers – Infinite consumers with the willingness and ability to buy the product at a certain price, Infinite producers with the willingness and ability to supply the product at a certain price.
- Zero Entry/Exit Barriers – It is relatively easy to enter or exit as a business in a perfectly competitive market.
- Perfect Information-Prices and quality of products are assumed to be known to all consumers and producers.
- Transactions are Costless-Buyers and sellers incur no costs in making an exchange.
- Firms Aim to Maximize Profits-Firms aim to sell where marginal costs meet marginal revenue, where they generate the most profit.
- Homogeneous Products – The characteristics of any given market good or service do not vary across suppliers.

Some subset of these conditions is presented in most textbooks as defining perfect competition. More advanced textbooks try to reconcile these conditions with the definition of perfect competition as equilibrium price taking; that is whether or not firms treat price as a parameter or a choice variable. It is this distinction which differentiates perfectly competitive markets from imperfectly competitive ones. It should be noted that a general rigorous proof that the above conditions indeed suffice to guarantee price taking is still lacking (Kreps 1990, p. 265).

The importance of perfect competition derives from the fact that price taking by the firm guarantees that when firms maximize profits (by choosing quantity they wish to produce, and the combination of

Factors of production to produce it with) the market price will be equal to marginal cost. An implication of this is that a factor's price (wage, rent, etc.) equals the factor's marginal revenue product. This allows for derivation of the supply curve on which the neoclassical approach is based (note that this is also the reason why "a monopoly does not have a supply curve"). The abandonment of price taking creates considerable difficulties to the demonstration of existence of a general equilibrium except under other, very specific conditions such as that of monopolistic competition.

Approaches and Conditions

Historically, in neoclassical economics there have been two strands of looking at what perfect competition is. The first emphasis is on the inability of any one agent to affect prices. This is usually justified by the fact that any one firm or consumer is so small relative to the whole market that their presence or absence leaves the equilibrium price very nearly unaffected. This assumption of negligible impact of each agent on the equilibrium price has been formalized by Aumann (1964) by postulating a continuum of infinitesimal agents. The difference between Aumann's approach and that found in undergraduate textbooks is that in the first, agents have the power to choose their own prices but do not individually affect the market price, while in the second it is simply assumed that agents treat prices as parameters. Both approaches lead to the same result.

The second view of perfect competition conceives of it in terms of agents taking advantage of – and hence, eliminating – profitable exchange opportunities. The faster this arbitrage takes place, the more competitive a market is. The implication is that the more competitive a market is under this definition, the faster the average market price will adjust so as to equate supply and demand (and also equate price to marginal costs). In this view "perfect" competition means that this adjustment takes place instantaneously. This is usually modelled via the use of the Walrasian auctioneer. The widespread recourse to the auctioneer tale appears to have favoured an interpretation of perfect competition as meaning price taking *always*, i.e. also at non-equilibrium prices; but this is rejected e.g. by Arrow (1959) or Mas-Colell et al.

Steve Keen notes, following George Stigler, that if firms do not react strategically to one another, the slope of the demand curve that a firm faces is the same as the slope of the market demand curve. Hence, if firms are to produce at a level that equates marginal cost and marginal revenue, the model of perfect competition must include at least an infinite number of firms, each producing an output quantity of zero. As noted above, an influential model of perfect competition in neoclassical economics assumes that the number of buyers and sellers are both of the power of the continuum, that is, an infinity even larger than the number of natural numbers. K. Vela Velupillai quotes Maury Osborne as noting the inapplicability of such models to actual economies since money and the commodities sold each have a smallest positive unit.

Thus nowadays the dominant intuitive idea of the conditions justifying price taking and thus rendering a market perfectly competitive is an amalgam of several different notions, not all present, nor given equal weight, in all treatments. Besides product homogeneity and absence of collusion, the notion more generally associated with perfect competition is the negligibility of the size of agents, which makes them believe that they can sell as much of the good as they wish at the equilibrium price but nothing at a higher price (in particular, firms are described as each one of them facing a horizontal demand curve). However, also widely accepted as part of the notion of perfectly competitive market are perfect information about price distribution and very quick adjustments (whose joint operation establish the law of one price), to the point sometimes of identifying perfect competition with an essentially instantaneous reaching of equilibrium between supply and demand. Finally, the idea of free entry with free access to technology is also often listed as a characteristic of perfectly competitive markets, probably owing to a difficulty with abandoning completely the older conception of free competition. In recent decades it has been rediscovered that free entry can be a foundation of absence of market power, alternative to negligibility of agents (Novshek and Sonnenschein 1987.)

Free entry also makes it easier to justify the absence of collusion: any collusion by existing firms can be undermined by entry of new firms. The necessarily long-period nature of the analysis (entry requires time!) also allows a reconciliation of the horizontal demand curve facing each firm according to the theory, with the feeling of businessmen that "contrary to economic theory, sales are by no means unlimited at the current market price". Sraffian economists see the assumption of free entry and exit as characteristic of the theory of free competition in Classical economics, an approach that is not expressed in terms of schedules of supply and demand.

Results

In the short-run, it is possible for an individual firm to make a profit. This situation is shown in this diagram, as the price or average revenue, denoted by P, is above the average cost denoted by C.

However, in the long period, positive profit cannot be sustained. The arrival of new firms or expansion of existing firms (if returns to scale are constant) in the market causes the (horizontal) demand curve of each individual firm to shift downward, bringing down at the same time the price, the average revenue and marginal revenue curve. The final outcome is that, in the long run, the firm will make only normal profit (zero economic profit). Its horizontal demand curve will touch its average total cost curve at its lowest point.

In a perfectly competitive market, a firm's demand curve is perfectly elastic.

As mentioned above, the perfect competition model, if interpreted as applying also to short-period or very-short-period behaviour, is approximated only by markets of homogeneous products produced and purchased by very many sellers and buyers, usually organized markets for agricultural products or raw materials. In real-world markets, assumptions such as perfect information cannot be verified and are only approximated in organized double-auction markets where most agents wait and observe the behaviour of prices before deciding to exchange (but in the long-period interpretation perfect information is not necessary, the analysis only aims at determining the average around which market prices gravitate, and for gravitation to operate one does not need perfect information).

In the absence of externalities and public goods, perfectly competitive equilibria are Pareto-efficient, i.e. no improvement in the utility of a consumer is possible without a worsening of the utility of some other consumer. This is called the First Theorem of Welfare Economics. The basic reason is that no productive factor with a non-zero marginal product is left unutilized, and the units of each factor are so allocated as to yield the same indirect marginal utility in all uses, a basic efficiency condition (if this indirect marginal utility were higher in one use than in other ones, a Pareto improvement could be achieved by transferring a small amount of the factor to the use where it yields a higher marginal utility).

A simple proof assuming differentiable utility functions and production functions is the following. Let w_j be the 'price' (the rental) of a certain factor j, let MP_{j1} and MP_{j2} be its marginal product in the production of goods 1 and 2, and let p_1 and p_2 be these goods' prices. In equilibrium these prices must equal the respective marginal costs MC_1 and MC_2; remember that marginal cost equals factor 'price' divided by factor marginal productivity (because increasing the production of good i by one very small unit through increase of the employment of factor j requires increasing the factor employment by $1/MP_{ji}$ and thus increasing the cost by w_j/MP_{ji}, and through the condition of cost minimization that marginal products must be proportional to factor 'prices' it can be shown that the cost increase is the same if the output increase is obtained by optimally varying all factors). Optimal factor employment by a price-taking firm requires equality of factor rental and factor marginal revenue product, $w_j=p_iMP_{ji}$, so we obtain $p_1=MC_1=w_j/MP_{j1}$, $p_2=MC_2=w_j/MP_{j2}$.

Now choose any consumer purchasing both goods, and measure his utility in such units that in equilibrium his marginal utility of money (the increase in utility due to the last unit of money spent on each good), $MU_1/p_1=MU_2/p_2$, is 1. Then $p_1=MU_1$, $p_2=MU_2$. The indirect marginal utility of the factor is the increase in the utility of our consumer achieved by an increase in the employment of the factor by one (very small) unit; this increase in utility through allocating the small increase in factor utilization to good 1 is $MP_{j1}MU_1=MP_{j1}p_1=w_j$, and through allocating it to good 2 it is $MP_{j2}MU_2=MP_{j2}p_2=w_j$ again. With our choice of units the marginal utility of the amount of the factor consumed directly by the optimizing consumer is again w, so the amount supplied of the factor too satisfies the condition of optimal allocation.

Monopoly violates this optimal allocation condition, because in a monopolized industry market price is above marginal cost, and this means that factors are underutilized in the monopolized industry, they have a higher indirect marginal utility than in their uses in competitive industries. Of course this theorem is considered irrelevant by economists who do not believe that general equilibrium theory correctly predicts the functioning of market economies; but it is given great importance by neoclassical economists and it is the theoretical reason given by them for combating monopolies and for antitrust legislation.

Profit

In contrast to a monopoly or oligopoly, it is impossible for a firm in perfect competition to earn economic profit in the long run, which is to say that a firm cannot make any more money than is necessary to cover its economic costs. In order not to misinterpret this zero-long-run-profits thesis, it must be remembered that the term 'profit' is also used in other ways. Neoclassical theory defines profit as what is left of revenue after all costs have been subtracted, including normal interest on capital plus the normal excess over it required to cover risk, and normal salary for managerial activity. Classical economists on the contrary defined profit as what is left after subtracting costs except interest and risk coverage; thus, if one leaves aside risk coverage for simplicity, the neoclassical zero-long-run-profit thesis would be re-expressed in classical parlance as profits coinciding with interest in the long period, i.e. the rate of profit tending to coincide with the rate of interest. Profits in the classical meaning do not tend to disappear in the long period but tend to normal profit. With this terminology, if a firm is earning abnormal profit in the short term, this will act as a trigger for other firms to enter the market. They will compete with the first firm, driving the market price down until all firms are earning normal profit only.

It is important to note that perfect competition is a sufficient condition for allocative and productive efficiency, but it is not a necessary condition. Laboratory experiments in which participants have significant price setting power and little or no information about their counterparts consistently produce efficient results given the proper trading institutions.

The Shutdown Point

When a firm is making a loss, it will have to decide whether to continue production or not. This decision will, in fact, depend on the different total costs levels and whether the firm is operating in the short run or in the long run.

If the firm is in the short run, and is Making a loss Where by:

- Total costs (TC) is greater than total revenue (TR)
- and whereby total revenue is greater or equal to total variable cost (TVC).

it is advisable for the firm to continue production. If it fails to achieve these conditions, it is advised to close down so that the only costs the firm will have to pay will be the fixed costs.

Even if the firm stops producing, it will have to continue to meet the level of fixed costs. Since whether the firm produces or not, it will have to pay fixed costs, it is better for it to continue production in an attempt to decrease total costs and increase total revenue, thus making profits. This can be done by:

- Increasing productivity. The most obvious methods involve automation and computerization which minimize the tasks that must be performed by employees. All else constant, it benefits a business to improve productivity, which over time lowers cost and (hopefully) improves ability to compete and make profit.
- Adopting new methods of production like Just In Time or lean manufacturing in an attempt to reduce costs and wastages.

In the long run, the condition to continue producing requires the price P to be higher than the ATC, i.e. the line representing market price should be above the minimum point of the ATC curve.

If P is equal to ATC, the firm is indifferent between shutting down and continuing to produce. This case is different from the short run shut down case because in long run there's no longer a fixed cost (everything is variable).

Short-run Supply Curve

The short run supply curve for a perfectly competitive firm is the MC curve at and above the shutdown point. Portions of the marginal cost curve below the shut down point are not part of the SR supply curve because the firm is not producing in that range. Technically the SR supply curve is a discontinuous function composed of the segment of the MC curve at and above minimum of the average variable cost curve and a segment that runs with the vertical axis from the origin to but not including a point "parallel" to minimum average variable costs.

Examples

Perhaps the closest thing to a perfectly competitive market would be a large auction of identical goods with all potential buyers and sellers present. By design, a stock exchange resembles this, not as a complete description (for no markets may satisfy all requirements of the model) but as an approximation. The flaw in considering the stock exchange as an example of Perfect Competition is the fact that large institutional investors (e.g. investment banks) may solely influence the market price. This, of course, violates the condition that "no one seller can influence market price".

Free software works along lines that approximate perfect competition. Anyone is free to enter and leave the market at no cost. All code is freely accessible and modifiable, and individuals are free to behave independently. Free software may be bought or sold at whatever price that the market may allow.

Some believe that one of the prime examples of a perfectly competitive market anywhere in the world is street food in developing countries. This is so since relatively few barriers to entry/exit exist for street vendors. Furthermore, there are often numerous buyers and sellers of a given street food, in addition to consumers/sellers possessing perfect information of the product in question. It is often the case that street vendors may serve a homogenous product, in which little to no variations in the product's nature exist.

Another very near example of perfect competition would be the fish market and the vegetable or fruit vendors who sell at the same place.

1) There are large number of buyers and sellers.
2) There are no entry or exit barriers.
3) There is perfect mobility of the factors, i.e buyers can easily switch from one seller to the other.
4) The products are homogenous.

Criticisms

The use of the assumption of perfect competition as the foundation of price theory for product markets is often criticized as representing all agents as passive, thus removing the active attempts to increase one's welfare or profits by price undercutting, product design, advertising, innovation, activities that-the critics argue-characterize most industries and markets. These criticisms point to the frequent lack of realism of the assumptions of product homogeneity and impossibility to differentiate it, but apart from this the accusation of passivity appears correct only for short-period or very-short-period analyses, in long-period analyses the inability of price to diverge from the natural or long-period price is due to active reactions of entry or exit.

A frequent criticism is that it is often not true that in the short run differences between supply and demand cause changes in price; especially in manufacturing, the more common behaviour is alteration of production without nearly any alteration of price (Lee 1998). Anyway, the critics of the assumption of perfect competition in product markets seldom question the basic neoclassical view of the working of market economies for this reason. The Neo-Austrian school insists strongly on this criticism, and yet the neoclassical view of the working of market economies as fundamentally efficient, reflecting consumer choices and assigning to each agent his/her contribution to social welfare, is esteemed to be fundamentally correct (Kirzner 1981). Some non-neoclassical schools, like Post-Keynesians, reject the neoclassical approach to value and distribution, but not because of their rejection of perfect competition as a reasonable approximation to the working of most product markets; the reasons for rejection of the neoclassical 'vision' are different views of the determinants of income distribution and of aggregate demand (Petri 2004). In particular, the rejection of perfect competition does not generally entail the rejection of free competition as characterizing most product markets; indeed it has been argued (Clifton 1977) that competition is stronger nowadays than in 19th century capitalism, owing to the increasing capacity of big conglomerate firms to enter any industry: therefore the classical idea of a tendency toward a uniform rate of return on investment in all industries owing to free entry is even more valid today; and the reason why General Motors, Exxon or Nestle do not enter the computers or pharmaceutical industries is not insurmountable barriers to entry but rather that the rate of return in the latter industries is already sufficiently in line with the average rate of return elsewhere as not to justify entry. On this few economists, it would seem, would disagree, even among the neoclassical ones. Thus when the issue is normal, or long-period, product prices, differences on the validity of the perfect competition assumption do not appear to imply important differences on the existence or not of a tendency of rates of return toward uniformity as long as entry is possible, and what is found fundamentally lacking in the perfect competition model is the absence of marketing expenses and innovation as causes of costs that do enter normal average cost. The issue is different with respect to factor markets. Here the acceptance or denial of perfect competition in labour markets does make a big difference to the view of the working of market economies. One must distinguish neoclassical from non-neoclassical economists.

For the former, absence of perfect competition in labour markets, e.g. due to the existence of trade unions, impedes the smooth working of competition, which if left free to operate would cause a decrease of wages as long as there were unemployment, and would finally ensure the full employment of labour: labour unemployment is due to absence of perfect competition in labour markets.

Most non-neoclassical economists deny that a full flexibility of wages would ensure the full employment of labour and find a stickiness of wages an indispensable component of a market economy, without which the economy would lack the regularity and persistence indispensable to its smooth working. This was, for example, Keynes's opinion.

Particularly radical is the view of the Sraffian school on this issue: the labour demand curve cannot be determined hence a level of wages ensuring the equality between supply and demand for labour does not exist, and economics should resume the viewpoint of the classical economists, according to whom competition in labour markets does not and cannot mean indefinite price flexibility as long as supply and demand are unequal, it only means a tendency to equality of wages for similar work, but the level of wages is necessarily determined by complex sociopolitical elements; custom, feelings of justice, informal allegiaces to classes, as well as overt coalitions such as trade unions, far from being impediments to a smooth working of labour markets that would be able to determine wages even without these elements, are on the contrary indispensable because without them there would be no way to determine wages (Garegnani 1990).

"Bizarre" Assumptions

A frequent criticism of perfect competition and the standard model is the absurdity of its assumptions. However, the reality of the assumptions is not the test of the validity of a scientific theory. It is whether the assumptions lead to refutable hypotheses that can survive empirical testing.

Some of the basic assumptions of perfect competition in its most pristine form are:

1. Consumers' sole motivation is to maximize utility-the satisfaction derived from the consumption of goods and services.
2. Producers maximize profits.
3. All economic actors are completely rational.
4. Only circumstances that can be quantified count.
5. All economic actors have perfect knowledge-they are omniscient and omnipresent.
6. All economic actors act independently; they are not affected by the actions of others.
7. Economic actors communicate only through price.
8. There are an infinite number of consumers and producers and infinite "supplies" of factors of production.
9. There are no barriers to entry, competition or mobility.
10. No market power

10a. No advertising

10b. No control over resources

10c. No proprietary technology,

10d. No patents

10e. No trademarks

10f. No copyrights

10g. No geographical advantages

10h. No customer loyalty

10i. No branding or marketing

10j. No government regulation

10k. No collusion

10l. No labour contracts or trade unions

10m. No research and development costs

10n. No sunk c©1 osts

10o. No stocks of inputs

10p. No distribution networks

10q. No middle-men

10r. No economies of scale

10s. Each producer produces an infinitely small quantity of goods or services.

11. Free entry and exit-there is no need to build factories-they just pop up wherever needed. In fact, there are no factories, no workers and no consumers in any material physical sense-production materials, inputs (labour, materials, capital), are instantaneously transformed into products which are instantaneously consumed.
12. Free mobility of factors of production
13. No inventories
14. All goods are instantaneously consumed-all products are instantaneously produced.
15. All goods and services are perfectly homogeneous.
16. No government
17. Time does not exist.
18. System is closed and deterministic.
19. No transaction costs
20. No information costs
21. All economic activities are flows rather than stocks-production is similar to gauging the flow of a river past a point (i.e. gallons per minute).
22. The system's preferred state is equilibrium in all markets.
23. All economic activities-production, exchange, distribution and consumption-are perfectly efficient.
24. No externalities-good or bad.

Monopolistic Competition

Monopolistic competition is a common market structure where many competing producers sell products that are differentiated from one another (ie. the products are substitutes, but are not exactly alike). Many markets are monopolistically competitive, common examples include the markets for restaurants, cereal, clothing, shoes and service industries in large cities. The "founding father" of the theory of monopolistic competition was Edward Hastings Chamberlin, in his pioneering book on the subject, *Theory of Monopolistic Competition* (1933).

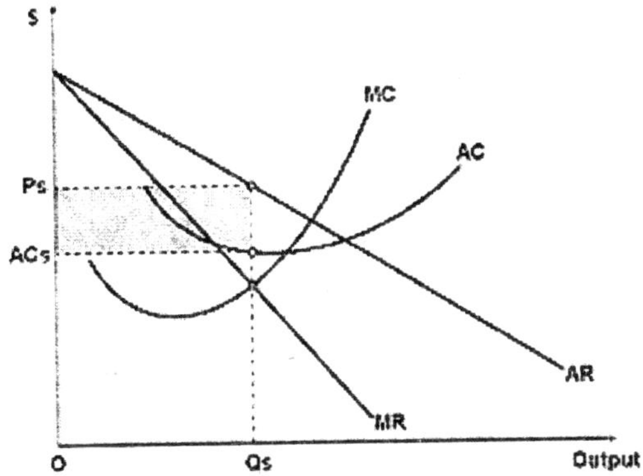

Short-run equilibrium of the firm under monopolistic competition

Monopolistically Competitive Markets have the Following Characteristics:

- There are many producers and many consumers in a given market, and no business has total control over the market price.
- Consumers perceive that there are non-price differences among the competitors' products.
- There are few barriers to entry and exit.
- Producers have a degree of control over price.

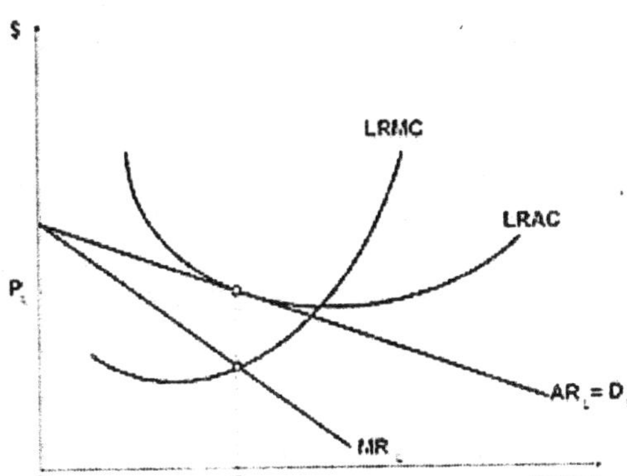

Long-run equilibrium of the firm under monopolistic competition

The characteristics of a monopolistically competitive market are almost the same as in perfect competition, with the exception of monopolistic competition having heterogeneous products, and that monopolistic competition involves a great deal of non-price competition (based on subtle product differentiation). A firm making profits in the short run will break even in the long run because demand will decrease and average total cost will increase. This means in the long run, a monopolistically competitive firm will make zero economic profit. This gives the amount of influence over the market; because of brand loyalty, it can raise its prices without losing all of its customers. This means that an individual firm's demand curve is downward sloping, in contrast to perfect competition, which has a perfectly elastic demand schedule.

Major Characteristics

There are six Characteristics of Monopolistic Competition (MC)

- product differentiation
- many firms
- free entry and exit in long run
- Independent decision making
- Market Power
- Buyers and Sellers have perfect information.

Product Differentiation

MC firms sell products that have real or perceived non-price differences. However, the differences are not so great as to eliminate goods as substitutes. Technically the cross price elasticity of demand between goods would be positive. In fact the XED would he high. MC goods are best described as close but imperfect subsitutes. The goods perform the same basic functions. The differences are in "qualities" and circumstances such as type, style, quality, reputation, appearance and location that tend to distinguish goods. For example, the function of motor vehilces is basically the same-to get from point A to B in reasonable comfort and safety. Yet there are many different types of motor vehicles, motor scooters, motor cycles, trucks, cars and SUV"s.

Many Firms

There are many firms in each MC product group and many firms on the side lines prepared to enter the market. A product group is a "collection of similar products" The fact that there are "many firms" gives each MC firm the freedom to set prices without engaging in strategic decision making. The requirements assures that each firm's actions have a negligible impact on the market. For example. a firm could cut prices and increase sales without fear that its actions will prompt retaliatory responses from competitors.

How many firms will an MC market structure support at market equilibrium? The answer depends on factors such as fixed costs, economies of scale and the degree of product differentiation. For example, the higher the fixed costs the fewer firms the market will support.. Also the greater the degree of product differentiation-the more the firm can separate itself from the pack-the fewer firms there will be in market equilibrium.

Free Entry and Exit

In the long run there is free entry and exit. There are numerous firms awaiting to enter the market each with its own "unique" product or in pursuit of positive profits and any firm unable to cover its costs can leave the market without incurring liquidation costs. This assumption implies that there are low start up costs, no sunk costs and no exit costs.

Independent Decision Making

Each MC firm independently sets the terms of exchange for its product. The firm gives no consideration to what effect its decision may have on competitors. The theory is that any action will have such a negligible effect on the overall market demand that an MC firm can act without fear of prompting hightened competition. In other words each firm feels free to set prices as if it were a monopoly rather than an oligopoly.

Market Power

MC firms have some degree of market power. Market power means that the firm has control over the terms and conditions of exchange. An MC firm can raise it prices without losing all its customers. The firm can also lower prices without triggering a potentially ruinous price war with competitors.

The source of an MC firm's market power is not barriers to entry since there are none. An MC firm derives it's market power from the fact that it has relatively few competitors, do not engage in strategic decision making and the firms sells differentiated product. Market power also means that an MC firm faces a downward sloping demand curve. The demand curve is highly elastic although not "flat".

Perfect Information

Buyers know exactly what goods are being offered, where the goods are being sold, all differentiating characteristics of the goods, the good's price, whether a firm is making a profit and if so how much.

Comparing Market Structures

Number of Firms

- PC: Infinite number of sellers
- MC: Many seller within each product group
- M: One seller.

Market Power

- PC: None
- MC: Some
- M: High.

Elasticity of Demand

- PC: Perfectly elastic
- MC: Highly elastic
- M:Relatively inelastic.

Product Differentiation

- PC: None
- MC:high
- M: Absolute.

Excess Profits

- PC: No
- MC: No
- M: Yes.

Efficiency

- PC: Yes
- MC: No
- M: No.

Profit Maximization Condition

- PC p =MR = MC
- MC MR = MC
- M MR = MC.

Ability to set Price

- PC Price taker
- MC price setter
- M price setter.

Inefficiency

There are two sources of inefficiency in the MC market structure. First, at its optimum output the firm charges a price that exceeds marginal costs, The MC firm maximizes profits where MR = MC. Since the MC firm's demand curve is downward sloping this means that the firm will be charging a price that exceeds marginal costs. The monopoly power possessed by an MC firm means that at its profit maximizing level of production there will be a net loss of consumer (and producer) surplus. The second source of inefficiency is the fact that MC firms operate with excess capacity. That is, the MC firm's profit maximizing output is less than the output associated with minimum average cost. Both a PC and MC firm will operate at a point where demand or price equals average cost. For a PC firm this equilibrium condition occurs where the perfectly elastic demand curve equals minimum average cost. An MC firm's demand curve is not flat but is downward sloping. Thus in the long run the demand curve will be tangent to the long run average cost curve at a point to the left of its minimum. The result is excess capacity.

Problems

While monopolistically competitive firms are inefficient, it is usually the case that the costs of regulating prices for every product that is sold in monopolistic competition by far exceed the benefits; the government would have to regulate all firms that sold heterogeneous products—an impossible proposition in a market economy. A monopolistically competitive firm might be said to be marginally inefficient because the firm produces at an output where average total cost is not a minimum. A monopolistically competitive market might be said to be a marginally inefficient market structure because marginal cost is less than price in the long run. Another concern of critics of monopolistic competition is that it fosters advertising and the creation of brand names. Critics argue that advertising induces customers into spending more on products because of the name associated with them rather than because of rational factors. This is disputed by defenders of advertising who argue that (1) brand names can represent a guarantee of quality, and (2) advertising helps reduce the cost to consumers of weighing the tradeoffs of numerous competing brands. There are unique information and information processing costs associated with selecting a brand in a monopolistically competitive environment. In a monopoly industry, the consumer is faced with a single brand and so information gathering is relatively inexpensive. In a perfectly competitive industry, the consumer is faced with many brands. However, because the brands are virtually identical, again information gathering is relatively inexpensive. Faced with a monopolistically competitive industry, to select the best out of many brands the consumer must collect and process information on a large number of different brands. In many cases, the cost of gathering information necessary to selecting the best brand can exceed the benefit of consuming the best brand (versus a randomly selected brand).

Evidence suggests that consumers use information obtained from advertising not only to assess the single brand advertised, but also to infer the possible existence of brands that the consumer has, heretofore, not observed, as well as to infer consumer satisfaction with brands similar to the advertised brand.

Examples

In many U.S. markets, producers practice product differentiation by altering the physical composition, using special packaging, or simply claiming to have superior products based on brand images and/or advertising. Toothpastes and toilet papers are examples of differentiated products.

Oligopoly

An oligopoly is a market form in which a market or industry is dominated by a small number of sellers (oligopolists). The word is derived, by analogy with "monopoly", from the Greek *oligoi* 'few' and *poleein* 'to sell'. Because there are few sellers, each oligopolist is likely to be aware of the actions of the others. The decisions of one firm influence, and are influenced by, the decisions of other firms. Strategic planning by oligopolists needs to take into account the likely responses of the other market participants. This causes oligopolistic markets and industries to be a high risk for collusion.

Description

Oligopoly is a common market form. As a quantitative description of oligopoly, the four-firm concentration ratio is often utilized. This measure expresses the market share of the four largest firms in an industry as a percentage (e.g. Target, Walmart and Bestbuy are viewed by some as having an oligopoly over their respective trades).

Oligopolistic competition can give rise to a wide range of different outcomes. In some situations, the firms may employ restrictive trade practices (collusion, market sharing etc.) to raise prices and restrict production in much the same way as a monopoly. Where there is a formal agreement for such collusion, this is known as a cartel. A primary example of such a cartel is OPEC which has a profound influence on the international price of oil.

Firms often collude in an attempt to stabilize unstable markets, so as to reduce the risks inherent in these markets for investment and product development. There are legal restrictions on such collusion in most countries. There does not have to be a formal agreement for collusion to take place (although for the act to be illegal there must be actual communication between companies)-for example, in some industries, there may be an acknowledged market leader which informally sets prices to which other producers respond, known as price leadership.

In other situations, competition between sellers in an oligopoly can be fierce, with relatively low prices and high production. This could lead to an efficient outcome approaching perfect competition. The competition in an oligopoly can be greater than when there are more firms in an industry if, for example, the firms were only regionally based and did not compete directly with each other.

Thus the welfare analysis of oligopolies is sensitive to the parameter values used to define the market's structure. In particular, the level of dead weight loss is hard to measure. The study of product differentiation indicates that oligopolies might also create excessive levels of differentiation in order to stifle competition. Oligopoly theory makes heavy use of game theory to model the behaviour of oligopolies:

- Stackelberg's duopoly. In this model the firms move sequentially.
- Cournot's duopoly. In this model the firms simultaneously choose quantities.
- Bertrand's oligopoly. In this model the firms simultaneously choose prices.

Characteristics

Profit maximization conditions: An oligopoly maximizes profits by producing where marginal revenue equals marginal costs.

Ability to set price: Oliopolies are price setters rather than price takers.

Entry and Exit: Barriers to entry are high. The most important barriers are economies of scale, patents, access to expensive and complex technology and strategic actions by incumbent firms designed to discourage or destroy nascent firms.

Number of firms: "Few"-a "handful" of sellers. There are so few firms that the actions of one firm can influence the actions of the other firms.

Long Run Profits: Oligopolies can retain long run positive profits. High barriers of entry prevent sideline firms from entering market to capture excess profits.

Product differentiation: Product may be standardized, steel, or differentiated, automobiles.

Perfect Knowledge Assumptions about perfect knowledge vary but the knowledge of various economic actors can be generally described as selective. Oligopolies have perfect knowledge of their own cost and demand functions but their inter-firm information may be incomplete. Buyers have only imperfect knowledge as to price, cost and product quality.

Interdependence: The distinctive feature of a monopoly is interdependence. Oligopolies are typically composed of a few large firms. Each firm is so large that its actions affect market conditions. Therefore the competing firms will be aware of a firm's market actions and will respond appropriately. This means that in contemplating a market action a firm must take into consideration the possible reactions of all competing firms and the firm's countermoves. It is very much like a game of chess or pool in which a player must anticipate a whole sequence of moves and countermoves in determining how to achieve his objectives. For example, an oligopoly that is considering a price reduction may wish to estimate the likelihood that competing firms would also lower their prices and possibly trigger a ruinous price war. Or if the firm is considering a price increase it may want to know whether other firms will also increase prices or hold existing prices constant.

This high degree of interdependence and need to be aware of what the other guy is doing or might do is to be contrasted with lack of interdependence in other market structures. In a PC market there is zero interdependence because no firm is large enough to affect market price. All firm's in a PC market are price takers information which they robotically follow in maximizing profits. In a monopoly there is quite simply no competitors to be concerned about. In a monopolistically competitive market each firm's effects on market conditions is so negligible as to be safely ignored by competitors.

Modelling

There is no single model describing the operation of an oligopolistic market. The variety and complexity of the models is due to the fact that you can have two to 102 firms competing on the basis of price, quantity, technological innovations, marketing, advertising and reputation. Fortunately, there are a series of simplified models that attempt to describe market behaviour under certain circumstances. Some of the better known models are the dominant firm model, the Cournot-Nash model, the Bertrand model and the kinked demand model

Dominant Firm Model

In some markets there is a single firm that controls a dominant share of the market and a group of smaller firms. The dominant firm sets prices which are simply taken by the smaller firms in determining their profit maximizing levels of production. This type market is practically a monopoly and an attached perfectly competitive market in which price is set by the dominant firm rather than the market. The demand curve for the dominant firm is determined by subtracting the supply curves of all the small firms from the industry demand curve. After estimating its net demand curve (market demand less the supply curve of the small firms) the dominant firm maximizes profits by following the normal p-max rule of producing where marginal revenue equals marginal costs. The small firms maximize profits by acting as PC firms-equating price to marginal costs.

Cournot-Nash Model

The Cournot-Nash model is the simplest oligopoly model. The models assumes that there are two "equally positioned firms"; the firms compete on the basis of quantity rather than price and each firms makes an "output decision assuming that the other firm's behaviour is fixed." The market demand curve is assumed to be linear and marginal costs are constant. To find the Cournot-Nash equilibrium one determines how each firm reacts to a change in the output of the other firm. The path to equilibrium is a series of actions and reactions. The pattern continues until a point is reached where neither firm desires "to change what it is doing, given how it believes the other firm will react to any change." K 326. The equilibrium is the intersection of the two firm's reaction functions. The reaction function shows how one firm reacts to the quantity choice of the other firm. For example, assume that the firm 1's demand function is $P = (60- Q_2)- Q_1$ where Q_2 is the quantity produced by the other firm and Q_1 is the amount produced by firm 1. Assume that marginal cost is 12. Firm 1 wants to know its maximizing quantity and price. Firm 1 begins the process by following the profit maximization rule of equating marginal revenue to marginal costs. Firm 1's total revenue function is $PQ = Q_1(60- Q_2- Q_1) = 60Q_1- Q_1Q_2 - Q_1^2$. The marginal revenue function is $MR = 60 - Q_2 - 2Q$..

$MR = MC$

$60 - Q_2 - 2Q = 12$

$2Q = Q_2 - 60$

$Q_1 = 30 - 0.5Q_2$ [1.1]

$Q_2 = 30 - 0.5Q_1$ [1.2]

Equation 1.1 is the reaction function for firm 1. Equation 1.2 is the reaction function for firm 2.

To determine the Cournot-Nash equilibrium you can solve the equations simultaneously. The equilibrium quantities can also be determined graphically. The equilibrium solution would be at the intersection of the two reaction functions. Note that if you graph the functions the axes represent quantities. The reaction functions are not necessarily symmetric. The firm's may face differing cost functions in which case the reaction functions would not be identical nor would the equilibrium quantities.

Bertrand Model

The Bertrand model is essentially the Cournot-Nash model except the strategic variable is price rather than quantity.

The Model Assumptions are:

There are two firms in the market.

They produce a homogeneous product.

They produce at a constant marginal cost.

Firms choose prices P_A and P_B simultaneously.

Firms outputs are perfect substitutes.

Sales are split evenly if $P_A = P_B$.

The only Nash equilibrium is $P_A = P_B = MC$.

Neither firm has any reason to change strategy if the firm raises prices it will lose all its customers. If the firm lowers price $P < MC$ then it will be losing money on every unit sold.

The Bertrand equilibrium is the same as the competitive result. Each firm will produce where P = marginal costs and there will be zero profits.

The Kinked Demand Curve Model

According to this model, each firm faces a demand curve kinked at the existing price. The conjectural assumptions of the model are (1) if a firm raises its price above the existing price competitor will not follow and the acting firm will lose market share (2) if a firm lowers price below the existing price then competitors will follow to preserve their market share and the acting frim's output will increase only slightly.

If the Assumptions Hold Then

The firm's marginal revenue curve is discontinuous, has a gap, at the kink.

For prices above the prevailing price the curve is relatively elastic.

For prices below the point the curve is relatively inelastic.

The gap in the marginal revenue curve means that marginal costs can fluctuate without changing equilibrium price and quantity. Thus prices tend to be rigid.

Examples

In industrialized economies, barriers to entry have resulted in oligopolies forming in many sectors, with unprecedented levels of competition, fueled by increasing globalization. Market shares in an oligopoly are typically determined by product development and advertising. For example, there are now only a small number of manufacturers of civil passenger aircraft, though Brazil (Embraer) and Canada (Bombardier) have participated in the small passenger aircraft market sector. Oligopolies have also arisen in heavily regulated markets such as wireless communications: in some areas only two or three providers are licensed to operate.

Australia

- Most media outlets are owned either by News Corporation, Time Warner, or by Fairfax Media
- Retailing is dominated by Coles Group and Woolworths.

Canada

- Three companies (Rogers Wireless, Bell Mobility and Telus) share over 94% of Canada's wireless market. United Kingdom
- Four companies (Tesco, Sainsbury's, Asda and Morrisons) share 74.4% of the grocery market
- Scottish & Newcastle, Molson Coors, and Inbev control two thirds of the beer brewing industry.
- The detergent market is dominated by two players, Unilever and Procter & Gamble.

United States

- Anheuser-Busch and MillerCoors control about 80% of the beer industry.
- Many media industries today are essentially oligopolies. Six movie studios receive 90% of American film revenues, and four major music companies receive 80% of recording revenues. There are just six major book publishers, and the television industry was an oligopoly of three networks—ABC, CBS, and NBC—from the 1990s. through the 1970s. Television has diversified since then, especially because of cable, but today it is still mostly an oligopoly of five companies: Disney/ABC,

CBS Corporation, NBC Universal, Time Warner, and News Corporation.

- Healthcare insurance in the United States consists of very few insurance companies controlling major market share in most states. For example, Calfornia's insured population of 20 million is the most competitive in the nation and 44% of that market is dominated by two insurance companies, Anthem and Kaiser Permanante.

Worldwide

- The accountancy market is controlled by Price Waterhouse Coopers, KPMG, Deloitte Touche Tohmatsu, and Ernst & Young (commonly known as the Big Four)
- Three leading food processing companies, Kraft Foods, PepsiCo and Nestle, together achieve a large proportion of global processed food sales. These three companies are often used as an example of "The rule of 3", which states that markets often become an oligopoly of three large firms.
- Boeing and Airbus have a duopoly over the airliner market.

Demand Curve

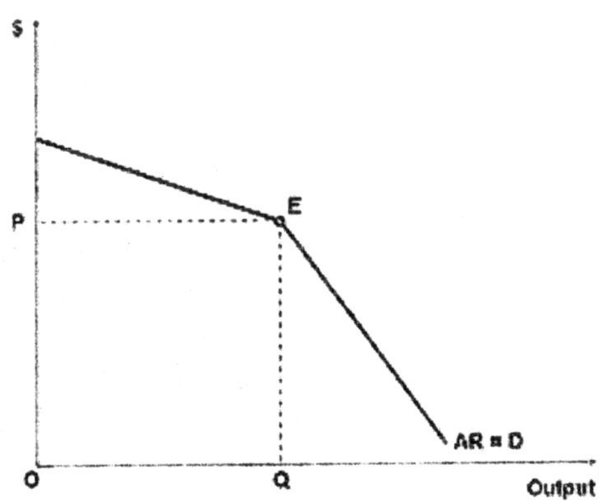

Above the kink, demand is relatively elastic because all other firms' prices remain unchanged. Below the kink, demand is relatively inelastic because all other firms will introduce a similar price cut, eventually leading to a price war. Therefore, the best option for the oligopolist is to produce at point E which is the equilibrium point and the kink point. This is a theoretical model proposed in 1947, which has failed to receive conclusive evidence for support.

In an oligopoly, firms operate under imperfect competition. With the fierce price competitiveness created by this sticky-upward demand curve, firms use non-price competition in order to accrue greater revenue and market share. "Kinked" demand curves are similar to traditional demand curves, as they are downward-sloping. They are distinguished by a hypothesized convex bend with a discontinuity at the bend-the "kink." Thus the first derivative at that point is undefined and leads to a jump discontinuity in the marginal revenue curve.

Classical economic theory assumes that a profit-maximizing producer with some market power (either due to oligopoly or monopolistic competition) will set marginal costs equal to marginal revenue. This idea can be envisioned graphically by the intersection of an upward-sloping marginal cost curve and a downward-sloping marginal revenue curve (because the more one sells, the lower the price must be, so the less a producer earns per unit). In classical theory, any change in the marginal cost structure (how much it costs to make each additional unit) or the marginal revenue structure (how much people will pay for each additional unit) will be immediately reflected in a new price and/or quantity sold of the item. This result does not occur if a "kink" exists. Because of this jump discontinuity in the marginal revenue curve, marginal costs could change without necessarily changing the price or quantity.

The motivation behind this kink is the idea that in an oligopolistic or monopolistically competitive market, firms will not raise their prices because even a small price increase will lose many customers. This is because competitors will generally ignore price increases, with the hope of gaining a larger market share as a result of now having comparatively lower prices. However, even a large price decrease will gain only a few customers because such an action will begin a price war with other firms. The curve is therefore more price-elastic for price increases and less so for price decreases. Firms will often enter the industry in the long run.

Oligopsony

An oligopsony is a market form in which the number of buyers is small while the number of sellers in theory could be large. This typically happens in market for inputs where a small number of firms are competing to obtain factors of production. It contrasts with an oligopoly, where there are many buyers but just a few sellers. An oligopsony is a form of imperfect competition.

The terms monopoly (one seller), monopsony (one buyer), and bilateral monopoly have a similar relationship.

One example of an oligopsony in the world economy is cocoa, where three firms (Cargill, Archer Daniels Midland, and Callebaut) buy the vast majority of world cocoa bean production, mostly from small farmers in third-world countries. Likewise, American tobacco growers face an oligopsony of cigarette makers, where three companies (Altria, Brown & Williamson, and Lorillard Tobacco Company) buy almost 90% of all tobacco grown in the US.

In each of these cases, the buyers have a major advantage over the sellers. They can play off one supplier against another, thus lowering their costs. They can also dictate exact specifications to suppliers, for delivery schedules, quality, and (in the case of agricultural products) crop varieties. They also pass off much of the risks of overproduction, natural losses, and variations in cyclical demand to the suppliers.

Monopoly

In economics, a monopoly exists when a specific individual or an enterprise has sufficient control over a particular product or service to determine significantly the terms on which other individuals shall have access to it. Monopolies are thus characterized by a lack of economic competition for the good or service that they provide and a lack of viable substitute goods. The verb "monopolize" refers to the *process* by which a firm gains persistently greater market share than what is expected under perfect competition.

A monopoly must be distinguished from monopsony, in which there is only one *buyer* of a product or service ; a monopoly may also have monopsony control of a sector of a market. Likewise, a monopoly should be distinguished from a cartel (a form of oligopoly), in which several providers act together to coordinate services, prices or sale of goods. Monopolies can form naturally or through vertical or horizontal mergers. A monopoly is said to be coercive when the monopoly firm actively prohibits competitors from entering the field.

In many jurisdictions, competition laws place specific restrictions on monopolies. Holding a dominant position or a monopoly in the market is not illegal in itself, however certain categories of behaviour can, when a business is dominant, be considered abusive and therefore be met with legal sanctions. A government-granted monopoly or *legal monopoly*, by contrast, is sanctioned by the state, often to provide an incentive to invest in a risky venture or enrich a domestic constituency. The government may also reserve the venture for itself, thus forming a government monopoly.

Economic Analysis

In economics, the study of market structures under imperfect competition begins with the analysis of Monopoly. If there is a single seller in a certain industry and there are no close substitutes for the goods being produced, then the market structure is that of a "pure monopoly". Sometimes, there are many sellers in an industry and/or there exist many close substitutes for the goods being produced, but nevertheless firms retain some market power. This is called monopolistic competition, whereas oligopoly refers to the case where the main theoretical framework revolves around firm's strategic interactions.

Basic Market Structures

There are four basic types of market structures under traditional economic analysis, perfect competition, monopolistic competition, oligopoly and monopoly. A Monopoly is a market structure is which a single supplier produces and sells the product.

Characteristics of a Monopoly

- *Single Seller:* In a monopoly there is one seller of the monopolized good who produces all the output. The firm and industry are identical. In a PC market there are an infinite number of sellers each producing an infinitesimally small quantity of output.
- *Market Power:* Market Power is the ability to affect the terms and conditions of exchange. It is the ability to set your own price. Although a monopoly's market power is high it is not absolute. A monopoly faces a negatively sloped demand curve not a perfectly inelastic curve. Consequently, any price increase will result in the loss of some customers. The monopoly's objective is to maximize profits.

- *High Barriers to Entry and Competition:* Monopolies derive their market power from barriers to entry-circumstances that prevent or greatly impede a potential competitor's entry into the market or ability to compete in the market. There are three major types of barriers to entry; economic, legal and deliberate.

Economic Barriers: Economic barriers include economies of scale, capital requirements, cost advantages and technological superiority.

Economies of Scale: Monopolies are characterized by declining costs over a relatively large range of production. Declining costs coupled with large start up costs give monopolies an advantage over would be competitors. Monopolies are often in a position to cut prices below a new entrant's operating costs and drive them out of the industry. Further the size of the industry relative to the minimum efficient scale may limit the number of firms that can effectively compete within the industry. If for example the industry is large enough to support one firm of minimum efficient scale then other firms entering the industry will operate at a size that is less than MES meaning that these firms cannot produce at an average cost that is competitive with the dominant industry.

Capital Requirements: Production processes that require large investments of capital, or large research and development costs or substantial sunk costs limit the number of firms in an industry. Large fixed costs also make it difficult for a small firm to enter an industry and expand.

Technological Superiority: A monopoly may be better able to acquire, integrate and use the best possible technology in producing its goods while entrants do not have the size or fiscal muscle to use the best available technology. In plain English one large firm can sometimes produce goods cheaper than several small firms.

No Substitute Goods: A monopoly sells a good for which there is no close substitutes. The absence of substitutes makes the demand for the good relatively inelastic enabling monopolies to extract positive profits.

Control of Natural Resources: A prime source of monopoly power is the control of resources that are critical to the production of a final good.

Legal Barriers: Legal rights can provide opportunity to monopolize the market in a good. Intellectual property rights, including patents and copyrights, give a monopolist exclusive control over the production and selling of certain goods. Property rights may give a firm the exclusive control over the materials necessary to produce a good.

Deliberate Actions: A firm wanting to monopolize a market may engage in various types of deliberate action to exclude competitors or eliminate competition. Such actions include collusion, lobbying governmental authorities, and force.

In addition to barriers to entry and competition, barriers to exit may be a source of market power. Barriers to exit are market conditions that make it difficult or expensive for a firm to leave the market. High liquidation costs are a primary barrier to exit. Market exit and shutdown are separate events. The decision whether to shut down or operate is not affected by exit barriers. A firm will shut down if price falls below minimum average variable costs.

Monopoly Versus Competitive Markets

While monopoly and perfect competition mark the extremes of market structures there are many point of similarity. The cost functions are the same. Both monopolies and perfectly competitive firms minimize cost and maximize profit. The shutdown decisions are the same. Both are assumed to face perfectly competitive factors markets. There are distinctions, some of the more important of which are as follows:

Market Power-market power is the ability to control the terms and condition of exchange. Specifically market power is the ability to raise prices without losing all one's customers to competitors. Perfectly competitive (PC) firms have zero market power when it comes to setting prices. All firms in a PC market are price takers. The price is set by the interaction of demand and supply at the market or aggregate level. Individual firms simply take the price determined by the market and produce that quantity of output that maximize the firm's profits. If a PC firm attempted to raise prices above the market level all its "customers" would abandon the firm and purchase at the market price from other firms. A monopoly has considerable although not unlimited market power. A monopoly has the power to set prices or quantities although not both. A monopoly is a price maker. The monopoly is the market and prices are set by the monopolist based on his circumstances and not the interaction of demand and supply. The two primary factors determining monopoly market power are the firm's demand curve and its cost structure.

Product Differentiation: There is zero product differentiation in a perfectly competitive market. Every product is perfectly homogeneous and a perfect substitute. With a monopoly there is high to absolute product differentiation in the sense that there is no available substitute for a monopolized good. The monopolist is the sole supplier of the good in question. A customer either buys from the monopolist on her terms or does without.

Number of Competitors: PC markets are populated by an infinite number of buyers and sellers. Monopoly involves a single seller.

Barriers to Entry-Barriers to entry are factors and circumstances that prevent entry into market by would be competitors and impediments to competition that limit new firm's from operating and expanding within the market. PC markets have free entry and exit. There are no barriers to entry, exit or competition. Monopolies have relatively high barriers to entry. The barriers must be strong enough to prevent or discourage any potential competitor from entering the market.

PED; the price elasticity of demand is the percentage change in demand caused by a one percent change in relative price. A successful monopoly would face a relatively inelastic demand curve. A high coefficient of elasticity is indicative of effective barriers to entry. A PC firm faces what it perceives to be perfectly elastic demand curve. The coefficient of elasticity for a perfectly competitive demand curve is infinite.

Excess Profits-Excess or positive profits are profit above the normal expected return on investment. A PC firm can make excess profits in the short run but excess profits attract competitors who can freely enter the market and drive down prices eventually reducing excess profits to zero. A monopoly can preserve excess profits because barriers to entry prevent competitors from entering the market.

Profit Maximization-A PC firm maximizes profits by producing where price equals marginal costs. A monopoly maximizes profits by producing where marginal revenue equals marginal costs. The rules are equivalent. The demand curve for a PC firm is perfectly elastic-flat. The demand curve is identical to the average revenue curve and the price line. Since the average revenue curve is constant the marginal revenue curve is also constant and equals the demand curve, Average revenue is the same as price (AR = TR/Q = P x Q/Q = P). Thus the price line is also identical to the demand curve. In sum, D = AR = MR = P.

P-Max quantity, price and profit: if a monopolist took over a perfectly competitive industry he would raise prices cut production and realize positive economic profits.

The most significant distinction between a PC firm and a monopoly is that the monopoly faces a downward sloping demand curve rather than the "perceived" perfectly elastic curve of the PC firm. Practically all the variations above mentioned relate to this fact. If there is a downward sloping demand curve then by necessity there is a distinct marginal revenue curve. The implications of this fact are best made manifest with a linear demand curve, Assume that the inverse demand curve is of the form x = a-by. Then the total revenue curve is TR = ay-by2 and the marginal revenue curve is thus MR = a-2by. From this several things are evident. First the marginal revenue curve has the same y intercept as the inverse demand curve. Second the slope of the marginal revenue curve is twice that of the inverse demand curve. Third the x intercept of the marginal revenue curve is half that of the inverse demand curve. What is not quite so evident is that the marginal revenue curve lies below the inverse demand curve at all points. Since all firms maximize profits by equating MR and MC it must be the case that at the profit maximizing quantity MR and MC are less than price which further implies that a monopoly produces less quantity at a higher price than if the market were perfectly competitive.

A company with a monopoly does not undergo price pressure from competitors, although it may face pricing pressure from potential competition. If a company raises prices too high, then others may enter the market if they are able to provide the same good, or a substitute, at a lower price. The idea that monopolies in markets with easy entry need not be regulated against is known as the "revolution in monopoly theory".

A monopolist can extract only one premium, and getting into complementary markets does not pay. That is, the total profits a monopolist could earn if it sought to leverage its monopoly in one market by monopolizing a complementary market are equal to the extra profits it could earn anyway by charging more for the monopoly product itself. However, the one monopoly profit theorem does not hold true if customers in the monopoly good are stranded or poorly informed, or if the tied good has high fixed costs.

A pure monopoly follows the same economic rationality of firms under perfect competition, i.e. to optimize a profit function given some constraints. Under the assumptions of increasing marginal costs, exogenous inputs' prices, and control concentrated on a single agent or entrepreneur, the optimal decision is to equate the marginal cost and marginal revenue of production. Nonetheless, a pure monopoly can-unlike a competitive firm-alter the market price for her own convenience: a decrease in the level of production results in a higher price. In the economics' jargon, it is said that pure monopolies "face a downward-sloping demand". An important consequence of such behaviour is worth noticing: typically a monopoly selects a higher price and lower quantity of output than a price-taking firm; again, less is available at a higher price.

There are important points for one to remember when considering the monopoly model diagram (and its associated conclusions) displayed here. The result that monopoly prices are higher, and production output lower, than a competitive firm follow from a requirement that the monopoly not charge different prices for different customers. That is, the monopoly is restricted from engaging in price discrimination (this is called first degree price discrimination, where all customers are charged the same amount).

If the monopoly were permitted to charge individualized prices (this is called third degree price discrimination), the quantity produced, and the price charged to the *marginal* customer, would be identical to a competitive firm, thus eliminating the deadweight loss; however, all gains from trade (social welfare) would accrue to the monopolist and none to the consumer. In essence, every consumer would be just indifferent between (1) going completely without the product or service and (2) being able to purchase it from the monopolist.

As long as the price elasticity of demand for most customers is less than one in absolute value, it is advantageous for a firm to increase its prices: it then receives more money for fewer goods. With a price increase, price elasticity tends to rise, and in the optimum case above it will be greater than one for most customers.

Monopoly and Efficiency

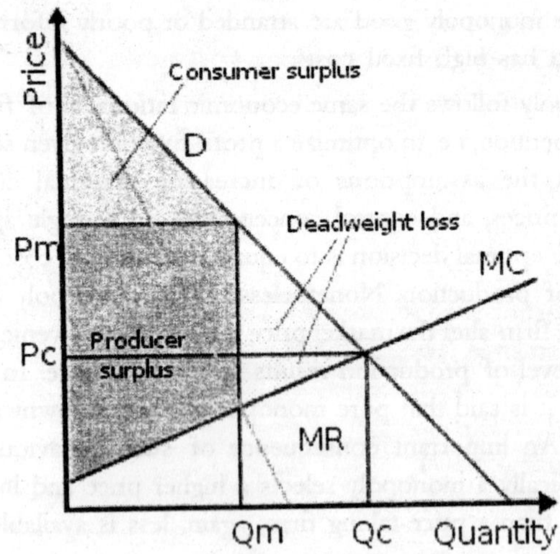

Surpluses and Deadweight loss Created by Monopoly price Setting

According to the standard model, in which a monopolist sets a single price for all consumers, the monopolist will sell a lower quantity of goods at a higher price than would firms under perfect competition. Because the monopolist ultimately forgoes transactions with consumers who value the product or service more than its cost, monopoly pricing creates a deadweight loss referring to potential gains that went neither to the monopolist or to consumers. Given the presence of this deadweight loss, the combined surplus (or wealth) for the monopolist and consumers is necessarily less than the total surplus obtained by consumers under perfect competition. Where efficiency is defined by the total gains from trade, the monopoly setting is less efficient than perfect competition.

It is often argued that monopolies tend to become less efficient and innovative over time, becoming "complacent giants", because they do not have to be efficient or innovative to compete in the marketplace. Sometimes this very loss of psychological efficiency can raise a potential competitor's value enough to overcome market entry barriers, or provide incentive for research and investment into new alternatives The theory of contestable markets argues that in some circumstances (private) monopolies are forced to behave *as if* there were competition because of the risk of losing their monopoly to new entrants. This is likely to happen where a market's barriers to entry are low. It might also be because of the availability in the longer term of substitutes in other markets. For example, a canal monopoly, while worth a great deal in the late eighteenth century United Kingdom, was worth much less in the late nineteenth century because of the introduction of railways as a substitute.

Natural Monopoly

A natural monopoly is a firm which experiences increasing returns to scale over the relevant range of output. A natural monopoly occurs where the average cost of production "declines throughout the relevant range of product demand." The relevant range of product demand is where the average cost curve is below the demand curve. When this situation occurs it is always cheaper for one large firm to supply the market than multiple smaller firms, In fact, absent government intervention such markets will naturally evolve into a monopoly. An early market entrant who takes advantage of the cost structure and can expand rapidly can exclude smaller firms from entering and can drive or buy out other firms. A natural monopoly suffers from the same inefficiencies as any other monopoly. Left to its own devices a profit seeking natural monopoly will produce where marginal revenue equals marginal costs. Regulation of natural monopolies is problematic. Breaking up such monopolies is counter productive. The most frequently used methods dealing with natural monopolies is government regulations and public ownership. Government regulation generally consists of regulatory commissions charged with the principal duty of setting prices. To reduce prices and increase output regulators often use average cost pricing. Under average cost pricing the price and quantity are determined by the intersection of the average cost curve and the demand curve. This pricing scheme eliminates any positive economic profits since price equals average cost. Average cost pricing in not perfect. Regulators must estimate average costs. Firms have a reduced incentive to lower costs. And regulation of this type has not been limited to natural monopolies.

Breaking up Monopolies

When monopolies are not broken through the open market, sometimes a government will step in, either to regulate the monopoly, turn it into a publicly owned monopoly environment, or forcibly break it up. Public utilities, often being naturally efficient with only one operator and therefore less susceptible to efficient breakup, are often strongly regulated or publicly owned. AT&T and Standard Oil are debatable examples of the breakup of a private monopoly: When AT&T was broken up into the "Baby Bell" components, MCI, Sprint, and other companies were able to compete effectively in the long distance phone market.

Law

The existence of a very high market share does not always mean consumers are paying excessive prices since the threat of new entrants to the market can restrain a high-market-share firm's price increases. Competition law does not make merely having a monopoly illegal, but rather abusing the power a monopoly may confer, for instance through exclusionary practices. First it is necessary to determine whether a firm is dominant, or whether it behaves "to an appreciable extent independently of its competitors, customers and ultimately of its consumer." As with collusive conduct, market shares are determined with reference to the particular market in which the firm and product in question is sold.

Under EU law, very large market shares raises a presumption that a firm is dominant, which may be rebuttable. If a firm has a dominant position, then there is "a special responsibility not to allow its conduct to impair competition on the common market". The lowest yet market share of a firm considered "dominant" in the EU was 39.7%. Certain categories of abusive conduct are usually prohibited under the country's legislation, though the lists are seldom closed. The main recognized categories are:

- Predatory pricing
- Tying (commerce) and product bundling
- Limiting supply
- Price discrimination
- Refusal to deal and exclusive dealing.

Despite wide agreement that the above constitute abusive practices, there is some debate about whether there needs to be a causal connection between the dominant position of a company and its actual abusive conduct. Furthermore, there has been some consideration of what happens when a firm merely attempts to abuse its dominant position.

Historical Monopolies

The term "monopoly" first appears in Aristotle's *Politics*, wherein Aristotle describes Thales of Miletus' cornering of the market in olive presses as a monopoly (*μουπωγλιν*).

Common salt (sodium chloride) historically gave rise to natural monopolies. Until recently, a combination of strong sunshine and low humidity or an extension of peat marshes was necessary for winning salt from the sea, the most plentiful source. Changing sea levels periodically caused salt "famines" and communities were forced to depend upon those who controlled the scarce inland mines and salt springs, which were often in hostile areas (the Sahara desert) requiring well-organized security for transport, storage, and distribution. The "Gabelle", a notoriously high tax levied upon salt, played a role in the start of the French Revolution, when strict legal controls were in place over who was allowed to sell and distribute salt.

Robin Gollan argues in *The Coalminers of New South Wales* that anti-competitive practices developed in the Newcastle coal industry as a result of the business cycle. The monopoly was generated by formal meetings of the local management of coal companies agreeing to fix a minimum price for sale at dock. This collusion was known as "The Vend."

The Vend collapsed and was reformed repeatedly throughout the late nineteenth century, cracking under recession in the business cycle. "The Vend" was able to maintain its monopoly due to trade union support, and material advantages (primarily coal geography). In the early twentieth century as a result of comparable monopolistic practices in the Australian coastal shipping business, the vend took on a new form as an informal and illegal collusion between the steamship owners and the coal industry, eventually going to the High Court as Adelaide Steamship Co. Ltd v. R. & AG.

Examples of Legal (and or) Illegal Monopolies

- The salt commission, a legal monopoly in China formed in 758.
- British East India Company; created as a legal trading monopoly in 1600.
- Standard Oil; broken up in 1911, two of its surviving "baby companies" are ExxonMobil and the Chevron Corporation.

- Major League Baseball; survived U.S. anti-trust litigation in 1922, though its special status is still in dispute as of 2009.
- Microsoft; settled anti-trust litigation in the U.S. in 2001; fined by the European Commission in 2004 for 497 million Euros, which was upheld for the most part by the Court of First Instance of the European Communities in 2007. The fine was 1.35 Billion USD in 2008 for noncompliance with the 2004 rule.
- Joint Commission; has a monopoly over whether or not US hospitals are able to participate in the Medicare and Medicaid programs.

Monopsony

In economics, a monopsony "single" is a market form in which only one buyer faces many sellers. It is an example of imperfect competition, similar to a monopoly, in which only one seller faces many buyers. As the only purchaser of a good or service, the "monopsonist" may dictate terms to its suppliers in the same manner that a monopolist controls the market for its buyers.

The term was first introduced by Joan Robinson in her influential book, *The Economics of Imperfect Competition*. Robinson credits classics scholar Bertrand Hallward of Peterhouse College, Cambridge with coining the term.

A single-payer health care system, in which the government is the only "buyer" of health care services, is an example of a monopsony. It has also been argued that Wal-Mart, in the United States, functions as a monopsony in certain market segments, as its buying power for a given item may dwarf the remaining market.

Overview

The term "monopsony power", in a manner similar to "monopoly power" is used by economists as a short hand reference to buyers who face an upwardly sloping supply curve but that are not the only buyer;. better, but more cumbersome terms may be oligopsony or monopsonistic competition. A monopsonist may at the same time be a monopolist.

A monopsonist has market power, because it can affect the market price of the purchased good by varying the quantity bought. Formally, this is so because a monopsonist faces a supply curve with a *finite* (and generally positive) price elasticity. However, one can find this condition– and hence monopsony power – also in markets with more than one buyer. In all such cases the resulting market form is called an oligopsony.

For most practical purposes, what matters is monopsony power as such, whether it is exercised by one or more subjects. In standard microeconomics, where monopsonists or oligopsonists are assumed to be profit-maximizing firms, monopsony power leads to a market failure, due to a *restriction of the quantity purchased* relative to the (Pareto) optimal competitive outcome. Moreover, markets with monopsony power are predicted to react differently to public price regulations. Monopsony power is thus relevant from both the normative and positive points of view. The practical importance of its effects depends however on its actual *intensity*, measured by the size of the deviation from competitive outcomes.

Traditional microeconomics tended to assume that in most modern cases such intensity was small enough to be ignored, justifying as an acceptable approximation the general use of much simpler competitive models. The only and oft-quoted exception to this principle was assumed to be the labour markets of the nineteenth-century "company towns", which were isolated mining centres with only one employer (the mining company) for almost everybody.

This view has however been variously questioned by the more recent literature devoted to the actual *measurement* of monopsony power in observed markets. On the one hand, econometric exercises on the available data have apparently ruled out significant labour monopsony for the typical West Virginia "company towns" of the early twentieth century. On the other hand, many observations appear to suggest significant monopsony power in various *contemporary* labour markets, from baseball players to nurses, college professors and many others. There have also been attempts to measure possible monopsony power in some non-labour markets as well.

Reasoning *a priori*, the specific dynamics of labour markets – and particularly search behaviour by workers – may indeed formally produce upward-sloping labour supply curves faced by most individual firms *in the short run*. On the longer-run supply behaviour of dynamic models, however, it is much more difficult to get simple general results on purely theoretical grounds, so that any firm conclusion must come from case-by-case empirical analysis.

A wide and useful survey of both the theoretical and empirical literature on monopsony in labour markets may be found in Boal and Ransom (1997). The large bibliography provided at the end of Manning (2003).

Static Monopsony in a Labour Market

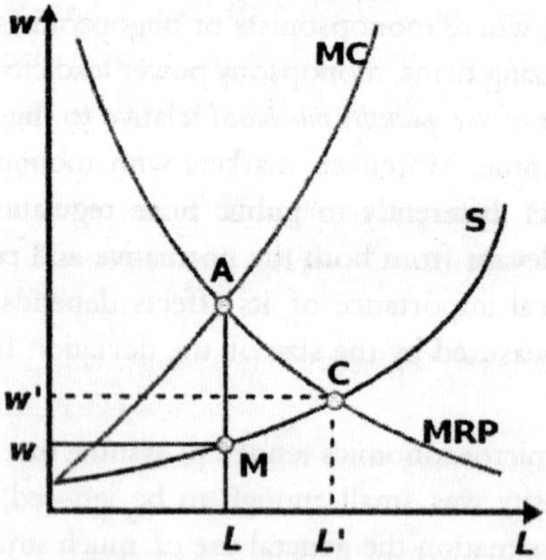

A monopsonist employer maximizes profits with employment *L*, that equates demand, given by the *MRP* curve, to marginal cost *MC* at point *A*. The wage is then determined on the supply curve, at point *M*, and is equal to *w*.

By contrast, a competitive labour market would reach equilibrium at point *C*, where supply *S* equals demand. This would lead to employment *L'* and wage *w'*.

The standard textbook monopsony model refers to static partial equilibrium in a labour market with just one employer who pays the same wage to all its workers. In this model, the employer is assumed to be a firm facing an upward-sloping *labour supply curve* (as generally contrasted with an infinitely elastic labour supply curve), represented by the *S* blue curve in the diagram on the right. This curve relates the wage paid, *w*, to the level of employment, *L*, and is denoted as the increasing function *w*(*L*). Total labour costs are then given by *w*(*L*)*L*. Assume now that the firm has a total revenue *R*, which increases with *L* according to the concave function *R*(*L*). It wants to choose *L* to maximize profits, which are given by:

$$R(L) - w(L)L \cdot$$

This leads to the first-order condition:

$$R'(L) = w(L) + w'(L)L \, .$$

The left-hand side of this expression is the *marginal revenue product* of labour (roughly, the extra revenue produced by an extra worker) and is represented by the red *MRP* curve in the diagram. The right-hand side is the *marginal cost* of labour (roughly, the extra cost due to an extra worker) and is represented by the green *MC* curve in the diagram. It should be noticed that this marginal cost is *higher* than the wage $w(L)$ paid to the new worker by the amount

$$w'(L)L \, .$$

This is because the firm has to increase the wage paid to all the workers it already employs whenever it hires an extra worker. In the diagram, this leads to an *MC* curve that is *above* the supply curve *S*.

The first-order condition for maximum profit is then satisfied at point *A* of the diagram, where the *MC* and *MRP* curves intersect. This determines the profit-maximising employment as *L* on the horizontal axis. The corresponding wage *w* is then obtained from the supply curve, through point *M*.

The monopsonistic equilibrium at *M* should now be contrasted with the equilibrium that would obtain under competitive conditions. Suppose a competitor employer entered the market and offered a wage higher than that at *M*.

Then every employee of the first employer would choose instead to work for the competitor. Moreover, the competitor would gain all the former profits of the first employer, minus a less-than-offsetting amount from the wage increase of the first employer's employees, plus profits arising from additional employees who decided to work in the market because of the wage increase.

But the first employer would respond by offering an even higher wage, poaching the new rival's employees, and so forth. In other words, a group of perfectly competitive firms would be forced, through competition, to intersection *C* rather than *M*. Just as a monopoly is thwarted by the competition to win sales, minimizing prices and maximizing output, competition for employees between the employers in this case would maximize both wages and employment, as shown in the graph.

Welfare Implications

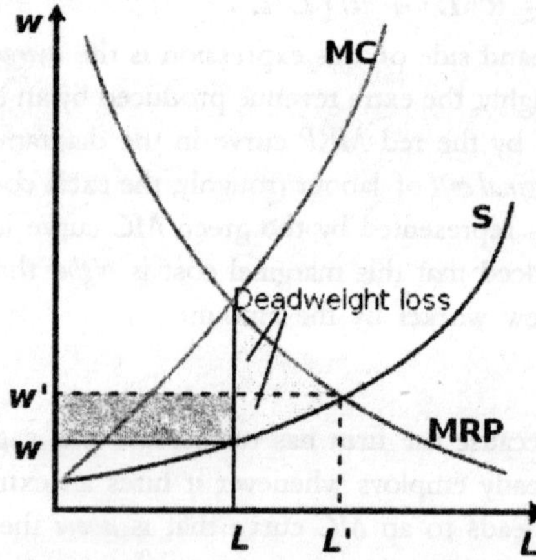

The grey rectangle is a measure of the amount of economic welfare transferred from the workers to their employer(s) by monopsony power. The yellow triangle shows the *overall deadweight loss* inflicted on both groups by the monopsonistic restriction of employment. It is thus a measure of the *market failure* caused by monopsony.

The lower employment and wage caused by monopsony power has two distinct effects on the economic welfare of the people involved. First, it redistributes welfare away from workers and to their employer(s). Secondly, it reduces the aggregate (or social) welfare enjoyed by both groups taken together, as the employers' net gain is smaller than the loss inflicted on workers. The diagram on the right illustrates both effects, using the standard approach based on the notion of economic surplus. According to this notion, the workers' economic surplus (or net gain from the exchange) is given by the area between the *S* curve and the horizontal line corresponding to the wage, up to the employment level. Similarly, the employers' surplus is the area between the horizontal line corresponding to the wage and the *MRP* curve, up to the employment level. The *social* surplus is then the sum of these two areas.

Following such definitions, the grey rectangle in the diagram is the part of the competitive social surplus that has been redistributed from the workers to their employer(s) under monopsony. By contrast, the yellow triangle is the part of the competitive social surplus that has been lost by *both* parties, as a result of the monopsonistic restriction of employment. This is a net social loss and is called *deadweight loss*. It is a measure of the market failure caused by monopsony power, through a wasteful misallocation of resources.

As the diagram suggests, the size of both effects increases with the difference between the marginal revenue product *MRP* and the market wage determined on the supply curve *S*. This difference corresponds to the vertical side of the yellow triangle, and can be expressed as a proportion of the market wage, according to the formula:

$$e = \frac{R'(w) - w}{w}.$$

The ratio *e* has been called the rate of exploitation, and it can be easily shown that it equals the reciprocal of the elasticity of the labour supply curve faced by the firm. Thus the rate of exploitation is zero under competitive conditions, when this elasticity tends to infinity. Empirical estimates of *e* by various means are a common feature of the applied literature devoted to the measurement of observed monopsony power. Finally, it is important to notice that, while the gray-area redistribution effect could be reversed by fiscal policy (i.e., taxing employers and transferring the tax revenue to the workers), this is not so for the yellow-area deadweight loss. The market failure can only be addressed in one of two ways: either by breaking up the monopsony through anti-trust intervention, or by regulating the wage policy of firms. The most common kind of regulation is a binding minimum wage higher than the monopsonistic wage.

Minimum Wage

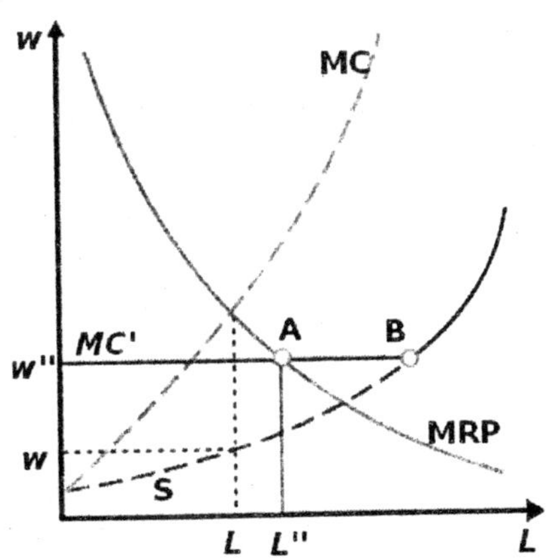

With a binding minimum wage of w'' the marginal cost to the firm becomes the horizontal black MC' line, and the firm maximises profits at A with a higher employment L''. However in this example the minimum wage is higher than the competitive one, leading to ***involuntary unemployment*** equal to the segment AB. A binding minimum wage can be introduced either by law or through collective bargaining, and its possible effects in a special case are shown in the diagram on the right.

Here the minimum wage is w'', higher than the monopsonistic w. At this given wage the firm can now hire all the workers it wants, up to the supply curve, so that in the relevant employment range its marginal cost of labour becomes effectively constant and equal to w'', as shown by the new black horizontal line MC'. Hence the firm maximizes profits at the new intersection point A, choosing the employment level L'', which is higher than the monopsonistic level L. As the reader can check, the rate of exploitation has been reduced to zero. More generally, a binding minimum wage modifies the form of the supply curve faced by the firm, which becomes:

$$w = \begin{cases} w_{min}, & \text{if } w_{min} \geq w(L) \\ w(L), & \text{if } w_{min} \leq w(L) \end{cases}$$

where $w(L)$ is the original supply curve and w_{min} is the minimum wage. The new curve has thus a horizontal first branch and a kink at the point

$$w(L) = w_{min}$$

as is shown in the diagram by the kinked black curve $MC'S$. The resulting equilibria can then fall into one of three classes or regimes, according to the value taken by the minimum wage, as is seen by the following table:

Minimum-wage regimes in monopsonistic labour markets

	Minimum wage	**Resulting equilibrium**
First regime	not higher than monopsony wage	unchanged from monopsony
Second regime	higher than monopsony wage but not higher than competitive wage	at kink of supply curve
Third regime	higher than competitive wage	at intersection where minimum wage equals *MRP*

As it is now seen, the example illustrated by the diagram belongs to the third regime. As a result, there is an excess supply of labour – i.e. *involuntary unemployment* – equal to the segment *AB*. So, although the exploitation rate has vanished, there is still a deadweight loss to society. This illustrates the problems that may arise when the proper level of the binding minimum wage is not exactly known, or cannot be enforced for political reasons.

Yet, even when it is sub-optimal, a minimum wage higher than the market rate raises the level of employment anyway. This is a highly remarkable result, because it only follows under monopsony. Indeed, under competitive conditions any minimum wage higher than the market rate would actually *reduce* employment, according to classical economic models. Thus, spotting the effects on employment of newly introduced minimum wage regulations is among the indirect ways economists use to pin down monopsony power in selected labour markets.

Wage Discrimination

Just like a monopolist, a monopsonistic employer may find that its profits are maximized if it *discriminates* prices. In this case this means paying different wages to different groups of workers even if their MRP is the same, with lower wages paid to the workers who have a lower elasticity of supply of their labour to the firm.

Some researchers have tried to use this fact to explain at least part of the observed wage differentials whereby women earn often less than men, even after controlling for observed productivity differentials. However, all such attempts have had to contend with the statistical fact that in most cases women actually display a *higher* labour supply elasticity than men.

Some authors have argued informally that, while this is so for *market* supply, the reverse may somehow be true of the supply to individual firms. In particular, Manning and others have shown that, in the case of the UK Equal Pay Act, implementation has led to higher employment of women. Since the Act was effectively minimum wage legislation for women, this might perhaps be interpreted as a symptom of monopsonistic discrimination.

Dynamic Problems

In many real-world situations a monopsonist firm will have to maximise its profits *through time*, rather than instantaneously as in the previous static model. In all such cases, any short-run outcomes will have to be balanced against longer-run ones, and the resulting equilibrium may differ.

The simplest dynamic model to bring out this idea, used in Boal and Ransom (1997), is one where the supply of labour to the firm reacts to wage changes with a lag, due for instance to information costs and search behaviour. Assume hence that the supply function has a distributed-lag specification, leading to:

$$L_t = L(w_t, L_{t-1}),$$

where the subscript refers to the time period and L is increasing in both arguments. Inverting this function gives:

$$w_t = w_t(L_t, L_{t-1}),$$

with

$$\frac{\partial w_t}{\partial L_t} \geq 0 \text{ and } \frac{\partial w_t}{\partial L_{t-1}} \leq 0.$$

If the firm has a time-discount rate r, the present value of profits is now given by:

$$\sum_{t=1}^{\infty} [R_t(L_t) - w_t(L_t, L_{t-1})L_t] \left(\frac{1}{1+r}\right)^{t-1}.$$

The tth first-order condition to maximise this present value is:

$$\frac{dR_t}{dL_t} - w_t - \frac{\partial w_t}{\partial L_t} L_t - \frac{\partial w_{t+1}}{\partial L_t} \frac{L_{t+1}}{1+r} = 0.$$

Define next the short-run simultaneous and lagged inverse supply elasticities respectively as:

$$\epsilon_{SR}^{-1} \stackrel{\text{def}}{=} \frac{\partial w_t}{\partial L_t} \frac{L_t}{w_t}, \qquad \epsilon_{SRL}^{-1} \stackrel{\text{def}}{=} \frac{\partial w_{t+1}}{\partial L_t} \frac{L_t}{w_{t+1}}.$$

Now, assume these elasticities to be constant over time. Assume further a steady state, with $L_t = L_{t+1}$ and $w_t = w_{t+1}$. Then the first-order condition gives the exploitation rate as:

$$\epsilon_t \stackrel{\text{def}}{=} \frac{MRP_t - w_t}{w_t} = \epsilon_{SR}^{-1} + \frac{\epsilon_{SRL}^{-1}}{1+r}.$$

Finally, the steady-state long-run inverse elasticity, ϵ_{LR}^{-1}, is given by the sum of the two short-run inverse elasticities defined above, and so one has:

$$e_t = \epsilon_{SR}^{-1}\left(\frac{r}{1+r}\right) + \epsilon_{LR}^{-1}\left(\frac{1}{1+r}\right).$$

The exploitation rate is thus a weighted average of the short-and long-run inverse supply elasticities, where the weight of the long-run one is much bigger, because *r* is much smaller than unity even when the discounting period is one year. It follows that, as the long-run (direct) supply elasticity of labour tends to be much higher than the short-run one, this very simple dynamic model predicts an exploitation rate which is much smaller than the one produced by static analysis.

However, less simplified dynamic models tell less simple stories. Even the employment effect of minimum wages is not as clear cut as static models would have.

Empirical Problems

The simplified dynamics sketched above suggests that the frequent observation of short-run relative inelasticity of labour supply to individual firms may not be very relevant to the diagnosis of significant monopsony power. Efforts to measure the size of the exploitation rate in specific labour markets have hence taken various forms:

- direct measurement of wage and MRP
- estimates of the long-run supply elasticity of labour to firms
- cross-sectional comparisons of wages and employer concentration
- correlations between wages and workers' mobility
- structural estimation of equilibrium search models
- employment effects of minimum wages.

The results of these empirical works are rarely unambiguous. However, even in cases such as coal miners or nurses, most US studies suggest rates of exploitation probably lower than marginal tax rates on workers' incomes, or union relative wage effects.

The better documented instances of significant exploitation are found in the probably rare cases of explicit collusion, such as US baseball before the reserve clause.

The Sources of Labour Monopsony Power

The simpler explanation of monopsony power in labour markets is barriers to entry on the *demand* side. In all such cases, oligopsony would result from oligopoly in the product markets of the industries that use that type of labour as input. If the hypothesis was generally true, one would then find a positive statistical correlation between exploitation, on one side, and industry concentration and firm size on the other. However, numerous statistical studies document significant positive correlations between firm or establishment size and *wages*. These results, by themselves inconsistent with the oligopoly-oligopsony hypothesis, may be due to the prevalence of other factors, such as efficiency wages.

However, monopsony power might also be due to circumstances affecting entry of workers on the *supply* side, directly reducing the elasticity of labour supply to firms. Paramount among these are moving costs for workers, which are also a cause of differentiation among potential employees, possibly leading to discrimination. But a similar effect might also be produced by all the institutional factors that limit labour mobility between firms, including job protection legislation. The requirement that employees in the government or the defence sector is another source of monopsonistic competition, as are requirements for professional certification, for example, a medical degree. Finally, as already noticed, a significant reduction in the short-run elasticity of supply may come from information costs and search behaviour.

An alternative that has been suggested as a source of monopsony power is worker preferences over job characteristics (Bhaskar and To, 1999; Bhaskar, Manning and To, 2002). Such job characteristics can include distance from work, type of work, location, the social environment at work, etc. If different workers have different preferences, employers have local monopsony power over workers that strongly prefer working for them.

Monopsony in Public Administration and Product Markets

The same or similar empirical difficulties dog attempts to identify significant monopsony in non-labour markets, and specifically in markets for intermediate goods bought as inputs by very large firms. Among the most likely US candidates, one finds in the literature:

- trade in technological knowledge: Rodriguez (1975)

- tomatoes for tomato processing: Just and Chern (1980)
- beef for the beef packing industry: Schroeter (1988)
- western coal for electric utilities: Atkinson and Kerkvliet (1989)
- pulpwood and sawlogs: Murray (1995)
- sophisticated weaponry (i.e. jet fighters, tanks, artillery, etc.)
- global warming research funding.

A related issue is the role of monopsony power from the point of view of anti-trust policy affecting vertical integrations. It has been argued that vertical integration by a monopsony – whereby the production of the previously bought input becomes an in-house operation – may reduce or eliminate the inefficiencies due to monopsonistic restriction of purchases.

In Australia, the Pharmaceutical Industry can be viewed as a kind of monopsony, as the Commonwealth government is the principal buyer of products through the Pharmaceutical Benefits Scheme (PBS)

In the US, several, including *Harper's* and the PBS program *Frontline*, have made the case that Wal-Mart is a monopsonist, dictating terms to suppliers, whilst at the same time a monopolist dictating terms to consumers-at least in certain market segments.

Bilateral Monopoly

In a bilateral monopoly there is both a monopoly (a single seller) and monopsony (a single buyer) in the same market.

In such, market price and output will be determined by the non economic forces like bargaining power of both buyer and seller. A bilateral monopoly model is often used in situations where the switching costs of both sides are prohibitively high.

Bilateral monopoly situations are commonly analysed using the theory of Nash bargaining games.

An example of a bilateral monopoly would be when a labour union and a monopolist negotiate.

Industrial Organization-Areas of Study

Price Discrimination

Price discrimination exists when sales of identical goods or services are transacted at different prices from the same provider. In a theoretical market with perfect information, no transaction costs or prohibition on secondary exchange (or re-selling) to prevent arbitrage, price discrimination can only be a feature of monopoly and oligopoly markets, where market power can be exercised.

Otherwise, the moment the seller tries to sell the same good at different prices, the buyer at the lower price can arbitrage by selling to the consumer buying at the higher price but with a tiny discount.

However, market frictions in oligopolies such as the airlines and even in fully competitive retail or industrial markets allow for a limited degree of differential pricing to different consumers. Price discrimination also occurs when it costs more to supply one customer than it does another, and yet the supplier charges both the same price.

The effects of price discrimination on social efficiency are unclear; typically such behaviour leads to lower prices for some consumers and higher prices for others.

Output can be expanded when price discrimination is very efficient, but output can also decline when discrimination is more effective at extracting surplus from high-valued users than expanding sales to low valued users. Even if output remains constant, price discrimination can reduce efficiency by misallocating output among consumers.

Price discrimination requires market segmentation and some means to discourage discount customers from becoming resellers and, by extension, competitors. This usually entails using one or more means of preventing any resale, keeping the different price groups separate, making price comparisons difficult, or restricting pricing information. The boundary set up by the marketer to keep segments separate are referred to as a *rate fence*. Price discrimination is thus very common in services, where resale is not possible; an example is student discounts at museums.

Price discrimination can also be seen where the requirement that goods be identical is relaxed. For example, so-called "premium products" (including relatively simple products, such as cappuccino compared to regular coffee) have a price differential that is not explained by the cost of production. Some economists have argued that this is a form of price discrimination exercised by providing a means for consumers to reveal their willingness to pay.

Types of Price Discrimination

First Degree Price Discrimination

In first degree price discrimination, price varies by customer's willingness or ability to pay. This arises from the fact that the value of goods is subjective. A customer with low price elasticity is less deterred by a higher price than a customer with high price elasticity of demand. As long as the price elasticity (in absolute value) for a customer is less than one, it is very advantageous to increase the price: the seller gets more money for fewer goods. With an increase of the price elasticity tends to rise above one. One can show that in the optimum the price, as it varies by customer, is inversely proportional to one minus the reciprocal of the price elasticity of that customer at that price. This assumes that the consumer passively reacts to the price set by the seller, and that the seller knows the demand curve of the customer. In practice however there is a bargaining situation, which is more complex: the customer may try to influence the price, such as by pretending to like the product less than he or she really does or by threatening not to buy it.

An alternative way to understand First Degree Price Discrimination is as follows: This type of price discrimination is primarily theoretical because it requires the seller of a good or service to know the absolute maximum price that every consumer is willing to pay. As above, it is true that consumers have different price elasticities, but the seller is not concerned with such. The seller is concerned with the maximum willingness to pay (or reservation price) of each customer. By knowing the reservation price, the seller is able to absorb the entire market surplus, thus taking all consumer surplus from the consumer and transforming it into revenues. From a social welfare perspective, first degree price discrimination is not undesirable. That is, the market is still entirely efficient and there is no deadweight loss to society. However, it is the complete opposite of a perfectly competitive market. In a perfectly competitive market, the consumers receive the bulk of surplus. In a market with first degree price discrimination, the seller(s) capture all surplus. Efficiency is unchanged but the wealth is transferred. This type of market does not much exist in reality, hence it is primarily theoretical. Examples of where this might be observed are in markets where consumers bid for tenders, though still, in this case, the practice of collusive tendering undermines efficiency.

Second Degree Price Discrimination

In second degree price discrimination, price varies according to quantity sold. Larger quantities are available at a lower unit price. This is particularly widespread in sales to industrial customers, where bulk buyers enjoy higher discounts.

Additionally to second degree price discrimination, sellers are not able to differentiate between different types of consumers. Thus, the suppliers will provide incentives for the consumers to differentiate themselves according to preference. As above, quantity "discounts", or non-linear pricing, is a means by which suppliers use consumer preference to distinguish classes of consumers. This allows the supplier to set different prices to the different groups and capture a larger portion of the total market surplus.

Third Degree Price Discrimination

In third degree price discrimination, price varies by attributes such as location or by customer segment, or in the most extreme case, by the individual customer's identity; where the attribute in question is used as a proxy for ability/willingness to pay.

Additionally to third degree price discrimination, the supplier(s) of a market where this type of discrimination is exhibited are capable of differentiating between consumer classes. Examples of this differentiation are student or senior discounts.

For example, a student or a senior consumer will have a different willingness to pay than an average consumer, where the reservation price is presumably lower because of budget constraints.

Thus, the supplier sets a lower price for that consumer because the student or senior has a more elastic price elasticity of demand. The supplier is once again capable of capturing more market surplus than would be possible without price discrimination.

Note that it is not always advantageous to the company to price discriminate even if it is possible, especially for second and third degree discrimination.

In some circumstances, the demands of different classes of consumers will encourage suppliers to simply ignore one/some class(es) and target entirely to the other(s). Whether it is profitable to price discriminate is determined by the specifics of a particular market.

Price Skimming

In price skimming, price varies over time. Typically a company starts selling a new product at a relatively high price then gradually reduces the price as the low price elasticity segment gets satiated. Price skimming is closely related to the concept of yield management.

Combination

These types are not mutually exclusive. Thus a company may vary pricing by location, but then offer bulk discounts as well. Airlines use several different types of price discrimination, including:

- Bulk discounts to wholesalers, consolidators, and tour operators
- Incentive discounts for higher sales volumes to travel agents and corporate buyers
- Seasonal discounts, incentive discounts, and even general prices that vary by location. The price of a flight from say, Singapore to Beijing can vary widely if one buys the ticket in Singapore compared to Beijing (or New York or Tokyo or elsewhere). In online ticket sales this is achieved by using the customer's credit card billing address to determine his location.
- Discounted tickets requiring advance purchase and/or Saturday stays. Both restrictions have the effect of excluding business travellers, who typically travel during the workweek and arrange trips on shorter notice.
- First degree price discrimination based on customer. It is not accidental that hotel or car rental firms may quote higher prices to their loyalty program's top tier members than to the general public.

Modern Taxonomy

The first/second/third degree taxonomy of price discrimination is due to Pigou (*Economics of Welfare*, 4th edition, 1932). However, these categories are not mutually exclusive or exhaustive. Ivan Png (*Managerial Economics*, 2nd edition, 2002) suggests an alternative taxonomy:

- Complete discrimination — where each user purchases up to the point where the user's marginal benefit equals the marginal cost of the item;
- Direct segmentation — where the seller can condition price on some attribute (like age or gender) that *directly* segments the buyers;

- Indirect segmentation — where the seller relies on some proxy (eg, package size, usage quantity, coupon) to structure a choice that *indirectly* segments the buyers.

The hierarchy—complete/direct/indirect—is in decreasing order of:

- profitability and.
- information requirement.

Complete price discrimination is most profitable, and requires the seller to have the most information about buyers. Indirect segmentation is least profitable, and requires the seller to have the least information about buyers.

Explanation

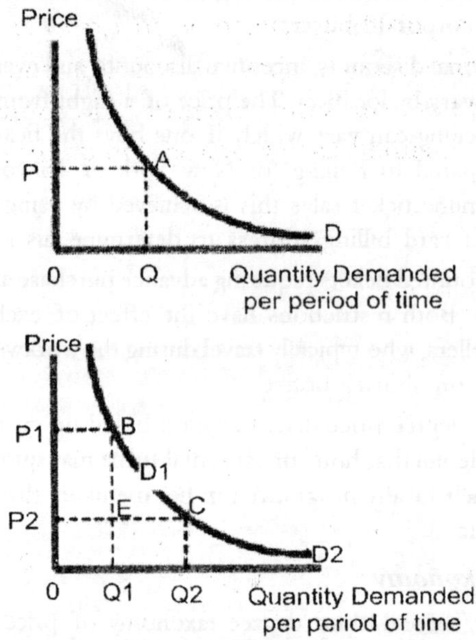

Sales Revenue Without and with Price Discrimination

The purpose of price discrimination is generally to capture the market's consumer surplus. This surplus arises because, in a market with a single clearing price, some customers (the very low price elasticity segment) would have been prepared to pay more than the single market price. Price discrimination transfers some of this surplus from the consumer to the producer/marketer. Strictly, a consumer surplus need not exist, for example where some below-cost selling is beneficial due to fixed costs or economies of scale. An example is a high-speed internet connection shared by two consumers in a single building; if one is willing to pay less than half the cost, and the other willing to make up the rest but not to pay the entire cost, then price discrimination is necessary for the purchase to take place.

It can be proved mathematically that a firm facing a downward sloping demand curve that is convex to the origin will always obtain higher revenues under price discrimination than under a single price strategy. This can also be shown diagrammatically. In the top diagram, a single price (P) is available to all customers. The amount of revenue is represented by area P, A,Q, O. The consumer surplus is the area above line segment P, A but below the demand curve (D).

With price discrimination, (the bottom diagram), the demand curve is divided into two segments (D1 and D2). A higher price (P1) is charged to the low elasticity segment, and a lower price (P2) is charged to the high elasticity segment. The total revenue from the first segment is equal to the area P1,B, Q1,O. The total revenue from the second segment is equal to the area E, C,Q2,Q1. The sum of these areas will always be greater than the area without discrimination assuming the demand curve resembles a rectangular hyperbola with unitary elasticity. The more prices that are introduced, the greater the sum of the revenue areas, and the more of the consumer surplus is captured by the producer.

Note that the above requires both first and second degree price discrimination: the right segment corresponds partly to different people than the left segment, partly to the same people, willing to buy more if the product is cheaper. It is very useful for the price discriminator to determine the optimum prices in each market segment. This is done in the next diagram where each segment is considered as a separate market with its own demand curve. As usual, the profit maximizing output (Qt) is determined by the intersection of the marginal cost curve (MC) with the marginal revenue curve for the total market (MRt).

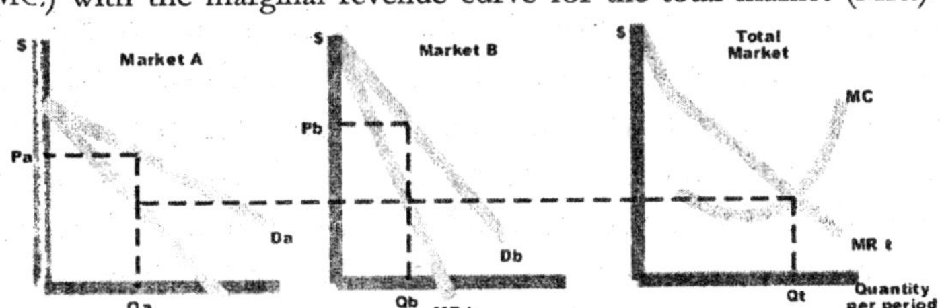

Multiple Market Price Determination

The firm decides what amount of the total output to sell in each market by looking at the intersection of marginal cost with marginal revenue (profit maximization). This output is then divided between the two markets, at the equilibrium marginal revenue level. Therefore, the optimum outputs are Qa and Qb. From the demand curve in each market we can determine the profit maximizing prices of Pa and Pb.

It is also important to note that the marginal revenue in both markets at the optimal output levels must be equal, otherwise the firm could profit from transferring output over to whichever market is offering higher marginal revenue.

Given that Market 1 has a price elasticity of demand of E1 and Market of E2, the optimal pricing ration in Market 1 versus Market 2 is $P1/P2 = [1 - 1/E2]/[1 - 1/E1]$.

Examples of Price Discrimination

Retail Price Discrimination

In certain circumstances, it is a violation of the Robinson-Patman Act, (a 1936 Federal U.S. antitrust statute) for manufacturers of goods to sell their products to similarly situated retailers at different prices based solely on the volume of products purchased.

Travel Industry

Airlines and other travel companies use differentiated pricing regularly, as they sell travel products and services simultaneously to different market segments. This is often done by assigning capacity to various booking classes, which sell for different prices and which may be linked to fare restrictions. The restrictions or "fences" help ensure that market segments buy in the booking class range that has been established for them. For example, schedule-sensitive business passengers who are willing to pay $300 for a seat from city A to city B cannot purchase a $150 ticket because the $150 booking class contains a requirement for a Saturday night stay, or a 15-day advance purchase, or another fare rule that discourages, minimizes, or effectively prevents a sale to business passengers.

Notice however that in this example "the seat" is not really always the same product. That is, the business person who purchases the $300 ticket may be willing to do so in return for a seat on a high-demand morning flight, for full refundability if the ticket is not used, and for the ability to upgrade to first class if space is available for a nominal fee. On the same flight are price-sensitive passengers who are not willing to pay $300, but who are willing to fly on a lower-demand flight (say one leaving an hour earlier), or via a connection city (not a non-stop flight), and who are willing to forgo refundability.

On the other hand, an airline may also apply differential pricing to "the same seat" over time, e.g. by discounting the price for an early or late booking (without changing any other fare condition). This could present an arbitrage opportunity in the absence of any restriction on reselling. However, passenger name changes are typically prevented or financially penalized by contract.

Since airlines often fly multi-leg flights, and since no-show rates vary by segment, competition for the seat has to take in the spatial dynamics of the product. Someone trying to fly A-B is competing with people trying to fly A-C through city B on the same aircraft. This is one reason airlines use yield management technology to determine how many seats to allot for A-B passengers, B-C passengers, and A-B-C passengers, at their varying fares and with varying demands and no-show rates.

With the rise of the Internet and the growth of low fare airlines, airfare pricing transparency has become far more pronounced. Passengers discovered it is quite easy to compare fares across different flights or different airlines. This helped put pressure on airlines to lower fares. Meanwhile, in the recession following the September 11, 2001, attacks on the U.S., business travellers and corporate buyers made it clear to airlines that they were not going to be buying air travel at rates high enough to subsidize lower fares for non-business travellers. This prediction has come true, as vast numbers of business travellers are buying airfares only in economy class for business travel.

There are sometimes group discounts on rail tickets and passes. This may be in view of the alternative of going by car together.

Premium Pricing

For certain products, premium products are priced at a level (compared to "regular" or "economy" products) that is well beyond their marginal cost of production. For example, a coffee chain may price regular coffee at $1, but "premium" coffee at $2.50 (where the respective costs of production may be $0.90 and $1.25). Economists such as Tim

Harford in the Undercover Economist have argued that this is a form of price discrimination: by providing a choice between a regular and premium product, consumers are being asked to reveal their degree of price sensitivity (or willingness to pay) for comparable products. Similar techniques are used in pricing business class airline tickets and premium alcoholic drinks, for example.

This effect can lead to (seemingly) perverse incentives for the producer. If, for example, potential business class customers will pay a large price differential only if economy class seats are uncomfortable while economy class customers are more sensitive to price than comfort, airlines may have substantial incentives to purposely make economy seating uncomfortable.

In the example of coffee, a restaurant may gain more economic profit by making poor quality regular coffee—more profit is gained from up-selling to premium customers than is lost from customers who refuse to purchase inexpensive but poor quality coffee. In such cases, the net social utility should also account for the "lost" utility to consumers of the regular product, although determining the magnitude of this foregone utility may not be feasible.

Segmentation by Age Group and Student Status

Many movie theatres, amusement parks, tourist attractions, and other places have different admission prices per market segment: typical groupings are Youth, Student, Adult, and Senior. Each of these groups typically have a much different demand curve. Children, people living on student wages, and people living on retirement generally have much less disposable income.

Discounts for Members of Certain Occupations

Many businesses, especially in the Southern United States, offer reduced prices to active military members. In addition to increased sales to the target group, businesses benefit from the resulting positive publicity, leading to increased sales to the general public. Less publicized are discounts to other service workers such as police; off-duty police customers in high-crime areas are said to constitute free security.

Employee Discounts

Discounts that businesses give to their own employees are also a form of price discrimination.

Retail Incentives

A variety of incentive techniques may be used to increase market share or revenues at the retail level. These include discount coupons, rebates, bulk and quantity pricing, seasonal discounts, and frequent buyer discounts.

Incentives for Industrial Buyers

Many methods exist to incentivize wholesale or industrial buyers. These may be quite targeted, as they are designed to generate specific activity, such as buying more frequently, buying more regularly, buying in bigger quantities, buying new products with established ones, and so on.

Thus, there are bulk discounts, special pricing for long-term commitments, non-peak discounts, on high-demand goods to incentivize buying lower-demand goods, rebates, and many others. This can help the relations between the firms involved.

Gender-Based Examples

Many gender-based price differences are held to be illegal in countries such as the United States and the United Kingdom.

"Ladies' Night"

Many North American or European nightclubs feature a "ladies' night" in which women are offered discount or free drinks, or are absolved from payment of cover charges. This differs from conventional price discrimination in that the primary motive is not, usually, to increase revenue at the expense of consumer surplus.

Dry Cleaning

Dry cleaners typically charge higher prices for the laundering of women's clothes than for men's. Some US communities, have reacted by outlawing the practice. Dry cleaners justify the price differences because women's clothes typically require far more time to press than men's clothes due to more pleating.

Haircutting

Women's haircuts are often more expensive than men's haircuts which in past times could be accounted for as women generally had longer, more complex hairstyles whereas men generally had shorter hairstyles. Nowadays men's and women's styles are more varied but the price discrimination continues. Some salons have modified their pricing to reflect "long hair" versus "short hair" or style instead of gender.

Financial Aid in Education

Financial aid as offered by U.S. colleges and universities is a form of price discrimination that is widely accepted, and completely legal.

Middle-and lower-income students may be offered discounts in the form of tuition waivers, scholarships, work-study programs that pay partly in free course hours, and government guaranteed loans.

Haggling

Many cultures involve haggling in market transactions — inflated prices are posted, but the customer can negotiate with the vendor. In the United States, haggling is rare to non-existent in retail, but common when automobiles and homes are sold. Negotiation often requires knowledge, confidence, and the ability to manage confrontational personalities, and vendors know that many customers will pay higher prices in order to avoid negotiating.

International Price Discrimination

Pharmaceutical companies may charge customers living in wealthier countries (such as the United States) a much higher price than for identical drugs in poorer nations, as is the case with the sale of anti-retroviral drugs in Africa. Since the purchasing power of African consumers is much lower, sales would be extremely limited without price discrimination. The ability of pharmaceutical companies to maintain price differences between countries is often reinforced by national drugs laws and regulations. (or lack thereof)

Another example is textbooks. Publishers such as Prentice Hall and Pearson have low cost editions of textbooks for countries such as India. The textbooks are often printed on cheaper paper, are paperbacks and priced at 15-20% of the dollar price. This pricing has largely eliminated the practice of photo copying these books.

Although not common in modern times, governments have traditionally raised revenues from tariffs. When these are not flat tariffs, the government effectively sets the prices of goods that are not produced locally and are only imported.

Even online sales for non material goods, which do not have to be shipped, may change according to the geographic location of the buyer. A song in Apple's iTunes costs 79 pence (1.49 USD) for Britons but only 99 cents for Americans. (~50% more for the same song) These differences may arise because of changes in exchange rates that occur much more frequently than changes in prices, or they may arise because the license-holders (in this case, record companies) are enforcing their existing pricing policy on new licensees or intermediaries.

Academic Pricing

Companies will often offer discounted software to students and faculty at K-12 and university levels. These may be labelled as academic versions, but perform the same as the full price retail software. Academic versions of the most expensive software suites may be priced as little as one fifth or less of retail price. Some academic software may have differing licenses than retail versions, usually disallowing their use in activities for profit or expiring the license after a given number of months. This also has the characteristics of an "initial offer"-that is, the profits from an academic customer may come partly in the form of future non-academic sales if they get "hooked" on the product.

Dual Pricing

Even within a country, differentiated pricing may be established to ensure that citizens receive lower prices than non-citizens; this is known as dual pricing. This is particularly common for goods that are subsidized or otherwise provided by the state (and hence paid by taxpayers). Thus Finns, Thais, and Indians (among others) may purchase special fare tickets for public transportation that are available only to citizens. Many countries also maintain separate admission charges for museums, national parks and similar facilities, the usually professed rationale being that citizens should be able to educate themselves and enjoy the country's natural wonders cheaply, but other visitors should pay the market rate.

Many publicly run universities in the United States are subsidized by taxpayers of the state in which they are located; residents of said state are frequently given a discount on tuition as a result.

Wage Discrimination

Wage discrimination is when the price of equivalent labour is discriminated among different groups of workers. This may be seen as just one kind of price discrimination or as an example of its inverse, one buyer buying identical goods at different rates.

Price Discrimination by Online Search Type

Some online stores and companies attempt to price discriminate between their customers by using information they gather about how a particular customer is searching for a product. For example, some travel firms have been shown to mark-up prices for all the holiday packages they list when a customer asks to see their holidays ranked with the most expensive package first (which suggests the customer may be price insensitive). The same packages may be available for less if the customer changes their search type. Variants of this behaviour have been reported on other e-commerce sites, where the more specific your search for a particular good, the lower price is displayed for that good.

Universal Pricing

Universal pricing is the opposite of price discrimination — one price is offered for the good or service. This is usually preferred by consumers over tiered pricing For example, the European Union is currently making efforts to set a single-price protocol for automobile sales.

Two Necessary Conditions for Price Discrimination

There are two conditions that must be met if a price discrimination scheme is to work. First the firm must be able to identify market segments by their price elasticity of demand and second the firms must be able to enforce the scheme. For example, airlines routinely engage in price discrimination by charging high prices for customers with relatively inelastic demand-business travellers-and discount prices for tourist who have relatively elastic demand, The airlines enforce the scheme by making the tickets non-transferable thus preventing a tourist from buying a ticket at a discounted price and selling it to a business traveller (arbitrage). Airlines must also prevent business travellers from directly buying discount tickets. Airlines accomplish this by imposing advance ticketing requirements or minimum stay requirements conditions that it would be difficult for average business traveller to meet.

Price Discrimination and Imperfect Competition

Firms frequently segment customers according to price sensitivity in order to price discriminate and increase profits. In some settings, consumer heterogeneity can be directly observed and a firm can base its pricing upon contractible consumer characteristics; in other settings, heterogeneity is not directly observable, but can be indirectly elicited by offering menus of products and prices and allowing consumers to self-select. In both cases, the firm seeks to price its wares as a function of each consumer's underlying demand elasticity, extracting more surplus and increasing sales to elastic customers in the process.

When the firm is a monopolist with market power, the underlying theory of price discrimination is now well understood, as explained, for example, by Varian (1989) in an earlier volume in this series. On the other extreme, when markets are perfectly competitive and firms have neither short-run nor long-run market power, the law of one price applies and price discrimination cannot exist. Economic reality, of course, largely lies somewhere in between the textbook extremes, and most economists agree that price discrimination arises in oligopoly settings. This chapter explores price discrimination in these imperfectly competitive markets, surveying the theoretical literature.

Price discrimination exists when prices vary across customer segments that cannot be entirely explained by variations in marginal cost. Stigler's (1987) definition makes this precise: a firm price discriminates when the ratio of prices is different from the ratio of marginal costs for two goods offered by a firm. Such a definition, of course, requires that one is careful in calculating marginal costs to include all relevant shadow costs. This is particularly true where costly capacity and aggregate demand uncertainty play critical roles, as discussed in section 8. Similarly, where discrimination occurs over the provision of quality, as reviewed in section 6, operationalizing this definition requires using the marginal prices of qualities and the associated marginal costs.

Even with this moderately narrow definition of price discrimination, there remains a considerable variety of theoretical models that address issues of rice discrimination and imperfect competition. We further limit attention in this survey to the straightforward setting of symmetric firms competing in a retail market; even here, there are numerous theories to explore. These include third-degree price discrimination (section 3), purchase-history price discrimination (section 4), intrapersonal price discrimination (section 5), second-degree price discrimination and nonlinear pricing (section 6), product bundling (section 7), and demand uncertainty and price rigidities (section 8). Unfortunately, we must prune a few additional areas of inquiry, leaving some models of imperfect competition and price discrimination unexamined. Among the more notable omissions in this chapter are price discrimination in vertical structures, imperfect information and costly search, the commitment effect of price discrimination policies, collusion and intertemporal price discrimination, and the strategic effect of product lines in imperfectly competitive settings.

It is well known that price discrimination is only feasible under certain conditions: (i) firm(s) have short-run market power, (ii) consumers can be segmented either directly or indirectly, and (iii) arbitrage across differently priced goods is infeasible. Given that these conditions are satisfied, an individual firm will typically have an incentive to price discriminate.

The form of price discrimination will depend importantly on the nature of market power, the form of consumer heterogeneity, and the availability of various segmenting mechanisms.

A firm can typically extract greater consumer surplus by varying the marginal price and screening consumers according to their revealed consumptions. This use of nonlinear pricing as a sorting mechanism is typically referred to as second-degree price discrimination.

More generally, in a richer setting with heterogeneity over observable and unobservable characteristics, we expect that the monopolist will practice some combination of direct and indirect price discrimination—offering P(q, _o), but using the price schedule to sort over unobservable characteristics.

While one can categorize price discrimination strategies as either direct or indirect, it is also useful to catalog strategies according to whether they discriminate across consumers (interpersonal price discrimination) or across units for the same consumer (intrapersonal price discrimination). Intrapersonal price discrimination is a variation of price/marginalcost ratios across the portfolio of goods purchased by a given consumer (i.e., cross-consumer heterogeneity is held constant). For example, suppose that there is no interconsumer heterogeneity so that _ is fixed. There will generally remain some intraconsumer heterogeneity over the marginal value of each unit of consumption so that a firm cannot extract all consumer surplus using a linear price. Here, a firm can capture the consumer surplus associated with intraconsumer heterogeneity, either by offering a nonlinear price schedule equal to the individual consumer's compensated demand curve or by offering a simpler two-part tariff. We will address these issues more in section 5.11 Elsewhere in this chapter, we will focus on interpersonal price discrimination, with the implicit recognition that intra-personal price discrimination often occurs simultaneously.

The methodology of monopoly price discrimination is both useful and misleading in illuminating the effects of discrimination by imperfectly competitive firms. It is useful because the monopoly methods can frequently be used to calculate each firm's best response to its competitors' policies. Just as one can solve for the best-response function in a Cournot quantity game by deriving a residual demand curve and proceeding as if the firm was a monopolist on this residual market, we can also solve for best responses in more complex price discrimination games by deriving residual market demand curves. Unfortunately, our intuitions from the monopoly models can be misleading, because we are ultimately interested in the equilibrium of the firms' best-response functions rather than a single optimal pricing strategy. For example, while it is certainly the case that, ceteris paribus, a single uniformpricing firm will weakly benefit by introducing price discrimination, if every firm were to switch from uniform pricing to price discrimination, profits may fall for the entire industry.

Whether profits fall depends upon whether the additional surplus extraction allowed by price discrimination (the standard effect in the monopoly setting) exceeds the additional competitive externality if discrimination increases the intensity of price competition. This comparison, in turn, depends upon the details of the markets, as will be explained. The pages that follow consist largely of evaluations of these interactions between price discrimination and imperfect competition.

When evaluating the impact of price discrimination in imperfectly competitive environments, two related comparisons are relevant. First, starting from a setting of imperfect competition and uniform pricing, what are the welfare changes from allowing firms to price discriminate? Second, starting from a setting of monopoly and price discrimination, what are the welfare effects of increasing competition? Because the theoretical predictions of the models often depend upon the nature of competition, consumer preferences and consumer heterogeneity, we shall pursue these questions by examining a collection of specialized models that illuminate the broad themes of this literature and illustrate how the implications of competitive price discrimination compare to uniform pricing and monopoly. In sections 2-7, we explore variations on these themes, by varying the forms of competition, preference heterogeneity, and segmenting devices. Initially in section 2, we begin with the benchmark of first-degree, perfect price discrimination. In section 3, we turn to the classic setting of third-degree price discrimination, applied to the case of imperfectly competitive firms. In section 4, we examine an important class of models that extends third-degree price discrimination to dynamic settings, where price offers may be conditioned on a consumer's purchase history from rivalsa form of price discrimination that can only exist under competition. In section 5, we study intrapersonal price discrimination. Section 6 brings together several diverse theoretical approaches to modelling imperfectly competitive second-degree price discrimination, comparing and contrasting the results to those under monopoly. Product bundling (as a form of price discrimination) in imperfectly competitive markets is reviewed in section 7. Models of demand uncertainty and price rigidities are introduced in section 8.

First-degree Price Discrimination

First-degree (or perfect) price discrimination—which arises when the seller can capture all consumer surplus by pricing each unit at precisely the consumer's marginal willingness to pay—serves as an important benchmark and starting point for exploring more subtle forms of pricing. When the seller controls a monopoly, the monopolist obtains the entire social surplus, and so profit maximization is synonymous with maximizing social welfare. How does the economic intuition of this simple model translate to oligopoly?

The oligopoly game of perfect price discrimination is quite simple to analyse, even in its most general form. Following Spulber (1979), suppose that there are n firms, each selling a (possibly differentiated) product, but that each firm has the ability to price discriminate in the first degree and extract all of the consumer surplus under its residual demand curve.

In this oligopoly game of perfect price discrimination, the marginal consumer purchases at marginal cost, so, under mild technical assumptions, social surplus is maximized. In this setting, unlike the imperfect price discrimination settings which follow, the welfare effect of price discrimination is immediate, just as in monopoly perfect price discrimination. A few differences exist, however.

First, while consumers obtain none of the surplus under the residual demand curves, it does not follow that consumers obtain no surplus at all; rather, for each firm i, they obtain no surplus from the addition of the ith firm's product to the current availability of n"1 other goods. If the goods are close substitutes and marginal costs are constant, the residual demand curves are highly elastic and consumers may nonetheless obtain considerable non-residual surplus from the presence of competition. The net effect of price discrimination on total consumer surplus requires an explicit treatment of consumer demand.

Second, it may be the case that each firm's residual demand curve is more elastic when its rivals can perfectly price discriminate than when they are forced to price uniformly.

Thus, while each firm prefers the ability to perfectly price discriminate itself, the total industry profit may fall when price discrimination is allowed, depending on the form of competition and consumer preferences.

We will see a clear example of this in the Hotelling demand model of These and Vives (1988) which examines discriminatory pricing based on observable location. In this simple setting, third-degree price discrimination is perfect, but firms are worse off and would prefer to commit collectively to uniform-pricing strategies.

Third, if n is endogenous, if entry with fixed costs occurs until long-run profits are driven to zero, and if consumer surplus is entirely captured by price discrimination, then price discrimination lowers social welfare compared to uniform pricing. This conclusion follows immediately from the fact that consumer surplus is zero and entry dissipates profits, leading to zero social surplus from the presence of the market. Uniform pricing typically leaves some consumer surplus (and hence positive social welfare). Again, whether consumer surplus is entirely captured by price discrimination requires a more explicit analysis of demand.

Rather than further explore the stylized setting of first-degree price discrimination, we instead turn to explicit analyses undertaken for each of the imperfect price discrimination strategies studied in the ensuing sections.

Third-degree price Discrimination

The classic theory of third-degree price discrimination by a monopolist selling to several distinct markets is straightforward: the optimal price-discriminating prices are found by applying the familiar inverse-elasticity rule to each market separately. If instead of monopoly, however, oligopolists compete in each market, then each firm applies the inverse-elasticity rule using its own residual demand curve—an equilibrium construction. Here, the crossprice elasticities of demand play a central role in determining equilibrium prices and outputs.

These cross-price elasticities, in turn, depend critically upon consumer preferences and the form of consumer heterogeneity.

Welfare Analysis

With third-degree price discrimination, there are three potential sources of social inefficiency.

First, aggregate output over all market segments may be too low if prices exceed marginal cost. To this end, we seek to understand the conditions for which price discrimination leads to an increase or decrease in aggregate output relative to uniform pricing.

Second, for a given level of aggregate consumption, price discrimination will typically generate interconsumer misallocations relative to uniform pricing; hence, aggregate output will not be efficiently distributed to the highest-value ends. And third, there may be inter-firm inefficiencies as a given consumer may be served by an inefficient firm, perhaps purchasing from a more distant or higher-cost firm to obtain a price discount. In the following, much is made of the relationship between aggregate output and welfare. If the same aggregate output is generated under uniform pricing as under price discrim-ination, then price discrimination must necessarily lower social welfare because output is allocated with multiple prices; with a uniform price, interconsumer misallocations are not possible. Therefore, holding production inefficiencies fixed, an increase in aggregate output is a necessary condition for price discrimination to increase welfare under monopoly. Varian (1985) made this point in the context of monopoly, but the economic logic applies more generally to imperfect competition, providing that the firms are equally efficient at production and the number of firms is fixed. Because we can easily make statements only about aggregate output for many models of third-degree price discrimination, this result will prove useful, giving us some limited power to draw welfare conclusions.

There are two common approaches to modelling imperfect competition: quantity competition with homogeneous goods and price competition with product differentiation. The simple quantity-competition model of oligopoly price discrimination is presented in section

We then turn to price-setting models of competition. Within price-setting games, we further distinguish two sets of models based upon consumer demands. In the first setting (section 3.3), all firms agree in their ranking of high-demand (or "strong") markets and low-demand (or "weak") markets. Here, whether the strong markets are more competitive than the weak markets is critical for many economic conclusions. In the second setting (section 3.4), firms are asymmetric in their ranking of strong and weak markets; e.g., firm a's strong market is firm b's weak market and conversely. With asymmetry, equilibrium prices can move in patterns that are not possible under symmetric rankings and different economic insights present themselves. Following the treatment of price-setting games, we take up the topics of third-degree price discrimination with endogenous entry (section 3.5) and private restrictions on price discrimination (section 3.6).

Several observations regarding the effects of competition follow immediately from this framework. First, it follows that marginal revenues are also equal across market segments, just as in monopoly. Second, under mild assumptions, as the number of firms increases, the markup over marginal cost decreases in each market segment. From this comparative static, it follows that each firm's profit also decreases and consumer surplus increases as n increases. Third, if each market segment has a constant elasticity of demand, relative prices across segments are constant in n and, therefore, an increase in firms necessarily decreases absolute price dispersion. Finally, in the spirit of monopolistic competition, one can introduce a fixed cost of production and allow entry to drive long-run profits to zero, thereby making the size of the market endogenous. In such a setting, both long-term market power and economic profit are zero, but fixed costs of entry generate short-run market power, short-run economic rents, and prices above marginal cost. Aside from the effects of competition, one can also inquire about the welfare effects of price discrimination relative to uniform pricing.

To this end, it is first helpful to review the setting of monopoly in Robinson (1933). In that work, Robinson concludes that whether aggregate output increases when a monopolist price discriminates depends upon the relative curvature of the segmented demand curves. Particularly in the case of two segments, if the "adjusted concavity" (an idea we will make precise below) of the more elastic market is greater than the adjusted concavity of the less elastic market at a uniform price, then output increases with price discrimination; when the reverse is true, aggregate output decreases.

When a market segment has linear demand, the adjusted concavity is zero. It follows that when demand curves are linear—providing all markets are served—price discrimination has no effect on aggregate output. In sum, to make a determination about the price discrimination effects on aggregate output under monopoly, one needs only to compare the adjusted concavities of each market segment.

A tale of two elasticities: best-response symmetry in price games
In her study of third-degree price discrimination under monopoly, Robinson (1933) characterizes a monopolist's two markets as "strong" and "weak." By definition, a price discriminating monopolist always sets the higher price in the strong market, and the lower price in the weak market. It is useful to extend this ranking to imperfectly competitive markets.

Suppose that there are two markets, i = 1, 2. We say that market i is "weak" (and the other is "strong") for firm j if, for any uniform price(s) set by the other firm(s), the optimal price in market i is always lower than the optimal price in the other segment. Formally, if BRj i (p) is the best-response function of firm j in market i, given that its rival sets the price p, then market 1 is weak (and 2 is strong) if and only if BRj

1(p) < BRj

2(p) for all

We say that the market environment satisfies best-response symmetry (following Corts (1998)) if the weak and strong markets of each firm coincide; alternatively, if the weak and strong markets of each firm differ, then the environment exhibits best-response asymmetry.

As we will see, when firms commonly agree on their rankings of markets from strong to weak (i.e., best-response symmetry), there exists a useful result from Holmes (1989) which predicts when aggregate output will rise or fall with the introduction of price discrimination, and therefore provides some indication about its ultimate welfare effects. This result is not available when best responses are asymmetric, which creates a crucial distinction in what follows. In this section, we assume that there exists best-response symmetry; in the following section, we study best-response asymmetry.

Borenstein (1985) and Holmes (1989) extend the analysis of third-degree price discrimination to settings of imperfect competition with product differentiation, under scoring the significance of cross-price elasticities in predicting changes in profits and surplus. Specifically,

Holmes (1989) builds upon the monopoly model of Robinson (1933) and demonstrates that under symmetric duopoly, it is crucial to know the ratio of market to cross-price elasticities, aside from the adjusted concavities of demand. The curvatures of the demand curves are insufficient, by themselves, to predict changes in aggregate output when markets are imperfectly competitive.

Several results follow from this comparison and the presence of the cross-price elasticity.

- Price effects. From the above formulation of the inverse-elasticity rules, competition clearly lowers prices in both markets compared to monopoly, ceteris paribus, and therefore we expect competition to increase welfare in this simple third-degree price discrimination setting. It is also immediate that the effect of competition on price dispersion across markets is ambiguous and depends upon the cross-price elasticities. If the goods are close substitutes and market competition is fierce, prices will be close to marginal cost and competition will reduce price differentials across the markets. Alternatively, if consumers in the weak market find the goods to be close substitutes (their next best alternative is consuming from a rival firm) while consumers in the strong market exhibit powerful brand loyalties (their next best alternative is the outside good), then the firms choose highly competitive prices in the weak market and close-to-monopoly prices in the strong market. These choices lead to greater price differentials across markets. Unfortunately, no testable implications for price dispersion arise from the theory without additional information regarding the cross-price elasticities in each market.

- Output (and welfare) effects. A recurring policy question in the price discrimination literature is whether to allow third-degree price discrimination or to enforce uniform pricing. A key ingredient to understanding this question in the context of imperfectly competitive markets is the impact of price discrimination on output.

We further assume that these marginal profit functions decrease in price for each market segment.

The first bracketed expression is a straightforward variation of Robinson's adjusted-concavity condition found in the case of monopoly. When demands are linear, the expression is zero. The second expression (the elasticity-ratio difference) is novel and due entirely to competition. If the strong market (market 2) is more sensitive to competition (i.e., "c 2/"m2 is larger in the strong market than the weak market), then price discrimination causes the output reduction in the strong market to be less than the output increase in the weak market; aggregate output rises accordingly. If this reduction in the strong market is sufficiently small relative to the weak market, then welfare will also rise.

The point most worth stressing is that the effect of competition depends upon the size of the cross-price elasticity relative to the industry elasticity. When demands are linear (and adjusted concavities are zero), the elasticity-ratio test gives a sufficient condition for increased output:

In words, price discrimination leads to an increase in output if the discrepancy in elasticities across the two markets is greater with respect to the outside option than with respect to the rival's good. Among other things, this condition implies that at the discriminating monopoly prices (where the left-hand ratio is 1), the strong market is "more competitive" than the weak market in the sense of cross-price elasticities.

Profit effects. The profit effects of price discrimination are more difficult to predict.

While any individual firm's profit rises when allowed to price discriminate, the entire industry profit may rise or fall when all firms add price discrimination to their strategic arsenals. Two papers have made significant findings in this direction. Holmes (1989) analyzes the case of linear demand functions and finds that when the elasticity ratio condition above is satisfied, profit (as well as output) increases. When the elasticity ratio is violated, however, the effect on profits is ambiguous although welfare necessarily falls. What is particularly interesting is that price discrimination decreases profits when the weak market has a higher cross-price elasticity but a lower market elasticity compared to the strong market. Because the market elasticity is lower in the weak market, a given increase in price would be more profitable (and more socially efficient) in the weak market than in the strong market. When profits fall due to price discrimination (which Holmes (1989) notes is never by more than a few percentage points), it is because the weak market's significantly higher cross-price elasticity outweighs its lower market elasticity, and therefore price discrimination reduces the weak-market price. From a profit perspective (and a social welfare perspective), this lower price is in the wrong market and thus profits decline relative to uniform pricing.

Related to this finding, Armstrong and Vickers (2001) consider a non-linear model of third-degree price discrimination in which each segment is a Hotelling linear market with uniformly distributed consumers, each of whom has identical downward-sloping demand.

The market segments differ only by the consumers' transportation costs. They demonstrate that when competition is sufficiently intense (specifically, each segment's transportation cost goes to zero while maintaining a constant cost ratio), industry profits increase under price discrimination and consumer surplus falls. This outcome suggests that Holmes's (1989) linear examples of slightly decreased profits from price discrimination may not be robust to nonlinear settings with intense competition. This finding, together with the other results of Holmes (1989), leads to a consensus that price discrimination increases profits in settings of best-response symmetry. In addition, Armstrong and Vickers (2001) find that when the segment with the lower market elasticity also has a sufficiently higher cross-price elasticity (i.e., low transportation costs), welfare falls under price discrimination. Interestingly, the economics underlying this result are similar to Holmes's (1989) linear model of decreased profits—price discrimination causes the prices to fall and rise in the wrong markets.

Inter-firm misallocations. The model examined in Holmes (1989) is symmetric across firms—no firm has a cost or product advantage over the other. This simplification obscures possibly significant, inter-firm misallocations that would arise in a model in which one firm has a comparative advantage in delivering utility to consumers. The change from uniform pricing to price discrimination may either mitigate or amplify these distortions. As an immediate illustration of this ambiguity, consider a duopoly setting in which both firms are local monopolists in the strong market and the strong-market demands are rectangular (although possibly different across firms). In the weak market, suppose that the firms are Hotelling (1929) duopolists in a market which is covered in equilibrium. Given these assumptions, the only social inefficiency is that some consumers in the weak market purchase from the "wrong" firm; this situation arises when the price differential across firms in the weak market is not equal to the difference in marginal costs. Under price discrimination, our assumption of rectangular demand curves implies that the strong-market, inter-firm price differential depends entirely on the consumer's valuations for each product. In the weak market, however, it is easy to see that the resulting price differential between the firms is smaller than the difference in marginal costs; the price discrimination equilibrium results in the high-cost firm serving too much of the market. Compare this outcome to the uniformprice setting: If the strong market is sufficiently important relative to the weak market, then the uniform-price differential will be close to the price-discriminating, inter-firm differential in the strong market. If the strong-market differential is close to the difference in marginal costs, then uniform pricing mitigates inefficiencies; if the differential in the strong market is smaller than the price-discriminating differential in the weak market, then uniform pricing amplifies the social distortions. In short, there are no robust conclusions regarding the effect of price discrimination on misallocated production.

When one firm's strength is a rival's weakness: best-response asymmetry in price games

The assumption that firms rank strong and weak markets symmetrically is restrictive, as it rules out most models with spatial demand systems in which price discrimination occurs over observable location; e.g., a weak (far away) market for firm a is a strong (close) market for firm b. The assumption of best-response symmetry in the previous analysis allowed us to conclude that the uniform price always lies between the strong market price and the weak market under discrimination. Without such symmetry, this conclusion does not exist. Indeed, it is possible that all prices rise or fall under price discrimination, depending on the underlying market demand curves.

A simple model to illustrate recurring themes. We begin with a simple example of differentiated duopoly drawn from These and Vives (1988) to illustrate some of the consequences of price discrimination when firms have dissimilar strengths and weaknesses across market segments. Consider a standard Hotelling (1929) model of duopoly in which two firms are located on the endpoints of a linear market. Each consumer has an observable location parameter, _ 2 (0, 1), which is drawn from a uniform distribution across the market; each consumer demands at most one unit of output.

Price Discrimination and Entry

The preceding analysis has largely taken the number of firms as exogenous. Given the possibility of entry with fixed costs, a new class of distortions arises: price discrimination may induce too much or too little entry relative to uniform pricing.

Monopolistic competition. If entry is unfettered and numerous potential entrants exist, entry occurs to the point where long-run profits are driven to zero. Under such models of monopolistic competition, social surplus is equated to consumer surplus. The question arises, with free entry does a change from uniform pricing to discrimination lead to higher or lower aggregate consumer surplus?

To answer this question, two effects must be resolved. First, by fixing the number of firms, does a change from uniform pricing to price discrimination lead to higher industry profits? We have already observed that price discrimination can either raise or lower industry profits, depending on the underlying system of demand. If price discrimination raises industry profits, then greater entry occurs; if price discrimination lowers profits, then fewer firms will operate in the market. Second, given that a move to price discrimination changes the size of the industry, will consumer surplus increase or decrease? Under uniform pricing, it is well known that the social and private values of entry may differ due to the effects of business stealing and product diversity; see, for example, Spence (1976) and Mankiw and Whinston (1986). Generally, when comparing price discrimination to uniform pricing, no clear welfare result about the social efficiency of free entry exists, although a few theoretical contributions are suggestive of the relative importance of various effects. Katz (1984), in a model of monopolistic competition with price discrimination, was one of the first to study how production inefficiencies from excessive entry may arise. He found that price discrimination's impact on social welfare is ambiguous and depends upon his model's demand parameters.

Rather than developing Katz's (1984) model, this ambiguity can be illustrated with a few simple examples. In our first example, price discrimination is shown to be beneficial through the extension of Hotelling's (1929) linear market to a circular setting, as in Salop (1979). Suppose that inelastic unit-demand consumers are uniformly distributed around a circular market. As entry occurs, assume firms automatically relocate equidistant from one another. When the market is covered, all potential consumers purchase a good from the nearest firm, so the optimal number of firms is that which minimizes the sum of transportation costs and the fixed costs of entry, K.

As a counter-example, suppose that consumer preferences are entirely observable so that a third-degree price-discriminating monopolist would capture more of the consumer surplus than a uniform-pricing monopolist. To model imperfect competition, assume along the lines of Diamond (1971) that goods are homogeneous, but consumers must bear a small search cost for each visit to a store to obtain a price quote. There is then an equilibrium in which all firms offer the monopoly price schedule and consumers purchase from the first store they visit, providing that the resulting consumer surplus exceeds the cost of search. All firms follow identical pricing strategies, so there is no value to search, and each sells to an equal fraction of consumers. Because of ex ante competition, firms enter this market until long-run profits are dissipated. Because more consumer surplus remains under uniform pricing than under price discrimination, welfare is higher under uniform pricing while too much entry occurs under price discrimination.

Unfortunately, as these two examples suggest, we are left without any clear guidance regarding the effects of price discrimination on entry and the associated changes in social welfare under monopolistic competition.

Entry deterrence Allowing price discrimination by symmetric firms can increase the profitability of serving a market, and thereby generate more entry as shown in Katz (1984). On the other hand, one might imagine that firms are situated asymmetrically, as in Armstrong and Vickers (1993), where an incumbent firm serves two market segments, and potential entry can occur only in one of the segments. Here, price discrimination has no strategic value to the entrant given its limited access to a single market, but it does allow the incumbent to price lower in the newly entered market, while still maintaining monopoly profits from its captive segment. Hence, the incumbent's best-response discriminating prices following entry will generally result in a lower price in the attacked market than if uniform pricing across segments were required.

For sufficiently high capital costs, entry is blockaded whether or not the incumbent can price discriminate. For sufficiently low costs of entry, occurs regardless of whether the incumbent can price discriminate. For intermediate values, however, the availability of price discrimination leads to blockaded entry, while uniform price restrictions accommodate the entrant. Under uniform pricing, in Armstrong and Vickers's (1993) model, the prices in both markets are lower with entry than they would be with price discrimination and deterrence. Entrant profits and consumer surplus are also higher, while incumbent profits fall. This result is robust, providing that the monopoly price in the captive market exceeds the optimal discriminatory price in the competitive market. Armstrong and Vickers (1993) further demonstrate that the net welfare effects of uniform price restrictions are generally ambiguous, as the efficiencies from reduced prices must be offset against the inefficiencies from additional entry costs.

The model in Armstrong and Vickers (1993) illustrates the possibility that uniform pricing reduces all prices relative to price discrimination, due entirely to entry effects. A restriction to uniform prices promotes entry, which in turn generates price reductions in both markets. A similar theme emerges in section 7 but for different economic reasons when we consider entry deterrence from bundling goods.

Restrictions Between Firms to Limit Price Discrimination

Using the example drawn from These and Vives (1988), we previously noted that when firms commit publicly to a pricing strategy (uniform or discriminating), it is possible that price discrimination becomes a dominant strategy and firms become trapped in a classic Prisoner's Dilemma—all firms would like to commit collectively to uniform pricing but, individually, each prefers to price discriminate. Of course, we have also seen settings in which price discrimination raises industry profits, as in Holmes (1989).28 At present, we do not have a general theory predicting when unilateral commitments to uniform pricing will be optimal. Such a theory would be directly useful for analyzing the conditions under which uniform pricing emerges without collective action. It would also be indirectly useful when studying strategic commitments in the face of entry. An incumbent monopolist may find, for example, that a commitment to uniform price is optimal if entry will occur regardless, but commitment to large price discounts (perhaps larger than the statically optimal price discriminating prices) will deter entry into the weak market.

We have more precise conclusions regarding collective restrictions, however, as well as a few useful insights regarding the control of price discrimination in vertical structures. We discuss each in turn.

Collective agreements to restrict price discrimination. It is difficult to obtain general results regarding the unilateral, multilateral and social incentives for price discrimination.

Fortunately, there are some clear cut cases: (i) best-response asymmetry with all-out competition, and (ii) best-response symmetry with linear demands. When all-out competition is present, price discrimination lowers prices and profits. Hence, a collective agreement by firms to restrict price discrimination has the effect of raising prices for all consumers, lowering aggregate output, and lowering consumer surplus and total welfare. In the second setting of best-response symmetry with linear demands, Holmes (1989) demonstrates that if the elasticity-ratio condition is satisfied, then price discrimination increases industry profits. Hence, with linear demands, firms have only a collective incentive to prohibit price discrimination if the elasticity-ratio condition fails. Given that demands are linear, violation of the elasticity-ratio condition implies that price discrimination lowers aggregate output and hence welfare. In this simple setting, it follows that welfare increases by allowing firms to agree collectively to limit price discrimination. There is still the possibility that the elasticity-ratio condition fails and welfare decreases, but industry profits still increase with price discrimination. Here, restrictions on welfare-reducing price discrimination must come from outside the industry. Winter (1997) considers a variation of Holmes's (1989) analysis in the context of collective agreements to limit (but not prohibit) price discrimination by restricting the difference between the high and low prices. His conclusion for linear demands is similar: when firms have a collective desire to restrict price discrimination, it is socially efficient for them to be allowed to do so. As an illustration, suppose an extreme case in which each half of the strong market is captive to one of the firms (therefore, "c 2 = 0), while the weak market has a positive cross-price elasticity of demand. In such a case, the elasticity-ratio test clearly fails. At the equilibrium prices, a slight restriction on price discrimination causes the weak-market price to rise slightly and the strong-market price to fall by a similar margin. Because the weak market price is below the collusive profit-maximizing price, this price increase helps the duopolists. Because the strong market's price is at the optimal monopoly price under discrimination (due to captive customers), a slight decrease causes only a second-order reduction in profits to the duopoly.

Hence, a slight restriction on price discrimination is jointly optimal for duopolists. In this case, where the elasticity-ratio condition is violated (and demands are linear), Holmes (1989) shows that Q0(r) < 0. As a consequence, a restriction on the price differential (a lowering of r) raises aggregate output. Since aggregate output increases and the price differential decreases, welfare necessarily increases. It follows that industry agreements to limit price discrimination arise only if price discrimination reduces welfare, providing that adjusted demand concavities are small. The results are less clear when demands are not linear and the adjusted concavity condition plays an important role.

In short, when profits are lower under price discrimination, firms in the industry would prefer to collude and commit to uniform pricing. Such collusion would decrease welfare if all-out competition would otherwise occur, and increase welfare when demand is linear and price discrimination would have reduced aggregate output. In more general settings, unfortunately, the results are ambiguous.

Vertical restraints and downstream price discrimination. Although this survey largely ignores the impact of price discrimination on competing vertical structures, it is worth mentioning a sample of work in this area.

We have already mentioned one strategic effect of price discrimination via secret price discounts by wholesalers to downstream firms: price discrimination may induce the upstream firm to flood the downstream market. A legal requirement that the wholesaler offer a single price to all retailers may instead help the upstream firm to commit to not over supply the retail market, thereby raising profits and retail prices. In other settings of wholesale price discrimination, if downstream market segments have different elasticities of demand but third-degree price discrimination is illegal or otherwise impractical because of arbitrage, vertical integration can be used as a substitute for price discrimination. Tirole (1988) gives a simple model of such a vertical price squeeze. A monopoly wholesaler, selling to a strong market at price p2 and to a weak market at price p1 < p2, may suffer from arbitrage as the firms in the weak downstream market resell output to the strong segment. By vertically integrating into one of the weak-segment downstream firms, the wholesaler can now supply all output at the strong-segment price of p2 while producing in the weak segment and using an internal transfer price no greater than p1.

Other firms in the weak market will be squeezed by the vertically integrated rival due to higher wholesale prices. The wholesaler effectively reduces competition in the weak segment to prevent arbitrage and implement a uniform wholesale price.

Consider instead the case where it is the downstream retail firms that are the source of price discrimination. How do the various tools of resale price maintenance (RPM) by the upstream manufacturer impact profits and welfare when retailers engage in third-degree price discrimination? As the previous discussions suggested, a manufacturer who sells to imperfectly competitive, price-discriminating retailers would prefer to constrain retailers from discounting their prices to consumers who are highly cross-elastic, as this is just a businessstealing externality. On the other hand, the manufacturer would like to encourage price discrimination across the full range of cross-price inelastic consumers as this action raises profits to the industry. Hence, the combination of competition and price discrimination generates a unique conflict in the vertical chain.

Price Discrimination by Purchase History

Consumer price sensitivities are often revealed by past purchase decisions. For example, consumers may suffer exogenous switching costs in firms, so past customers may have more inelastic demands than new customers. Here, purchase history is useful because an otherwise homogeneous good becomes differentiated ex post due to exogenous switching costs. In other cases, it may be that no exogenous switching costs exist but that the products are inherently differentiated, with consumers having strong preferences for one product or the other. It follows that a customer who reveals a preference for firm a's product at current prices is precisely the person to whom firm b would like to offer a price reduction. In this case, purchase history operates through a different conduit of differentiation because it informs about a consumer's exogenous brand preference. Regardless, the strategies of "paying customers to switch" (Chen (1997b)) or "consumer poaching" (Fudenberg and Tirole (2000)) can be profitable because purchase history provides a valuable variable for the basis of dynamic third-degree price discrimination. It is not surprising, therefore, that such pricing is a well-known strategy among marketers. As the examples suggest, two approaches to modelling imperfect competition and purchase-history price discrimination have been taken in the literature. The first set of models, e.g., Nilssen (1992), Chen (1997b), Taylor (2003), et al., assumes that the goods are initially homogeneous in period 1, but after purchase the consumers are partially locked in with their sellers; exogenous switching costs must be paid to switch to different firms in future periods. The immediate result is that although prices rise over time as firms exploit the lock-in effects of switching costs, firms ultimately compete away in period 1 the long-run profits due to lock-in.

The second set of models assumes that products are horizontally differentiated in the initial period (e.g., Caminal and Matutes (1990), Villas-Boas (1999), Fudenberg and Tirole (2000), et al.). In the simplest variant, brand preferences are constant over time. It follows that a consumer who prefers firm a's product and reveals this preference through his purchase in period 1 will become identified as part of a's "strong" market segment (and firm b's "weak" market segment) in period 2. As we will see, when firms cannot commit to long-term prices, this form of unchanging product differentiation will generate prices that decrease over time, and competition intensifies in each segment.

The resulting price paths in the above settings rest on the assumption that firms cannot commit to future prices. This assumption may be inappropriate. One could easily imagine that firms commit in advance to reward loyal customers in the future with price reductions or other benefits (such as with frequent flyer programs). Such long-term commitments can be thought of as endogenous switching costs and have been studied in the context of horizontal differentiation by Banerjee and Summers (1987), Caminal and Matutes (1990), Villas-Boas (1999) and Fudenberg and Tirole (2000). Two cases have been studied: preferences that change over time and preferences that are static. In the first case, most papers assume that consumer valuations are independently distributed across the periods. If preferences change from period to period and firms cannot commit to future prices, there is no value to using purchase history as it is uninformative about current elasticities. Public, longterm contracts between, say, firm a and a consumer, however, can raise the joint surplus of the pair by making firm b price lower in the second period to induce switching, as in the models of Caminal and Matutes (1990) and Fudenberg and Tirole (2000). In equilibrium, social welfare may decrease as long-term contracts induce too little switching. In the second category of price-commitment models, preferences are assumed to be fixed across periods.

When preferences are unchanging across time, Fudenberg and Tirole (2000) demonstrate a similar effect from long-term contracts: firm a locks in some of its customer base to generate lower second-period pricing for switching, and thereby encourages consumers to buy from firm a in the initial period. With long-term contracts, some inefficient switching still occurs but less than when firms cannot commit to long-term prices; hence welfare increases by allowing such contracts.

We consider both switching-cost and horizontal-differentiation models of pricing without commitment in the following two subsections. We then turn to the effects of long-term price commitments when discrimination on purchase history is allowed.

Exogenous Switching Costs and Homogeneous Goods

There are many important and subtle effects in switching-cost models. Farrell and Klemperer (2003), in this volume, provide a thorough treatment of switching costs, so we will limit our present attention to the very specific issues of price discrimination over purchase history under imperfect competition.

One of the first discussions of purchase-history discrimination in a model of switching costs appears in Nilssen (1992).31 Chen (1997b), building on this approach, introduces a distribution of switching costs in a two-period model, resulting in some measure of equilibrium switching. We present a variant of Chen's (1997b) model here.

Consider duopolists, j = a, b, selling identical homogeneous goods to a unit measure of potential consumers.

Discrimination over Revealed Preferences from First-period Choices

Instead of assuming exogenous switching costs arising after an initial purchase from either firm, one can suppose that consumers have exogenous preferences for brands that are present from the start, as in Fudenberg and Tirole (2000). To keep the analysis simple, they model such horizontal differentiation by imagining a Hotelling-style linear market of unit length with firms positioned at the endpoints, and by assuming that each consumer's uniformly distributed brand preference, _, remains fixed for both periods of consumption. Consumers have transportation costs of _ per unit distance, and firms produce with constant marginal and average costs of c per unit. In such a setting, consumers reveal information about their brand preference by their first-period choice, and firms set second-period prices accordingly.

Purchase-History Pricing with Long-term Commitment

Unlike the previous analyses which relied on short-term price agreements, we now ask what happens if a firm can write a long-term contract, committing to a second-period price so as to guarantee returning customers terms that differ from those offered to other customers.

Banerjee and Summers (1987) and Caminal and Matutes (1990) were among the first to explore the use of long-term contracts to induce loyalty and generate endogenous switching costs. Consider the setting of Caminal and Matutes (1990). As before, there are two firms and two periods of competition. The market in each period consists of a linear city of unit length, with firm a located at 0 and firm b located at 1, and consumers uniformly distributed across the interval. The difference with the previous models is that the location of each consumer is independently distributed across periods. Thus, a consumer's location in period 1, _1, is statistically independent of the consumer's location in period 2, _2.

This independence assumption implies that there is no relevant second-period information contained in a consumer's first-period choice. It follows that if firms cannot commit to long-term prices, there is no value from price discrimination based upon purchase history. Caminal and Matutes (1990) find a few noteworthy results. First, equilibrium prices decline over time. Remarkably, the second-period commitment price is below even marginal cost. The reasoning of this is subtle. Suppose, for example, that firm b's poaching price in the second period was independent of firm a's second-period loyalty price. Because the consumer's second-period location is unknown at the time of long-term contracting, firm a maximizes the joint surplus of a consumer and itself by setting pj 2j = c and pricing efficiently in the second period. Given that firm b's poaching price in reality does depend positively on firm a's second-period loyalty price, firm a can obtain a first-order gain in joint surplus by reducing its price slightly below cost and thereby reducing firm b's second-period price.

This slight reduction in price incurs only a corresponding second-order loss in surplus since pricing was originally at the efficient level. Hence, a firm will commit to a follow-on price below marginal cost in the second-period as a way to increase the expected surplus going to the consumer, and hence raise the attractiveness of purchasing from the firm initially.

In this sense, the price commitment is similar to the analysis of Diamond and Maskin (1979) and Aghion and Bolton (1987), in which contractual commitments are used to extract a better price from an outside party. Of course, as Caminal and Matures (1990) confirm, when both firms undertake this strategy simultaneously, profits fall relative to the no-commitment case and firms are worse off. Welfare is also lower as too little switching takes place from a social viewpoint.

What are the effects of the presence of this commitment strategy? As is by now a familiar theme, although an individual firm will benefit from committing to a declining price path for returning customers, the firms are collectively worse off with the ability to write longterm price contracts. With commitment, it is also the case that there is too much lock-in or inertia in the second-period allocations. Without commitment, social welfare would therefore be higher, as consumers would allocate themselves to firms over time to minimize transportation costs. The endogenous switching costs (created by the declining price path for returning consumers) decrease social welfare. As before, because market demand is inelastic in this model, there is an inherent bias against price discrimination, so we must carefully interpret the welfare conclusions.

Closely related to Caminal and Matutes (1990), Fudenberg and Tirole (2000) also consider an environment in which price commitments can be made through long-term contracts, using an interesting variation in which consumer preferences are fixed across periods (i.e., location _ between firms a and b does not change). In this setting, there are no exogenous switching costs, but long-term contracts with breach penalties can be offered which introduce endogenous switching costs in the sense of Caminal and Matutes (1990). While such contracts could be effectively used to lock consumers into a firm and prevent poaching, the firms choose to offer both long-term and spot contracts in equilibrium so as to segment the marketplace. In equilibrium, consumers with strong preferences for one firm will purchase long-term contracts, while those with weaker preferences will select short-term contracts and switch suppliers in the second period. The firm utilizes long-term contracts to generate lower poaching prices, which benefit consumers located near the centre of the market. The firm can extract concessions in the first period by locking in some customers with long-term contracts, thereby generating more aggressive second-period pricing (similar in spirit to Caminal and Matutes (1990).) In addition, the long-term contracts also generate a singlecrossing property that segments first-period consumers: in equilibrium, consumers located near the middle of the market are more willing to purchase short-term contracts and switch in the second period to a lower-priced rival than consumers located at the extreme.

It is worth noting that a multi-plant monopolist would accomplish a similar sorting by selling long-term contracts for aa, bb and the switching bundles ab and ba. The monopolist can therefore segment the market, charging higher prices to the non-switchers and lower prices to the consumers who are willing to switch. The optimal amount of monopoly switching in the second period (given a uniform distribution) can be shown to be one-half of the consumers. Here, long-term contracts serve a similar segmentation function. Interestingly, Fudenberg and Tirole (2000) show that if consumers are uniformly distributed, one-fourth of the consumers will switch in the long-term contracting equilibrium with duopoly—less switching than in the case of short-term contracts alone, and still less switching than under monopoly. Hence, given price discrimination is allowed, allowing firms to use long-term contracts improves social welfare. This finding emerges because demand is unchanging across periods, in contrast to Caminal and Matutes (1990), who find that long-term price commitments lead to too much lock-in and hence reduce social welfare when preferences vary over time.

Intrapersonal Price Discrimination

Intrapersonal price discrimination has received very little attention, partly because in the context of monopoly, the models and results are economically immediate. For example, consider a consumer with a known demand curve, p = D(q), and a constant marginal (and average) cost of production equal to c. Let q_ be the unique solution to c = D(q_). A monopolist can increase profits by offering any of a host of equally optimal but distinct mechanisms: a fixed bundle of q_ units at a bundle price of Rq_ 0 D(z)dz; a fully nonlinear tariff of P(q) = D(q); or a two-part tariff equal to P(q) = v(c)+cq where v(p) _ maxq u(q)" pq is the consumer's indirect utility of consuming at the linear price p. In all examples, the monopolist is effectively price discriminating in an intrapersonal manner: Different prices are charged to the same consumer for different units because the marginal values to the consumer for those units vary according to consumption. In this sense, it is closely related to third-degree price discrimination because the different units of consumption can be thought of as distinguishable market segments. Because there is no heterogeneity within each market segment—the reservation value is D(q) in the q-th unit market—price discrimination is perfect and social welfare is maximized.

When markets are imperfectly competitive, intrapersonal price discrimination using nonlinear prices allows firms to provide more efficiently a given level of consumer surplus and cover any fixed, per-consumer costs of production. This efficiency suggests that intrapersonal price discrimination may raise social welfare when firms compete. Following Armstrong and Vickers (2001), we address this possibility and related issues of consumer surplus and industry profit in the simplest discrete-choice setting in which there is a single market segment with homogeneous consumers.

Nonlinear Pricing (Second-Degree Price Discrimination)

Unlike the setting of third-degree price discrimination, indirect (second-degree) discrimination relies upon self-selection constraints, thus introducing an entirely new set of competitive issues.

In what follows we assume that firms compete via price schedules of the form Pj(qj), and consumers choose which (if any) firms to patronize and which product(s) from the offered lines they will purchase. To model imperfect competition we assume the product lines are differentiated. The theoretical literature on second-degree price discrimination under imperfect competition has largely focused on characterizing equilibrium schedules and the efficiency consequences of competition; less attention has been spent on the desirability of enforcing uniform pricing in these environments. This is due in part to the extra technical complexity of second-degree price discrimination, and, to a lesser degree, to the impracticality of requiring uniform pricing when q refers to quality rather than quantity.

The variety of consumer preferences and competitive environments make it useful to distinguish a few cases. First, two possible equilibrium configurations can arise: a consumer may purchase exclusively from one firm (referred to in the contract theory literature as exclusive agency) or may purchase different products from multiple firms (referred to as common agency). Second, within each setting, there are several possibilities regarding the unobservable heterogeneity of consumers. The two most common forms are what we will call vertical and horizontal heterogeneity. In the former, the consumer's marginal preferences for q (and absolute preferences for participating) are increasing in _ for each firm; in the latter, the consumer's marginal preferences for q and absolute preferences for participating are monotonic in _, but the direction varies across firms with the result that a high-demand type for firm j is a low-demand type for firm k and conversely. Under these definitions, vertical heterogeneity implies that firms agree in their ranking of type from high demand to low demand; under horizontal heterogeneity, two firms have reversed ranking for consumer types. In this sense, the taxonomy is similar in spirit to best-response symmetry and asymmetry under third-degree price discrimination.

Ideally, a general model of competition among second-degree price-discriminating firms should incorporate two dimensions of heterogeneity, one vertical and one horizontal, to capture both a common ranking of marginal valuations for quality among consumers (holding brand preferences fixed) and a variety of brand preferences (holding quality valuations fixed). Unfortunately, multidimensional self-selection models are considerably more difficult to study, as they introduce additional economic and technical subtleties. As a result, the economics literature has either relied upon one-dimensional models (either vertical or horizontal) for precise analytic results (e.g., Spulber (1989), Martimort (1992,1996), Stole (1991), Stole (1995), Martimort and Stole (2003a)), numerical simulations of multidimensional models (e.g., Borenstein (1985)), or further restrictions on preferences to simplify multidimensional settings to the point of analytical tractability (e.g., Armstrong and Vickers (2001), Rochet and Stole (2002a), Martimort and Ivaldi (1994)).

Before we survey the various approaches taken in the literature, we begin with a review of monopoly second-degree price discrimination to provide a benchmark and a vehicle to introduce notation.

3

Determinants of Financing Patterns

Distinguishing Factors

If these differences in styles and motivations exist, then there may be several characteristics of firms that will enable us to distinguish between family owned and managed and professionally managed enterprises. These are firm size, firm age, strategy and the use of internal control systems.

Firm Size. If managers act in their own self interest seeking personal gain rather than firm profits, it is likely that the professionally managed firm will be larger than the family firm. There are the reasons for this. First, large firms often have excess capacity (slack resources) which can be used to buffer the consequences of poor decisions or smooth out variations in performance-this will make them look more efficient than they really are. Second, executive compensation is often based on size and growth rather than on firm profitability. Third, in a growing firm, there will be more opportunities for managers to get ahead. This is not an important consideration for owner-operators, and dealing with the growth of family firms in fact can be difficult (Alcorn 1982).

Firm Age. The professionally managed firm is also likely to be an older, more established firm. This is because most family owned firms do not survive past the first generation, while professionally managed firms do not depend on succession plans controlled by the founder/family.

Firm Strategy. Professionally managed firms are likely to grow at a faster rate, thus there should be differences in strategy. This is related to the managerial culture: Professional managers are likely to follow more active, growth-oriented strategies because these fulfil their interests better.

Internal Control Systems. Professionally managed firms are likely to rely more on internal control systems to monitor firm operations in order to control the moral hazard and opportunism problems; these procedures can offset the effects of managers' self-interested actions. In contrast, less formalized systems characterize family owned and managed firms, where there is no need to account for actions to a "disinterested owner." Formal measurement procedures are also less likely while a centralized appraisal system is more likely.

Research Study

We performed a field survey to see whether these four measures do accurately differentiate between family and non-family firms, and the results were very good: nearly three quarters of the cases were correctly classified. Our sample included 486 small manufacturers in Indiana, randomly selected by two-digit SIC codes from the 1988 Harris' Industrial Directory. We made three requirements for inclusion: the firm must be primarily a manufacturer (SIC codes 20-39); have fewer than 500 employees; and have sales under $30 million. Fifty three percent of the sample were professionally managed; the reason this is less than the national average is most likely due to the size restraint and our concentration on manufacturing firms. The manufacturers in the sample were on average 43 years old, which is longer than the tenure of most founder/entrepreneurs. In addition, manufacturing usually requires larger amounts of capital, and getting such financing may involve a loss of family ownership and/or control.

Because we were interested in the agency problem which occurs when ownership is separate from control, we split the sample into two categories: family owned and managed (representing a unification of ownership and control) and professionally managed (capturing all other combinations where ownership and control are separated).

We used two separate methods to make this distinction. First, using the Harris directory, a firm with two or more individuals with the same last name listed as officers was designated as a family managed firm, while the others were designated as professionally managed firms. We checked the validity of this categorization by telephoning a random sample of 30 firms. Each was asked a structured set of questions in order to determine the ownership and management of the firm. Question (1) was "In 1988, were there top/key managers related to the owner working in the business?" If the answer was yes, the firm was categorized as a family owned and manged firm. If no, question (2) was asked: "Are there other managers who are not related to the owner?" If yes, the firm was categorized as a professionally managed firm. If no, the final question was asked: "Then there are no other managers?" If the response was in agreement, then the firm was classified as a family owned and managed one, following the argument that a firm managed by the owner may eventually pass on ownership and control to a family member not currently operating in a management capacity.

Results of both methods gave a high degree of convergence in correct categorization: 27 of the 30 firms sampled were in agreement with the original directory method.

Survey

Surveys were then sent to the owner/operator of each firm, with a follow-up letter sent four weeks later. Nine were returned as non-deliverable and therefore not included in the calculation of the response rate, which was 39% (186 surveys). The usable response rate was. (104 surveys) which included only returns from the individual directing the firm (54 owners of family firms; 32 presidents and 18 general managers of professionally managed firms). Hence we had representatives of both types of firm.

We found that organizational size was captured by the number of full time employees which was highly correlated with sales volume. Firm age was captured by number of years in business. The use of formal internal controls was assessed using six items: use of information systems, quality control, cost control, cost centres, profit centres and formal appraisal of personnel. We used Miles and Snow's (1978) typology of defender, prospector, analyzer and reactor to indicate firm strategy.

Results

As noted earlier, we had excellent results indicating that there are valid differences between family and nonfamily firms with respect to these four measures. As they do differentiate between the two ownership structures, the study will be of significant help to other family firm researchers by providing an efficient way of accessing and categorizing any given sample of firms. That is, firms can be categorized from an archival source such as the directory we used, and then further checked by means of a telephone follow up of a small subset.

We also found that professionally managed firms were larger, most likely due to the positive relationship between executive compensation and firm size and the need for these firms to grow so as to accommodate the advancement of managers through promotion. On the other hand, growth and development of family firms is likely to be stunted: they are likely to be dominated by a founder who is unwilling to allow the firm to grow if this means a loss of personal control-this inability to yield control to other capable people limits expansion. Unless there is a recognition of the need to involve others-either family or non-family-the family run firm cannot continue to grow.

Growth is a problem, and the reluctance of family firms to plan for the succession of the founder so as to remain family owned shows up in their higher mortality rates: only 30% survive past the first generation (Ward 1987). This problem does not apply to the professionally managed firms which survive beyond the working life of the founder; thus these firms will be older than family firms.

We also found that family run firms rely less on the use of formal internal control systems, probably due to the desire of the family to maintain personal control rather than use impersonal, formalized procedures. Use of the latter in professionally managed firms is also likely to be a function of their larger size.

Finally, there were differences in firm strategy. The most significant differences between the two groups were that family businesses were more highly concenrated in the defender category, while professionally managed firms were over-represented in the reactor category (which tend to have the lowest performance). In conclusion, this study marks a significant step in providing a methodology for research in family business. It has implications for the management of firms and by helping us understand the differences in operating techniques, may assist the survival of a significant element of American enterprise.

Journal Article Excerpt

Family Firms are Different

Is there a difference in the management styles of family firms as compared with businesses run by professional non-family managers?

The answer is likely to be yes, but strangely, there has not been too much research into this question until recently in spite of their numbers and importance. Part of the reason for this lack of research may be the difficulty of distinguishing firms which are family owned and operated from those which are not; the former tend to be small and difficult to gain access to for research purposes. We became interested in this question, and have suggested two ways of making the distinction. We also briefly discuss some of the reasons why differences in firm ownership and control affect organizational processes. This can be useful for improving managerial processes in general.

It has been suggested that one of the reasons why family firms have been relatively overlooked is the acceptance by social scientists of the Berle and Means thesis. This is the idea that the control of American businesses has shifted from their owners to professional managers. Recently, however, research into family firms has gained more attention due in part to their economic importance. They are the most prevalent form of enterprise in the US today, generating between 40 to 60 percent of GNP (Ward and Aronoff 1990).

Just because family firms are common does not automatically make them suitable subjects for research. Why are they interesting for research purposes? The reason is the possibility that differences in ownership and control of firms do affect the way they are run, but there are few explanations. One set of possible explanations derives from agency theory (e.g. Fama 1980). What this suggests is that family firms may be lower cost, and therefore by implication, more efficient. The reason is that professional managers (the agents) impose extra costs on the firm. The first type of cost is due to the different interests of owners and managers; the second is due to the moral hazard and potential for opportunism when control is separated from ownership. Owners obviously have a personal stake in the firm's success, but the professional manager's interest is limited to the specifics of the employment contract. Managers, in addition, seldom stay with one firm for their entire work life, and loss of a job or even failure of the business is unlikely to be as disastrous for the professional manager as for the founder-manager.

This distinction arises because the professional culture of managers is characterized by a unique set of values and beliefs based on individual motivation and achievement. This encourages a focus on monetary rewards and tangible benefits; personal gain comes through advancement and promotion within the organization and increased compensation rather than a sense of pride in the organization as such. Comparing top management compensation, organizational performance is correlated with compensation in owner-controlled firms but with size in professionally-managed firms. This in turn may help explain the shorter time horizon of professional managers compared to owner-managers.

Another distinction is noted in decision-making. Founder-run organizations tend to be more centralized, with one or a few individuals dominating a rather secretive decision-making process, and not encouraging dissension due to their desire to retain control.

Distinguishing Factors

If these differences in styles and motivations exist, then there may be several characteristics of firms that will enable us to distinguish between family owned and managed and professionally managed enterprises. These are firm size, firm age, strategy and the use of internal control systems.

Firm Size. If managers act in their own self interest seeking personal gain rather than firm profits, it is likely that the professionally managed firm will be larger than the family firm. There are the reasons for this. First, large firms often have excess capacity (slack resources) which can be used to buffer the consequences of poor decisions or smooth out variations in performance-this will make them look more efficient than they really are. Second, executive compensation is often based on size and growth rather than on firm profitability. Third, in a growing firm, there will be more opportunities for managers to get ahead. This is not an important consideration for owner-operators, and dealing with the growth of family firms in fact can be difficult (Alcorn 1982).

Firm Age. The professionally managed firm is also likely to be an older, more established firm. This is because most family owned...

Why do Firms Different and how does it Matter?

Discusses interfirm differences from an economists point of view. Economists tend to be interested in how industries work, or don't, and not in the actions of individual firms. A student of management however is more interested in the behaviour and performance of individual firms. The author wants to make a strong case for the economic significance of 'discretionary' differences between firms, this is contrary to traditional 'theorectical' thinking. 'Discretionary' indicates differences that arise though choices made by the firms. In traditional economics the differences in firms is largely ignored, economists focus on macro or environmental variables. By discretionary differences Nelson means the differences that occur as a results of different firm strategies, these are formed through decision making processes within firms.

The author argues that Porter, and others, have identified macro problems that affect firms but they do not explain "why do firms differ and how does it matter?". Probably not relevant but Nelson argues that classical economists tend to believe that if similar companies are faced with similar choices they will have no problem in chooosing the right course of action-not really the case in real life! This view tends to mean that economists do focus on the micro level of firms. So the general economics view is that discretionary differences in firms do not matter.

On page 66 Nelson introduces his concept of 'evolutionary' economics. He starts to reference Schumpeter who also talks about "an evolutionary process". This is a process where people and organisations have different views about possible innovations, and their relative, and would therefore 'bet' one way or another. Schumpeter then goes on to say there's a series of winners and losers through these decisions.

Schumpeter, J "Capitalsim, Socialism and Democracy"

Nelson "An Evolutionary Theory of Ecomonic Change"-book

Teece, Pisano & Shuen (1990) "Firm capabilities, resources, and the concept of strategy"-looks like a good reference, if I can find it!

Nelson now talks about his reference sources, not needed now but might come back to this later, page 67.

Nelson identifies the three main features of a firm that must be acknowledged if a firm is to be described accurately:

- Its strategy
- It's structure
- Its core capabilities.

Nelson states that major changes in the last two have major cost implications which implies that they are stable descriptors of a firm.

Strategy

In this context, strategy refers to the "broad commitments made by a firm that define and rationalise its objectives and how it intends to pursue them. A strategy adopted by a firm may be a combination of written word and culture within the firm. While many economists would argue that a firms strategy represents its intended method of delivering profit, Nelson has different perspective. Nelson argues the following:

- A firms strategy is more likely to be based on views of managements (Nelson="faith") and its traditions, rather than a specific defined, strategy
- The strategy a firm develops does not directly determine a firms actions, instead its a direction in which the company should be moving
- Nelson then argues a firms strategy may not even be beneficial to the company, and in some cases may be of detriment.

Structure

Nelson argues that the structure of a firm is influenced by its strategy. The structure of the firm moulds itself to adapt to the implementation of strategy, although it does not define the detail. The structure of a firm is defined by how it is organised and managed, and how decisions are made.

A change in strategy may also require a change in structure. Changing the structure of a firm is more difficult than it might seem. We are referring to how the company is managed, how it makes decisions, changes in org charts or buy outs etc. do not change culture, it is argued by Nelson that this is what influences structure more than formal reporting mechanisms. Nelson argues that to do this effectively is costly. It is recognised that it is easy to break existing structures, but also that it is far more difficult to put effective alternatives in place. So effecting a major change in strategy would be difficult due to impact on the structure of a firm.

Core Capabilities

As Nelson puts it "what an organisation can do well has something of a life of its own". A hierarchy of organisational routines is central to Nelsons concept of core capabilities. Routines that firms do often are generally things that they confident in doing, and hence do well. Such routines however must start in the higher echelons of a company and be adpated at lower levels to provide core capabilities. If lower oder routines do not exist, or are not done well, then these are not a core capability. However, it is not simply enough to do one thing well for a given set of processes, this will not allow the company to survive longer term. "To be successful for any length of time a firm must innovate."

In a firm that works well, all parts of the business e.g. procurement, marketing etc., combine to support its core capabilities and complement new products and processes. It is further key that firms leverage innovation to produce profit, through best use of its assets and activities. Innovation is useless without being able to take advantage of it. Nelson argues that firms must innovate the right things, and then learn how to take advantage of those innovations, this needs focus and structure and does not happen randomly. Also, innovation does not happen in isolation, innovation in one area tends to lead to other innovations.

The focus on innovation referred to here comes from a firms strategy. With the strategy defining a firms structure, it is possible then to define a structure that supports the innovation. By implementing routines around the defined structure the next step to develop the innovation into the core capabilities.

Evolutionary theory promotes the idea that it is not possible for a firm to define an actual best strategy, business is too complicated for that. While a firm will make good strategic decisions based on the information it has, it is also likely that they will make bad decisions. Due to the complex nature of business, and of the different skills and experience of senior management, it is inevitable that firms make different strategic choices. The different strategic choices then lead to different structures and different core capabilities. This leads to firms following different and being more or less successful that competitors. A collary argument is then possible, where firms core capabilities are significantly different, it can be argued that their patterns of innovation also differ significantly.

It is argued the idea that a firms core capabilities and its ability to innovate are linked is overlooked in much literature. While one company might be able to innovate and produce a certain new product, inherent differences in structure and strategy mean that is not easy for another company to innovate in the same manner. This leads to the idea that effective technology imitation is not simple, and requires the competitor to go through the same processes of development to produce the same outcome. So firms that resemble each other in terms of structure and strategy can more readily imitate each others developments. It can then be argued (by me) that to truely innovate the strategy and structure of a firm must differ from its competitors. However, Nelson argues that to replicate innovation companies must imitate their competitors, the idea of strategic diversity disappears.

Nelson goes onto discuss how technological advance and organisational need to develop in parallel with each other. Organisational change has been required to foster an innovative environment. However there is no great vision about the ultimate organsiational structure, it tends to develop over time. While technological advance has been apparent for many years, these advances would not have been possible without changes in organisations.

Nelson argues that it is organisational differences, particularly around innovation, that create a source of durable difference between, differences that cannot be easily imitated. So while in some circumstances innovation may try to be copied, if the structure does not lend itself to innovation, that innovation cannot be copied.

In evolutionary economic theory, firm diversity is an essential part of the process of creating economic progress. As such, if a monopoly exists where the barriers to entry are high, economic development is adversely affected as there will less, or no, innovation to drive development.

A Comparison of Different Investment Firms

In recent years, investment firms have made more money than traditional banks and other lending institutions. Consequently, there are a number of young investment firms out there. You might consider investing in one of these companies because of the proximity or personal attention you will receive. Also, some of the younger companies may be more willing to take risks than the more established companies.

Typically, however, most people will probably want to invest money with large companies with a long records of accomplishments and success. This is a brief description of four such companies. The firms are J.P. Morgan, Merrill Lynch, Morgan Stanley, and Citigroup, they are among the largest, and best know investment firms in the world.

J.P. Morgan-JPMorgan is an investment firm that focuses on "insight". This means that if JPMorgan is your investment firm, they will focus their professional expertise on the investment of your money. They have an investment strategy of combining insight and process to help you realize the biggest returns possible. This strategy seems to work, as JP Morgan is one of the largest and most successful investments companies in the world. Current investment performance shows 81% of mutual fund assets were under management in the 1st and 2nd quartiles over the past five years.

Merrill Lynch-Merrill Lynch is a company that was has been around for a long time. The company was founded in 1914 and is one of the oldest investment banks around. They are also one of the biggest, managing about 1.6 trillion dollars for clients around the world. They cite client relations to be among their greatest assets have worked hard to establish positive relationships through growth, innovation, and execution. The company did undergo some restructuring in the years preceding 2006. The result has been more value for clients in the 2006 and 2007 fiscal years.

Morgan Stanley-this company is a powerhouse in investment banking. They currently handle $717 billion dollars of investment moneys and have offices in 32 countries. In 1997, Morgan Stanley merged with Dean Witter and Discover card. Because of these mergers, the company focuses on several different types of business. This includes credit services and institutional securities as well as investment management. In spite of being spread among these different business aims, Morgan Stanley is still a front-runner for investment firms. This company has been commended on issues of diversity and culture and was names one of the 100 best companies for working mothers.

Citigroup-Citgroup dates back to 1812 when Citibank was formed. This is the oldest financial institution of these four candidates. However, Citigroup Inc. developed out of Citibank in 1998 to specialize in investment banking. This corporation has been extremely active since its inception. Primarily, the activity has been in expansion and the acquisition of other banking companies. This company is definitely on the move. In 2006 alone, 1,200 new branches opened globally. The company is also on the move socially; it has endorsed Hurricane Katrina support and made a commitment to reduce greenhouse gases.

When you are trying to choose an investment firm, you might consider the size of the company. Are there branch offices in your community? How easy is it to talk with a broker? Do you agree with the company with regard to their politics and social stands? Any of these big firms has become big through successful investments of client funds. The difference between the groups is often one of sustained growth. Going to each company's website may help you to decide which company is right for you.

Product Differentiation

In marketing, product differentiation (also known simply as "differentiation") is the process of distinguishing a product or offering from others, to make it more attractive to a particular target market. This involves differentiating it from competitors' products as well as one's own product offerings.

Differentiation is a source of competitive advantage. Although research in a niche market may result in changing your product in order to improve differentiation, the changes themselves are not differentiation. Marketing or product differentiation is the process of describing the differences between products or services, or the resulting list of differences. This is done in order to demonstrate the unique aspects of your product and create a sense of value. Marketing textbooks are firm on the point that any differentiation must be valued by buyers (e.g.). The term unique selling proposition refers to advertising to communicate a product's differentiation.

In economics, successful product differentiation leads to monopolistic competition and is inconsistent with the conditions for perfect competition, which include the requirement that the products of competing firms should be perfect substitutes.

The brand differences are usually minor; they can be merely a difference in packaging or an advertising theme. The physical product need not change, but it could. Differentiation is due to buyers perceiving a difference, hence causes of differentiation may be functional aspects of the product or service, how it is distributed and marketed, or who buys it. The major sources of product differentiation are as follows.

- Differences in quality which are usually accompanied by differences in price
- Differences in functional features or design

- Ignorance of buyers regarding the essential characteristics and qualities of goods they are purchasing
- Sales promotion activities of sellers and, in particular, advertising
- Differences in availability (e.g. timing and location).

The objective of differentiation is to develop a position that potential customers see as unique.

Differentiation primarily impacts performance through reducing directness of competition: As the product becomes more different, categorization becomes more difficult and hence draws fewer comparisons with its competition. A successful product differentiation strategy will move your product from competing based primarily on price to competing on non-price factors (such as product characteristics, distribution strategy, or promotional variables).

Most people would say that the implication of differentiation is the possibility of charging a price premium; however, this is a gross simplification. If customers value the firm's offer, they will be less sensitive to aspects of competing offers; price may not be one of these aspects. Differentiation makes customers in a given segment have a lower sensitivity to other features (non-price) of the product.

Discrete Choice Theory of Product Differentiation

Product differentiation-in quality, packaging, design, colour, and style-has an important impact on consumer choice. It also provides a rich source of data that has been largely unexplored because there has been no generally accepted way to model the information available. This important study shows that an understanding of product differentiation is crucial to understanding how modern market economies function and that differentiated markets can be analysed using discrete choice models of consumer behaviour. It provides a valuable synthesis of existing, often highly technical work in both differentiated markets and discrete choice models and extends this work to establish a coherent theoretical underpinning for research in imperfect competition.

The discrete choice approach provides an ideal framework for describing the demands for differentiated products and can be used for studying most product differentiation models in the literature. By introducing extra dimensions of product heterogeneity, the framework also provides richer models of firm location.

Product differentiation is a business level strategy in which firms attempt to create and exploit differences between their products and those offered by competitors. These differences may lead to competitive advantage if customers perceive the difference and have a preference for the difference.

A product differentiation strategy requires that a firm be able to effectively communicate with customers through advertising, public relations, sponsoring of events, etc. In fact, advertising usually plays a critical role in an effective product differentiation strategy. Ironically, a firm does not have to be able to create a product with actual differences if it can convince customers that differences exist. Firms that do create products with actual differences have a much easier time convincing customers that those differences exist. Nike's capabilities lie primarily in design and marketing.

The vast majority of Nike's production of shoes and clothing is outsourced to other firms. Nike's base of differentiation is not proprietary high-tech manufacturing of superior athletic shoes. Rather, Nike's base of differentiation is a well-orchestrated marketing effort that has spanned decades.

Bases of Differentiation

The notion of a base of differentiation is important because it allows a firm to focus its efforts on creating and exploiting a particular difference between its products and competitors' products. Managers need to understand their own bases of differentiation and the bases of differentiation of competitors so that they can make informed strategic choices. Almost anything could be a base of differentiation. The key is that some set of customers must find value in the base of differentiation.

Everything from tangible product characteristics to abstract intangible concepts like national or regional pride could potentially be a base of differentiation. Managers can create and exploit bases of differentiation from a seemingly infinite number of ideas. For example, "freedom fries" became a base of differentiation among some restaurants as a form of protest against the French who refused to join the U.S. in its war against Saddam Hussein's government in Iraq. The name change from French fries to freedom fries was the idea of small but very patriotic restaurateur. This base of differentiation was short-lived as the attention of Americans shifted from the lack of French participation to the war itself.

Differentiation based on:

Attributes of the Product or Service

- preferences are created by actual differences in the tangible product or service offered by the focal firm vis-a-vis competitors' offerings
- product features (Arm & Hammer's baking soda toothpaste)
- product complexity (new digital cameras compared to single use film cameras)
- timing of product introduction (release of movies during the Holiday and Summer seasons)
- location (Chevron's company-owned, combined c-stores & gas stations are situated in prime traffic locations)

Relationship Between the Focal firm and its Customers

- preferences are created as the focal firm develops and exploits relationships with customers based on what the focal firm's target customers want
- product customization (Dell Computers-customers get exactly the features desired)
- consumer marketing (Mountain Dew-changed the image of the product through marketing-product stayed the same)
- product reputation (Harley-Davidson Motorcycles-reputation is so strong that some people tattoo the logo on their bodies)

Linkages Within or Between Firms

- preferences are created as the focal firm combines the competencies of different functions within or across organizations to produce tangible and/or intangible differences between the focal firm's offerings and those of competitors
- linkages among functions within the focal firm (Ford Motor Company's combination of auto manufacturing and financing)
- linkages with other firms (Mattel toys in McDonald's Happy Meals)
- product mix (Cisco's wide range of Internet technology products)

- distribution channels (Coke & Pepsi vending machines)
- service and support (Lexus service).

Example: Chrysler Reintroduces the Hemi Engine

Chrysler has exploited several bases of differentiation with its reintroduction of the Hemi engine. Reintroduced in 2002, this engine was actually developed in the 1960's. It was used in Chrysler's muscle cars in the late 60's and 70's. In 1996, an engineering team headed by Robert E. Lee was assigned to develop a high power engine to use in Dodge pickups. At the time, Dodge pickups lagged behind Ford and GM pickups in power. Lee and his team decided to use the old Hemi design which gets its name from the hemispherical shape of the top of the engines cylinders. This hemispherical shape serves to concentrate the fuel and air at the top of the cylinder. Lee's team also used two spark plugs in each cylinder. The shape of the cylinder head and the two spark plugs makes the engine much more powerful and efficient than other engines the same size. They also designed the new Hemi to be even more fuel efficient on the highway by shutting down four of the eight cylinders at highway cruising speeds. These product features added very little cost to the engine.

Chrysler embarked on a marketing campaign that has met with huge success. This campaign attempts to tap into the nostalgia for the muscle cars of the 60's and 70's. Phrases from advertisements like "Well, it's a Hemi"; "That thing got a Hemi?; and "It's got a Hemi" have become popular, even among young people who had no idea what a Hemi engine was before the advertisements appeared.

The Hemi engine is a pricey option, but customers are clamoring for the engine. On a Dodge Magnum, the Hemi adds about $5,000 to the price tag. Remember, the incremental cost to Chrysler is miniscule. Most of that $5,000 is pure profit. Forty-one percent of the Chrysler 300's, 46% of Dodge Magnum's, 72% of the new Dodge Charger's, and 52% of the Dodge Durango's are sold with the Hemi. In 2004, Chrysler sold almost 300,000 cars and pickups with the Hemi engine. The company had profits of $1.9 billion in 2004, when Ford and GM had large losses.

The Hemi brand has become very popular. Chrysler decided to offer the engine in the Jeep Grand Cherokee, but it didn't put the Hemi badge on the car. Jeep customers began calling Chrysler asking for the badges so they could put one on their cars. In response, Chrysler now puts the Hemi badge on the Grand Cherokee. In fact, Chrysler recently increased the size of the Hemi badge.

Chrysler seems to have successfully differentiated its products by combining several bases of differentiation such as product features, links within the organization, reputation, and consumer marketing. Chrysler recognized that the full value of the product feature (Hemi engine) would not be realized without a focus on consumer marketing that played on the reputation of the product feature. Chrysler also realized that the value of the differentiated product could be increased by spreading the product feature and the reputation across multiple car lines (links with the organization).

Value of Differentiation

Neutralizing Threats. Here is a brief description of how product differentiation can neutralize the threats of the forces mentioned in the Five Forces Model along with an example of each one. If the focal firm's product differentiation strategy is effective:

Threat of Entry

- would-be entrants face the costs of overcoming customers' preferences for the focal firm's products and/or services
- Example: Toyota was protected from Hyundai's entry into the U.S. market because Hyundai had to enter at a low price and advertise heavily to attract customers away from Toyota's well-established Corolla.

Threat of Rivalry

- customers have, to some extent, segmented themselves based on their preferences for the products of the several competing firms in a market.

Thus, the rivalry is generally lower among firms competing in a market of differentiated products.

- *Example:* Allen Edmonds men's dress shoes sell for around $300. Most models have thick leather soles that conform comfortably to the foot. Once a customer wears Allen Edmonds shoes, he tends to be very loyal to the brand. Cole Hahn is a competitor at the high end of the market. Some people prefer Cole Hahn, some prefer Allen Edmonds and once the customer decides on a preference, there is little competition remaining between Cole Hahn and Allen Edmonds.

Product differentiation attenuates rivalry for Allen Edmonds because competition for customers is minimized due to customers' selfselected segmentation.

Threat of Substitutes

- customers will find the focal firm's products and services substantially more attractive than substitute products (i.e., customers are less inclined to even try the substitute product and the focal firm is therefore insulated from the threat of the substitute)

Example: Printing digital photographs on a personal printer at home may be viewed as a substitute for professional printing at a photo shop. Photo shops that advertise that their digital prints are superior to what can be printed at home are attempting to create a preference for their product. Shops that successfully convince customers that their product is superior are insulated from the competitive pressure of the in-home substitute.

Threat of Suppliers

- The power of suppliers may be mitigated in two ways. First, the focal firm will likely be able to pass supplier price increases along to customers who have a preference for the focal firm's differentiated product (customers with a preference for a differentiated product tend not to be price sensitive).

Second, a firm that enjoys the strong preference of customers will usually have more bargaining power with suppliers compared to competitors that do not have differentiated products and services.

- *Example:* Recent spikes in the price of beef are easily passed on to customers of high-end steak houses like Ruth's Chris and Spencer's. McDonald's, Wendy's, and Burger King's customers are more sensitive to price increases that make the $.99 burger a thing of the past.

Threat of Buyers

- The power of buyers is reduced because the focal firm enjoys a quasimonopoly. By definition, if a firm has a highly differentiated product, then the firm is the only firm in that market that can offer that particular product. Customers with a preference for the focal firm's products and services must buy from the focal firm, thus reducing the power of buyers.

- Daimler-Chrysler's Crossfire sports car has allowed dealers to enjoy a quasi-monopoly as evidenced by the "local market adjustment" (of about $5,000) that dealers are able to tack onto the price of the car. The car is different from other cars and a set of customers has a strong preference for the car. There are a limited number of the cars being built. These factors serve to greatly reduce the power of buyers of the Crossfire.

Exploiting Opportunities. A product differentiation strategy can be used to exploit opportunities in several different ways. The textbook focuses on how product differentiation can be used to exploit opportunities based on the type of industry in which the focal firm operates.

In addition to industry-type opportunities, there are many other opportunities that arise in the external environment that firms can exploit. In a sense, a firm is exploiting an opportunity in the external environment any time it is able to fill some customer need in a new or different way.

- Important Point: The value of product differentiation that comes from exploiting an opportunity in the external environment is a function of the benefit the differentiation creates for customers—either real or perceived. Product differentiation may create advantages for the focal firm vis-a-vis competitors, but these advantages all have their roots in benefits to customers.
- Important Point: Successful product differentiation results in two important outcomes that generate value for the focal firm. First, customers develop *preferences* for the focal firm's products and/or services. Second, when customers perceive a benefit to themselves they become willing to pay a premium for the differences that create that benefit.

If the benefit is great enough that customers are willing to pay a price that is above the focal firm's average total cost, then we can conclude that the product differentiation strategy has created value for the firm. The firm whose customers have a preference for its products and a willingness to pay a premium price for its products is in an enviable position.

Other Opportunities in the External Environment

Trends or Fads:

- firms can provide a differentiated product to satisfy the needs of customers who are responding to trends or fads
- custom wheel "spinners" are a current example

Government Policy:

- Changes in government policy can provide many opportunities for firms to develop differentiated products
- Significant tax incentives exist in the U.S. and Europe for highly efficient automobiles that help make cars like the Toyota Prius and the SMARTCAR attractive to customers

Social Causes:

- social causes can create demand for differentiated products that help people further their cause of choice
- credit cards issued by causes (in partnership with an issuer) have become a point of differentiation in the credit card business—World Wild Life Fund, alumni associations, etc.

Economic Conditions:

- almost any economic condition creates opportunities for product differentiation (high unemployment, low unemployment; high interest rates, low interest rates; high inflation, low inflation; etc.)
- first Hyundai and then Suzuki tried to differentiate their low priced cars by offering the "best" warranties in America in response to stagnating car sells brought on by economic conditions

Product Differentiation and Competitive Advantage

Having established the *V*alue of product differentiation, we next consider the *R*areness and *I*mitability of product differentiation. The answer to the question of rareness can safely be assumed to be affirmative at this point in the analysis. The assumption is that the focal firm has established a differentiated product, which implies that the product is rare. We therefore turn our attention to the question of imitability. If a product differentiation strategy is costly to imitate, the focal firm can reasonably expect to enjoy a competitive advantage.

- *Important Point:* Remember that the notion of 'costly to imitate' means that the cost of imitating the strategy would prove to be greater than the benefit of imitating the strategy. This implies that would-be imitators would rationally choose not to attempt imitation.
- *Important Point:* Only product differentiation strategies based on resources and capabilities that are the result of unique historical circumstances, causally ambiguous, and/or socially complex will be costly to imitate.

Easy to Duplicate

Product Features

- are easy for competitors to observe
- unless there is a patent, competitors face little cost in imitation
- may lead to temporary competitive advantage until competitors are able to imitate
- Example: Wrinkle-free, 100% cotton in shirts, blouses, and pants is a product feature that has been rapidly duplicated. This innovation meant that customers could enjoy the feel of 100% cotton without having to iron or professionally launder their clothing. Nordstrom was an early adopter with its SmartCare line. Most other department stores now have their own line of all cotton clothing that is wrinkle-free.

May be Costly to Duplicate

Product mix.

Links with other firms.

Product customization.

Product complexity.

Consumer marketing.

- these bases all entail a relationship and/or the need for coordination
- if any of these relationships and/or coordination efforts are

marked by unique historical circumstances, causal ambiguity, or more likely, social complexity, then it may be costly for other firms to imitate these relationships

- *Example:* iTunes is part of Apple's product mix. iTunes depends on links with several other firms in the music, entertainment, and technology industries. The product is customizable and, to some extent, complex. Consumer marketing is definitely a part of the iTunes strategy. As time goes on, the iTunes model is becoming increasingly costly to imitate as these relationships and coordination efforts mature. Customers face switching costs that imitators would have to overcome.
- these relationships could exist without being historically unique, causally ambiguous or socially complex, in which case, they could be easily imitate.

Usually Costly to Duplicate

- all have the common element of uniqueness in some way, most of the time (specific linkages can exist only in the focal firm, there is only one 'first mover', there is only one of a prime location, there is only one firm reputation, etc.)
- in many cases, it would be impossible for a competitor to duplicate the base of differentiation
- links, reputation, distribution channels, and service and support all depend on relationships
- these relationships are usually marked by historical uniqueness, social complexity, and often by causal ambiguity—making it very costly for competitors to duplicate the relationships
- differentiated service and support is usually the result of social complexity within the firm and between firm employees and customers
- the relationships that lead to happy employees, that in turn, lead to happy customers through differentiated service are costly, if not impossible, to imitate.

Example: What is the first brand name that comes to mind when you hear the phrase "high quality watch"?

Rolex is the answer most people give. The product differentiation that Rolex enjoys initially stemmed from several bases, including product

Toyota developed a manufacturing system that drove costs to a minimum. Toyota recognized that they could achieve low manufacturing costs and very high quality simultaneously with their system. Most American consumers initially viewed Toyota as a low cost alternative to higher priced American cars. In time, Toyota began to differentiate its products on quality. Its Lexus line is very much a differentiated product that is manufactured at a very competitive cost among luxury car makers.

Mercedes developed a strong reputation for high quality cars. For many years, cost was not a critical issue for Mercedes. The introduction of car lines like the Lexus and the rising popularity of SUVs has forced Mercedes to focus more on cost.

In other words, Mercedes is being forced to be concerned about cost. It remains to be seen if Mercedes will become competitive on cost or if Mercedes will further differentiate its cars on quality. Some industry analysts worry that Mercedes may hurt its reputation for quality if it tries to focus on cost too much.

Ford very successfully introduced the Taurus as described above. However, in 1996 Ford tried to move the Taurus up market. Other car makers had imitated many of the Taurus' most distinguishing features. Ford tried to differentiate the Taurus with even more 'rounding' of the body. The sticker price was raised about $2,500. This attempt to differentiate the Taurus was a failure. Many customers turned to the Toyota Camry and the Honda Accord. By 1996 the Taurus wasn't a cost leader and it wasn't highly differentiated. It seems to have become stuck in the middle.

K-Mart tried to differentiate itself by moving upscale in the mid-1990s. Having realized it couldn't compete with Wal-Mart on price, K-Mart seems to have decided to adopt a level of differentiation. Celebrities such as Kathy Ireland and Martha Stewart were used to try to generate more sales in clothing and household goods, respectively. Stores were remodeled.

Many were converted to "Big K" stores. Several years of financial performance, including a bankruptcy, suggest that this attempt at differentiation did not work. K-Mart seems to have tried to abandon cost leadership in favour of differentiation. In the end, it seems to have become stuck in the middle.

International Implementation of Product Differentiation

When a firm contemplates entering an international market, one of the main questions to be answered is: How much must the products and/or services of the focal firm be modified for the foreign market? The answer to this question depends primarily on two issues. First, the degree of necessary modification depends on whether the product or service in question lends itself to standardization across national boundaries. Second, the degree of modification depends on how similar the tastes and preferences of the foreign customers are to the tastes and preferences of customers in the firm's domestic market.

If a global standard exists for a product or service, then local tastes and preferences are not a major concern. This is often the case with electronics and high technology products. Such a situation calls for what is known as a global international expansion strategy. Firms using this strategy rely on centralized decision making and strive for efficiencies from being able to produce at global volumes. The business functions remain centralized at headquarters. In many ways, the logic of the global strategy is similar to the cost leadership strategy. Historically, Japanese companies like Sony and Hitachi have been successful with global strategies.

On the other hand, if a product does not have a global standard and there are significant differences in local tastes and preferences from country to country, then what is known as a multi-domestic strategy is used. This strategy consists of replicating business functions in multiple countries as needed. For example, a firm using this strategy might establish marketing and finance organizations in each country where it operates.

The implementation of this strategy is similar to the implementation of a product differentiation strategy in that managers and employees are given great latitude in responding to local tastes and preferences. Historically, European companies like Phillips, Siemens, and Unilever have been successful using the multi-domestic strategy. A hybrid of these two approaches, known as the transnational strategy, has been suggested as a way to exploit the benefits of both the global and multi-domestic strategies. The basic idea behind this strategy is that the local knowledge gleaned from *multi-domestic* operations can be transferred around the world through a *global* network of coordinated reporting relationships.

Summary of Product Differentiation

The main points from this discussion that students need to understand are:

1) successful product differentiation means that customers have a preference for the focal firm's products and/or services
2) customers' preferences will lead them to pay a premium price for the focal firm's products and/or services
3) there are many possible bases of differentiation—in fact, almost anything could be a base of differentiation
4) product differentiation may lead to competitive advantage if the base of differentiation meets the VRIO criteria
5) the value of a base of differentiation can be manifest by limiting a threat and/or exploiting an opportunity in the external environment
6) some bases of differentiation are easy to duplicate, some may be costly to duplicate, and some are usually costly to duplicate
7) a successful product differentiation strategy depends on the appropriate implementation of the strategy with respect to organizational structure, management controls, and compensation policies
8) firms can simultaneously pursue both cost leadership and product differentiation strategies but it is difficult to do.

Non-price Competition

Non-price competition is a marketing strategy "in which one firm tries to distinguish its product or service from competing products on the basis of attributes like design and workmanship" (McConnell-Brue, 2002, p. 437-438). The firm can also distinguish its product offering through quality of service, extensive distribution, customer focus, or any other sustainable competitive advantage other than price. It can be contrasted with price competition, which is where a company tries to distinguish its product or service from competing products on the basis of low price. Non-price competition typically involves promotional expenditures, (such as advertising, selling staff, sales promotions, coupons, special orders, or free gifts), marketing research, new product development, and brand management costs.

Firms will engage in non-price competition, in spite of the additional costs involved, because it is usually more profitable than selling for a lower price, and avoids the risk of a price war.

Although any company can use a non-price competition strategy, it is most common among oligopolies and monopolistic competition, because firms can be extremely competitive

Marketing

Marketing is the process associated with promoting for sale goods or services. It is considered a "social and managerial process by which individuals and groups obtain what they need and want through creating and exchanging products and values with others." It is an integrated process through which companies create value for customers and build strong customer relationships in order to capture value from customers in return.

Marketing is used to create the customer, to keep the customer and to satisfy the customer. With the customer as the focus of its activities, it can be concluded that *marketing management* is one of the major components of business management. The evolution of marketing was caused due to mature markets and overcapacities in the last decades. Companies then shifted the focus from production more to the customer in order to stay profitable.

The term *marketing concept* holds that achieving organisational goals depends on knowing the needs and wants of target markets and delivering the desired satisfactions. It proposes that in order to satisfy its organizational objectives, an organization should anticipate the needs and wants of consumers and satisfy these more effectively than competitors.

Further Definitions

Marketing is defined by the American Marketing Association as *"the activity, set of institutions, and processes for creating, communicating, delivering, and exchanging offerings that have value for customers, clients, partners, and society at large."* The term developed from the original meaning which referred literally to going to a market to buy or sell goods or services. Seen from a systems point of view, sales process engineering views marketing as *"a set of processes that are interconnected and interdependent with other functions, whose methods can be improved using a variety of relatively new approaches."*

The Chartered Institute of Marketing defines marketing as *"the management process responsible for identifying, anticipating and satisfying customer requirements profitably.*" A different concept is the *value-based marketing* which states the role of marketing to contribute to increasing shareholder value. In this context, marketing is defined as "*the management process that seeks to maximise returns to shareholders by developing relationships with valued customers and creating a competitive advantage.*"

Marketing practice tended to be seen as a creative industry in the past, which included advertising, distribution and selling. However, because the academic study of marketing makes extensive use of social sciences, psychology, sociology, mathematics, economics, anthropology and neuroscience, the profession is now widely recognized as a science, allowing numerous universities to offer Master-of-Science (MSc) programmes. The overall process starts with marketing research and goes through market segmentation, business planning and execution, ending with pre and post-sales promotional activities. It is also related to many of the creative arts. The marketing literature is also adept at re-inventing itself and its vocabulary according to the times and the culture.

Organizational Orientation

In this sense, a firm's marketing department is often seen as of prime importance within the functional level of an organization. Information from an organization's marketing department would be used to guide the actions of other departments within the firm. As an example, a marketing department could ascertain (via marketing research) that consumers desired a new type of product, or a new usage for an existing product. With this in mind, the marketing department would inform the R&D department to create a prototype of a product/service based on consumers' new desires. The production department would then start to manufacture the product, while the marketing department would focus on the promotion, distribution, pricing, etc. of the product. Additionally, a firm's finance department would be consulted, with respect to securing appropriate funding for the development, production and promotion of the product. Inter-departmental conflicts may occur, should a firm adhere to the marketing orientation. Production may oppose the installation, support and servicing of new capital stock, which may be needed to manufacture a new product. Finance may oppose the required capital expenditure, since it could undermine a healthy cash flow for the organization.

Mutually Beneficial Exchange

A further marketing orientation is the focus on a *mutually beneficial exchange*. In a transaction in the market economy, a firm gains revenue, which thus leads to more profits/market share/sales. A consumer on the other hand gains the satisfaction of a need/want, utility, reliability and value for money from the purchase of a product or service. As no one has to buy goods from any one supplier in the market economy, firms must entice consumers to buy goods with contemporary marketing ideals.

Herd Behaviour

Herd behaviour in marketing is used to explain the dependencies of customers' mutual behaviour. *The Economist* reported a recent conference in Rome on the subject of the simulation of adaptive human behaviour. It shared mechanisms to increase impulse buying and get people "to buy more by playing on the herd instinct."

The basic idea is that people will buy more of products that are seen to be popular, and several feedback mechanisms to get product popularity information to consumers are mentioned, including smart card technology and the use of Radio Frequency Identification Tag technology. A "swarm-moves" model was introduced by a Florida Institute of Technology researcher, which is appealing to supermarkets because it can "increase sales without the need to give people discounts."

Other recent studies on the "power of social influence" include an "artificial music market in which some 14,000 people downloaded previously unknown songs" (Columbia University, New York); a Japanese chain of convenience stores which orders its products based on "sales data from department stores and research companies;" a Massachusetts company exploiting knowledge of social networking to improve sales; and online retailers who are increasingly informing consumers about "which products are popular with like-minded consumers" (e.g., Amazon, eBay).

Further Orientations

- An emerging area of study and practice concerns *internal marketing*, or how employees are trained and managed to deliver the brand in a way that positively impacts the acquisition and retention of customers, see also *employer branding.*

- *Diffusion of innovations* research explores how and why people adopt new products, services and ideas.
- With consumers' eroding attention span and willingness to give time to advertising messages, marketers are turning to forms of *permission marketing* such as *branded content*, *custom media* and *reality marketing*.

Marketing Research

Marketing research involves conducting research to support marketing activities, and the statistical interpretation of data into information. This information is then used by managers to plan marketing activities, gauge the nature of a firm's marketing environment, attain information from suppliers, etc. Marketing researchers use statistical methods (such as quantitative research, qualitative research, hypothesis tests, Chi-squared tests, linear regression, correlation co-efficients, frequency distributions, Poisson and Binomial distributions, etc.) to interpret their findings and convert data into information. The marketing research process spans a number of stages including the definition of a problem, development of a research plan, collecting and interpretation of data and disseminating information formally in form of a report.

A distinction should be made between *marketing research* and *market research*. Market research pertains to research in a given market. As an example, a firm may conduct research in a target market, after selecting a suitable market segment. In contrast, marketing research relates to all research conducted within marketing. Thus, market research is a subset of marketing research.

Marketing Environment

The term *marketing environment* relates to all of the factors (whether internal, external, direct or indirect) that affect a firm's marketing decision-making or planning and is subject of the marketing research. A firm's marketing environment consists of two main areas, which are:

Macro Environment

On the macro environment a firm holds only little control. It consists of a variety of external factors that manifest on a large (or macro) scale. These are typically economic, social, political or technological phenomena. A common method of assessing a firm's macro-environment is via a PESTLE (Political, Economic, Social,

Technological, Legal, Ecological) analysis. Within a PESTLE analysis, a firm would analyse national political issues, culture and climate, key macroeconomic conditions, health and indicators (such as economic growth, inflation, unemployment, etc.), social trends/attitudes, and the nature of technology's impact on its society and the business processes within the society.

Micro Environment

A firm holds a greater amount (though not necessarily total) control of the micro environment. It comprises factors pertinent to the firm itself, or stakeholders closely connected with the firm or company. A firm's micro environment typically spans:

- Customers/consumers
- Employees
- Suppliers
- The Media.

By contrast to the macro environment, an organization holds a greater degree of control over these factors.

Market Segmentation

Market segmentation pertains to the division of a market of consumers into persons with similar needs and wants. As an example, if using Kellogg's cereals in this instance, Frosties are marketed to children. Crunchy Nut Cornflakes are marketed to adults. Both goods aforementioned denote two products which are marketed to two distinct groups of persons, both with like needs, traits, and wants. The purpose for market segmentation is conducted for two main issues.

First, a segmentation allows a better allocation of a firm's finite resources. A firm only possesses a certain amount of resources. Accordingly, it must make choices (and appreciate the related costs) in servicing specific groups of consumers.

Furthermore the diversified tastes of the contemporary Western consumers can be served better. With more diversity in the tastes of modern consumers, firms are taking noting the benefit of servicing a multiplicity of new markets.

Market segmentation can be defined in terms of the *STP* acronym, meaning *Segment*, *Target* and *Position*.

Segment

Segmentation involves the initial splitting up of consumers into persons of like needs/wants/tastes. Four commonly used criteria are used for segmentation, which include:

- Geographical (e.g. country, region, city, town, etc.)
- Psychographic (i.e. personality traits or character traits which influence consumer behaviour)
- Demographic (e.g. age, gender, socio-economic class, etc.)
- Behavioural (e.g. brand loyalty, usage rate, etc.).

Target

Once a segment has been identified, a firm must ascertain whether the segment is beneficial for them to service. The *DAMP* acronym, meaning *Discernible, Accessible, Measurable* and *Profitable*, are used as criteria to gauge the viability of a target market. DAMP is explained in further detail below:

- Discernable-How a segment can be differentiated from other segments.
- Accessible-How a segment can be accessed via Marketing Communications produced by a firm.
- Measurable-Can the segment be quantified and its size determined?
- Profitable-Can a sufficient return on investment be attained from a segment's servicing?

The next step in the targeting process is the level of differentiation involved in a segment serving. Three modes of differentiation exist, which are commonly applied by firms. These are:

- Undifferentiated-Where a company produces a like product for all of a market segment.
- Differentiated-In which a firm produced slight modifications of a product within a segment.
- Niche-In which an organisation forges a product to satisfy a specialised target market.

Position

Positioning concerns how to position a product in the minds of consumers. A firm often performs this by producing a perceptual map, which denotes products produced in its industry according to how consumers perceive their price and quality. From a product's placing on the map, a firm would tailor its marketing communications to suit meld with the product's perception among consumers.

Marketing Information System

A *marketing information system (MKIS)* is an information system that is commonly used by marketing management to analyse and view information pertaining to marketing activities. As the label suggests, an MKIS is a computer-based information system therefore used to input, store, process and output marketing information. An MKIS spans four subset components, which are detailed below:

Marketing Intelligence System

This sub-system stores information gathered from a firm's marketing intelligence activities. Marketing intelligence consists of actions a firm would undertake within its own market or industry, geared towards information existing within its markets. This can be obtained via communication with suppliers, consumers or other bodies within a market.

Internal Processes System

The internal processes system catalogues all internal marketing processes within a firm.

Marketing Research System

This section of the overall system contains data from a firm's marketing research activities.

Analytical System

The analytical system is the only sub-system which does not store data or information. It's function is to analyse and process data from the other three systems, into reliable, timely and relevant information for the perusal and use of marketing management.

Types of Marketing Research

Marketing research, as a sub-set aspect of marketing activities, can be divided into the following parts:

- Primary research (also known as field research), which involves the conduction and compilation of research for the purpose is was intended.

- Secondary research (also referred to as desk research), is initially conducted for one purpose, but often used to support another purpose or end goal.

By these definitions, an example of primary research would be market research conducted into health foods, which is used *solely* to ascertain the needs/wants of the target market for health foods. Secondary research, again according to the above definition, would be research pertaining to health foods, but used by a firm wishing to develop an unrelated product.

Primary research is often expensive to prepare, collect and interpret from data to information. Nonetheless, while secondary research is relatively inexpensive, it often can become outdated and outmoded, given it is used for a purpose other than for which is was intended. Primary research can also be broken down into quantitative research and qualitative research, which as the labels suggest, pertain to numerical and non-numerical research methods, techniques.

The appropriateness of each mode of research depends on whether data can be quantified (quantitative research), or whether subjective, non-numeric or abstract concepts are required to be studied (qualitative research).

Marketing Planning

The area of *marketing planning* involves forging a plan for a firm's marketing activities. A marketing plan can also pertain to a specific product, as well as to an organisation's overall marketing strategy. Generally speaking, an organisation's marketing planning process is derived from its overall business strategy. Thus, when top management are devising the firm's strategic direction or mission, the intended marketing activities are incorporated into this plan. Within the overall strategic marketing plan, the marketing planning process contains the following stages:

- Mission statement
- Corporate objectives-These are the broad-based objectives resulting from the firm's mission statement.
- Marketing audit-a marketing audit is an audit of all marketing processes within a firm. It's purpose is to highlight which areas require improvement, and which ones require modification, prior to the establishment of the marketing plan.

- SWOT analysis
- Assumptions arising from the marketing audit and SWOT analysis
- Marketing objectives derived from the assumptions
- An estimation of the expected results of the objectives
- Identification of alternative plans or mixes
- Budgeting for the marketing plan
- A first-year implementation program.

There are several levels of marketing objectives within an organization. As stated previously, the senior management of a firm would formulate a general business strategy for a firm. However, this general business strategy would be interpreted and implemented in different contexts throughout the firm.

Corporate

Corporate marketing objectives are typically broad-based in nature, and pertain to the general vision of the firm in the short, medium or long-term. As an example, if one pictures a group of companies (or a conglomerate), top management may state that sales for the group should increase by 25% over a ten year period.

Strategic Business Unit

An SBU is an autonomous entity within a firm, which produces a unique product/service. It could be a single product, a product line, or a subsidiary of a larger group of companies. The SBU would embrace the corporate strategy, and attune it to its own particular industry. For instance, an SBU may partake in the sports goods industry. It thus would ascertain how it would attain additional sales of sports goods, in order to satisfy the overall business strategy.

Functional

The functional level relates to departments within the SBUs, such as marketing, finance, HR, production, etc. The functional level would adopt the SBU's strategy and determine how to accomplish the SBU's own objectives in its market.

To use the example of the sports goods industry again, the marketing department would draw up marketing plans, strategies and communications to help the SBU achieve its marketing aims.

Product Life Cycle

The Product Life Cycle or *PLC* is a tool used by marketing managers to gauge the progress of a product, especially relating to sales or revenue accrued over time. The PLC is based on a few key assumptions, including that a given product would possess an *introduction*, *growth*, *maturity* and *decline* stage. Furthermore it is assumed that no product lasts perpetually on the market. Last but not least a firm must employ differing strategies, according to where a product is on the PLC.

Introduction

In this stage, a product is launched onto the market. To stimulate growth of sales/revenue, use of advertising may be high, in order to heighten awareness of the product in question.

Growth

The product's sales/revenue is increasing, which may stimulate more marketing communications to sustain sales. More entrants enter into the market, to reap the apparent high profits that the industry is producing.

Maturity

A product's sales start to level off, and an increasing number of entrants to a market produce price falls for the product. Firms may utilise sales promotions to raise sales.

Decline

Demand for a good begins to taper off, and the firm may opt to discontinue manufacture of the product. This is so, if revenue for the product comes from efficiency savings in production, over actual sales of a good/service. However, if a product services a niche market, or is complementary to another product, it may continue manufacture of the product, despite a low level of sales/revenue being accrued.

Marketing Strategy

The field of marketing strategy encompasses the strategy involved in the management of a given product.

A given firm may hold numerous products in the marketplace, spanning numerous and sometimes wholly unrelated industries. Accordingly, a plan is required in order to manage effectively such products. Such decisions consist of the following decisions:

- Should we (,i.e. the firm) enter a market/industry?
- Should we increase funding for our product(s)?
- Should we maintain funding for our product(s)?
- Should we divest or cease production of our product(s)?

Evidently, a company needs to weigh up and ascertain how to utilise effectively its finite resources. As an example, a start-up car manufacturing firm would face little success, should it attempt to rival immediately Toyota, Ford, Nissan or any other large global car maker. Moreover, a product may be reaching the end of its life-cycle. Thus, the issue of divest, or a ceasing of production may be made. With regard to the aforesaid questions, each scenario requires a unique marketing strategy to be employed. Below are listed some prominent marketing strategy models, which seek to propose means to answer the preceding questions.

Ansoff Matrix

The Ansoff Matrix was devised by Igor Ansoff, a Russian-born American pioneer of strategic planning.

Ansoff proposed his Matrix, as a means of identifying how a firm should market its product in differing scenarios. The labels are listed below:

- X-axis
- Existing markets
- Existing products
- Y-axis
- New markets
- New products.

Four quadrants can then be determined, which are:

- Market penetration
- Diversification
- Market development
- Product Development.

Each aforesaid category provides a unique marketing scenario, in which Ansoff denoted a given strategy.

Marketing mix

In the early 1960s, Professor Neil Borden at Harvard Business

School identified a number of company performance actions that can influence the consumer decision to purchase goods or services. Borden suggested that all those actions of the company represented a "Marketing Mix". Professor E. Jerome McCarthy, at the Michigan State University in the early 1960s, suggested that the Marketing Mix contained 4 elements product, price, place and promotion.

Product

The product aspects of marketing deal with the specifications of the actual goods or services, and how it relates to the end-user's needs and wants. The scope of a product generally includes supporting elements such as warranties, guarantees, and support.

Pricing

This refers to the process of setting a price for a product, including discounts. The price need not be monetary; it can simply be what is exchanged for the product or services, e.g. time, energy, or attention. Methods of setting prices optimally are in the domain of pricing science. A number of modes of pricing techniques exist, which span:

- Elasticities (whether Price Elasticity of Demand, Cross Elasticity of Demand, or Income Elasticity of Demand)
- Market skimming pricing
- Market penetration pricing.

Elasticities are a microeconomic concept, which gauges how elastic demand is for a given good/service. In a marketing context, its usefulness relates to the suitable level at which a product can be priced, in accordance with price, a product's complements and substitutes, and the level of income a consumer possesses.

Market skimming pertains to firm releasing a good in a "first to market" scenario. As an example, picture a company which releases a new type of personal media playing system. It may set the good at an initially high level, but reduce it over time, once the level of demand gradually rises. Market skimming is best operable within a first to market scenario, since there would be few competitors within the company's industry. This pricing strategy is also best implemented within a market of high entry barriers (such as a monopoly or an oligopoly). This is so since the high barriers to entry discourage competitors into the industry for the product.

Market penetration concerns pricing policies for late entrants to a market. As another example, a company could release a product into a market years after it is initially introduced, but at an artificially low price in order to stimulate demand. The result of such a pricing strategy would be to draw consumers from competitors and into purchasing its own product. Market penetration, in contrast to market skimming, best functions within a market form with low barriers to entry (such as perfect competition or monopolistic competition). Low barriers to entry facilitates a company's ability to sell goods at a price lower than its market clearing point.

Placement (or Distribution)

This refers to how the product gets to the customer; for example, point-of-sale placement or retailing. This third P has also sometimes been called *Place*, referring to the channel by which a product or service is sold (e.g. online vs. retail), which geographic region or industry, to which segment (young adults, families, business people), etc. also referring to how the environment in which the product is sold in can affect sales.

Promotion

This includes advertising, sales promotion, including promotional education, publicity, and personal selling. Branding refers to the various methods of promoting the product, brand, or company.

These four elements are often referred to as the marketing mix, which a marketer can use to craft a marketing plan. The four Ps model is most useful when marketing low value consumer products. Industrial products, services, high value consumer products require adjustments to this model. Services marketing must account for the unique nature of services. Industrial or B2B marketing must account for the long term contractual agreements that are typical in supply chain transactions. Relationship marketing attempts to do this by looking at marketing from a long term relationship perspective rather than individual transactions. As a counter to this, Morgan, in *Riding the Waves of Change* (Jossey-Bass, 1988), suggests that one of the greatest limitations of the 4 Ps approach "is that it unconsciously emphasizes the inside–out view (looking from the company outwards), whereas the essence of marketing should be the outside–in approach".

In order to recognize the different aspects of selling services, as opposed to Products, a further three Ps were added to make a range of *Seven Ps* for service industries:

- Process-the way in which orders are handled, customers are satisfied and the service is delivered.
- Physical Evidence-is tangible evidence of the service customers will receive (for example a holiday brochure).
- People-the people meeting and dealing with the customers.

As markets have become more satisfied, the 7 Ps have become relevant to those companies selling products, as well as those solely involved with services: customers now differentiate between sellers of goods by the service they receive in the process from the people involved. Some authors cite a further P-Packaging-this is thought by many to be part of Product, but in certain markets (Japan, China for example) and with certain products (perfume, cosmetics) the packaging of a product has a greater importance-maybe even than the product itself.

Marketing Communications

Marketing communications is defined by actions a firm takes to communicate with end-users, consumers and external parties. A simple definition of marketing communication is *"the means by which a supplier of goods, services, values and/or ideas represent themselves to their target audience with the goal of stimulating dialog leading to better commercial or other relationships"*. *Marcoms* is a frequently used short-form for marketing communications. Marketing communications can be seen as a part of the promotional mix, as the exact nature of how to apply marketing communications depends on the nature of the product in question.

Accordingly, a given product would require a unique communications mix, in order to convey successfully information to consumers. Some products may require a stronger emphasis on personal sales, while others may need more focus on advertising.

The process in which the differing modes of marketing communications are complemented and synthesised is called *integrated marketing communications (IMC)*.

It is used in order to create a single and coherent marketing communications process. As an example, a firm can advertise the existence of a sales promotion, via a newspaper, magazine, TV, radio, etc. The same promotion can also be communicated via direct marketing, or personal selling. The aim of IMC is to lessen confusion among a product's target market, and to lessen cost for the firm. Several different subsets of marketing communications can be distinguished.

Personal Selling

Oral presentation given by a salesperson who approaches individuals or a group of potential customers. Personal selling is often used in business to business (,i.e. "B2B") settings, in addition to business to consumer (,i.e. "B2C") scenarios in which a personal and face to face medium is required for the communication of the product. In B2B situations, personal selling is preferred if the product is technical in nature. Personal selling can compose of the use of presentations, in order to convey the benefits of a firm's good/service. In B2C settings, personal selling is utilised if the product requires to be tailored to the unique needs of an individual. Examples of this include car (and other vehicle) sales, financial services (such as insurance or investment), etc. Personal selling involves the following points:

- Live, interactive relationship
- Personal interest
- Attention and response
- Interesting presentation
- Clear and thorough.

Sales Promotion

Short-term incentives to encourage buying of products.

- Instant appeal
- Anxiety to sell

An example is coupons or a sale. People are given an incentive to buy, but this does not build customer loyalty or encourage future repeat buys. A major drawback of sales promotion is that it is easily copied by competition. It cannot be used as a sustainable source of differentiation. Sales promotions are typically used to heighten sales/ revenue, especially if a firm holds dead/excess stock, or if the market for a product has matured.

Public Relations

Public Relations (or PR, as an acronym) is the use of media tools by a firm in order to promote goodwill from an organization to a target market segment, or other consumers of a firm's good/service. PR stems from the fact that a firm cannot seek to antagonize or inflame its market base, due to incurring a lessened demand for its good/service. Organizations undertake PR in order to assure consumers, and to forestall negative perceptions towards it. PR can span:

- Interviews
- Speeches/Presentations
- Corporate literature, such as financial statements, brochures, etc.

Publicity

Publicity involves attaining space in media, without having to pay directly for such coverage. As an example, an organization may have the launch of a new product covered by a newspaper or TV news segment. This benefits the firm in question since it is making consumers aware of its product, without necessarily paying a newspaper or television station to cover the event.

Advertising

Advertising occurs when a firm directly pays a media channel to publicize its product. Common examples of this include TV and radio adverts, billboards, branding, sponsorship, etc.

Direct Marketing

Direct marketing is a process where a firm uses communication channels to attain and retain consumers for its product. It is a comparatively new mode of marketing communications (when compared with forms such as advertising, sales promotions, personal selling, etc.) Direct marketing involves carefully seeking out persons within a target market, and communicating to them about the nature of a product. This process is signified by brochures sent via the mail, e-mails from companies, etc. It can also constitute the use of telemarketing, in order to communicate with a target market.

International Marketing

International marketing can be defined as the application of marketing strategies, planning and activities to external or foreign markets. International marketing is of consequence to firms which operate in countries and territories other than their home country or the country in which they are registered in and have their head office. The factors influencing international marketing are culture, political and legal factors, a country's level of economic development and the mode of involvement in foreign markets.

The reasons why a firm would engage in international markets are numerous, including:

- Maturity within domestic markets
- To increase general market share, sales or revenue.

Culture

Social norms, attitudes towards buying foreign goods, and the working practices of foreign markets are all cultural factors when opting to invest in foreign markets. Social norms affect business practices, since social norms are one factor in the demand for a product. A company marketing pork would experience less sales in an Islamic country, than it would in China (which is the world's largest consumer of pork). In Western societies, sexuality and sexual topics are often used in marketing communications (such as advertising, for instance). However, in a comparatively more conservative society (such as India for instance) social attitudes may shun the use of sexual topics to advertise products.

Political and Legal Factors

The following political/legal factors are of bearing in international marketing:

- Government attitude to business
- The level of governmental regulations, red-tape and bureaucracy
- Monetary regulations
- Political stability.

Not all governments are as open to foreign investment as others, nor are all governments equally favourable to business. Typically, a firm may opt to invest in an economy in which the government is more inclined to support business activity in a country. In other words, the "business-friendliness" of a foreign government is paramount in this instance.

Additionally, some economies are more "liberal" and less regulated, by comparison to other economies. Excessive regulations can be a hindrance on a firm, since they contribute to additional costs to a firm. Conversely, regulations can aid in assisting firms, by easing the path of doing business. A firm seeking to invest in foreign markets must gauge the regulatory arrangement of the economy it is looking to invest in. Monetary regulations, akin to the above points, can hinder the ability to do business. A high level of monetary regulations can hamper foreign investment within an economy.

Lastly, the political stability of a country is also a key factor in foreign investment decisions. Nation-states experiencing continual coup-d'etat can appear unattractive to invest in, since the continual changes in political system can compound the inherent risk in investing. Typically, a firm would opt to invest in a country which had a stable mode of government, in which handovers of power were peaceful and non-violent. Even if a country is not a liberal democracy, the level of political stability within a country may supersede the political system (or, more accurately, the perceived immorality of a government's policies/ constitutional structure) of a given nation-state.

Level of Economic Development

The level of economic development of an economy can affect foreign investment decisions. Within the field of developmental economics, differing modes of economic development can be identified. These are:

- Developing economy
- Newly-Industrialised country
- Industrialised country (also known as a developed country, advanced economy or first world economy).

A developing economy has a comparatively low general living standard (as defined by material lifestyle/level of material possession). Moreover, a developing economy may also be at subsistence level, or possess a large share of its Gross Domestic Product in primary industries. Accordingly, a developing country would not be a profitable market for high-end consumer goods, or fast-moving consumer goods commonly found in developed/advanced economies. Exports of machinery (related to the extraction and processing of raw materials) may be viable for a developing economy, due to primary industries possessing a large share of national income.

A newly-industrialised economy is an economy which has experienced high recent economic growth, and thus has experienced a rise in general living standards. Coupled with the rapid economic growth, the emergence of a middle class leads to the development of a consumerist culture in the society. A newly-industrialised economy would consequently possess a small general demand for high-end consumer goods, but not to the extent of an advanced economy. A newly-industralised economy may export manufactured goods to other countries, and often possess secondary sector industries as a high percentage of its economic output.

An industrialised economy is typically identified via a high Gross Domestic Product per capita, a high United Nations Human Development Index rating and a high level of tertiary/quaternary/quinary sector industries in the context of its national income. Thus, the high general living standard denotes the highest generalised demand for goods and services within all modes of economic development. Commonly, developed/advanced economies are high exporters of high-tech manufactured goods, as well as service sector products (such as financial services, for instance).

Green Marketing

Green marketing can be defined as the marketing of products which are environmentally sound. The notion of green marketing is a comparatively new one within general marketing thought, as it has chiefly grown in acceptance since the 1990s. Nonetheless, as a contemporary branch of marketing thought, it can be seen as one of the fastest growing areas of marketing principles.

The rationale for the devising and emergence of green marketing is thus:

- A higher quantity of persons willing and able to buy green products.
- Heightened awareness among consumers, concerning the potentially negative aspects of global climate change.

Green marketers thus target persons who are more environmentally conscious. The segmentation and market research processes of numerous firms denote that the target market for green products has grown widely in numerous years. Accordingly, green marketers are willing to supply what persons are willing and able to buy.

It can also be stated that green products are often more expensive than "non-green" products, due perhaps to higher production costs. Nevertheless, green consumers are typically willing to pay higher prices, as a means of doing their part to safeguard the environment of the planet Earth.

Some drawbacks of green marketing are thus:

- The ideal of "green washing"
- Disputes and contention surrounding the exact meaning of a green product

Green washing pertains to when a firm misleadingly produces a product, with ostensible green characteristics, which is not actually environmentally sound. In addition to evident ethical issues concerning deceit, such conduct can undermine an organisation's drive to be deemed a "green" company. Accordingly, a firm must be sincere in its efforts to be environmentally sound, regarding its environmental practices and policies. Moreover, the extent and nature of a green product can be a moot point. To some, a product must be wholly green to be viewed as green. To others, a product may only possess a reduction in environmentally harmful inputs to be worthy of being labelled green. Nonetheless, a firm can enhance its green marketing efforts if it persuades consumers that the purchase of green products can enhance environmental protection.

Buying Behaviour

A marketing firm, in the course of its operations, must ascertain the nature of buying behaviour, if it is to market properly its product. In order to entice and persuade a consumer to buy a product, the psychological/behavioural process of how a given product is purchased.

Buying behaviour consists of two prime strands, namely being consumer (B2C) behaviour and organisational/industrial behaviour (B2B).

B2C Buying Behaviour

This mode of behaviour concerns consumers, in the purchase of a given product. The B2C buying process is as thus:

- Need/want recognition
- Information search
- Search for alternatives (to satisfy need/want)
- Purchase decision
- Post-purchase evaluation.

As an example, if one pictures a pair of sneakers, the desire for a pair of sneakers would be followed by an information search on available types/brands. This may include perusing media outlets, but most commonly consists of information gathered from family and friends.

If the information search is insufficient, the consumer may search for alternative means to satisfy the need/want. In this case, this may be buying leather shoes, sandals, etc. The purchase decision is then made, in which the consumer actually buys the product.

Following this stage, a post-purchase evaluation is often conducted, comprising an appraisal of the value/utility brought by the purchase of the sneakers. If the value/utility is high, then a repeat purchase may be bought. This could then develop into consumer loyalty, for the firm producing the pair of sneakers.

B2B buying Behaviour

B2B buying behaviour relates to organisational/industrial buying behaviour. B2C and B2B behaviour are not exact, as similarities and differences exist. Some of the key differences are listed below:

- Consumer behaviour
- Low in monetary value
- Low in volume/mass
- Swift purchase
- Transaction marketing-based
- Single buying instances
- Number of consumer is higher
- Individual/market-based demand
- Organisational behaviour
- High in monetary value
- High in volume/mass
- Lengthy purchase process
- Relationship marketing-based
- Multiple buying instances
- Number of consumers is lesser
- Demand is consumer derived (in that firms purchase goods to ultimately meet consumer demand) .

The organisational buying process is thush:

- Problem recognition
- Need description
- Product specification
- Supplier search
- Proposal solicitation
- Supplier selection
- Order routine specification
- Supplier performance review.

In a straight rebuy, the fourth, fifth and sixth stages are omitted. In a modified rebuy scenario, the fifth and sixth stages are precluded. In a new buy, all aforementioned stages are conducted.

The Decision Making Unit (DMU)

The DMU, in other terms, can be labelled as the Purchasing or Procurement departments of an organisation Accordingly, it is responsible for the purchasing of organisational items and assets. The persons comprising a DMU are as thus:

- Gatekeepers
- Users
- Buyers
- Decision Makers
- Influencers
- Initiators.

Areas of Marketing Specialization

- Agricultural marketing
- Article marketing
- Cause marketing
- Communal marketing
- Business marketing
- Database marketing
- Digital marketing
- Direct marketing
- Engagement marketing

- Ethical marketing
- Evangelism marketing
- Experiential marketing Global marketing
- Guerrilla marketing
- Integrated marketing
- International marketing
- Internet marketing
- Industrial marketing
- Macromarketing
- Mobile marketing
- Multichannel marketing
- Permission marketing
- Political marketing
- Product marketing
- Proximity marketing
- Public marketing
- Reality marketing
- Referral marketing
- Relationship marketing
- Reverse marketing
- Search engine marketing
- Shopper marketing
- Social media marketing
- Trade marketing
- Value-based marketing
- Wholesale marketing.

Market Segment

A market segment is a group of people or organizations sharing one or more characteristics that cause them to have similar product and/or service needs. A true market segment meets all of the following criteria: it is distinct from other segments (different segments have different needs), it is homogeneous within the segment (exhibits common needs); it responds similarly to a market stimulus, and it can be reached by a market intervention. The term is also used when consumers with identical product and/or service needs are divided up into groups so they can be charged different amounts. These can broadly be viewed as 'positive' and 'negative' applications of the same idea, splitting up the market into smaller groups.

"Positive" Market Segmentation

Market segmenting is dividing market into groups of individual with similar wants or needs that a company divides the market into distinct groups who have distinct needs, wants, behaviour or who might want different products & services.

Broadly, markets can be divided according to a number of general criteria, such as by industry or public versus private although industrial market segmentation is quite different from consumer market segmentation, both have similar objectives. All of these methods of segmentation are merely proxies for true segments, which don't always fit into convenient demographic boundaries.

Consumer-based market segmentation can be performed on a *product specific* basis, to provide a close match between specific products and individuals. However, a number of generic market segment systems also exist, e.g. the Nielsen Claritas PRIZM system provides a broad segmentation of the population of the United States based on the statistical analysis of household and geodemographic data.

The process of segmentation is distinct from targeting (choosing which segments to address) and positioning (designing an appropriate marketing mix for each segment).

The overall intent is to identify groups of similar customers and potential customers; to prioritize the groups to address; to understand their behaviour; and to respond with appropriate marketing strategies that satisfy the different preferences of each chosen segment. Revenues are thus improved.

Improved segmentation can lead to significantly improved marketing effectiveness. Distinct segments can have different industry structures and thus have higher or lower attractiveness (Michael Porter). With the right segmentation, the right lists can be purchased, advertising results can be improved and customer satisfaction can be increased leading to better reputation.

Successful Segmentation

Successful segmentation requires the following

- homogeneity within the segment
- heterogeneity between segments
- segments are measurable and substantial
- segments are differentiable
- segments are accessible and actionable
- target segment is large enough to be profitable.

Variables Used for Segmentation

- Geographic variables.
    - region of the world or country, East, West, South, North, Central, coastal, hilly, etc.
    - county size: Metropolitan Cities, small cities, towns.
    - Density of Area Urban, Semi-urban, Rural.
    - climate Hot, Cold, Humid, Rainy.
- Demographic variables.
    - age.
    - gender Male and Female.
    - family size.
    - family life cycle: young children, empty nest, etc.
    - education Primary, High School, Secondary, College, Universities.
    - income.
    - occupation.
    - socioeconomic status.
    - religion.
    - nationality/race (ethnic marketing).
    - language.
- Psychographic variables.
    - personality.
    - lifestyle.
    - value.
    - attitude.

- Behavioural variables.
  - benefit sought.
  - product usage rate.
  - brand loyalty.
  - product end use.
  - readiness-to-buy stage.
  - buying centre.
  - profitability.
  - income status.
- Technological segmentation variables.
  - motivations.
  - usage patterns.
  - attitudes about technology.
  - fundamental values.
  - lifestyle perspective.
  - standard of living.
  - profit is there in business from the existing clients.

When numerous variables are combined to give an in-depth understanding of a segment, this is referred to as depth segmentation. When enough information is combined to create a clear picture of a typical member of a segment, this is referred to as a buyer profile. When the profile is limited to demographic variables it is called a demographic profile (typically shortened to "a demographic"). A statistical technique commonly used in determining a profile is cluster analysis. Other techniques used to identify segments are algorithms such as CHAID and regression-based CHAID and discriminant analysis. Alternatively, segments can be modelled directly from consumer preferences via discrete choice methodologies such as choice-based conjoint and MaxDiff.

Positioning

Once a market segment has been identified (via segmentation), and targeted (in which the viability of servicing the market is determined), the segment is then subject to positioning. Positioning involves ascertaining how a product is perceived in the minds of consumers.

This part of the segmentation process consists of drawing up a perceptual map, which highlights rival goods within one's industry according to perceived quality and price. After the perceptual map has been devised, a firm would consider the marketing communications mix best suited to the product in question.

Top-Down and Bottom-UP

George S. Day (1980) describes model of segmentation as the top-down approach: *You start with the total population and divide it into segments.* He also identified an alternative model which he called the bottom-up approach.

In this approach, you start with a single customer and build on that profile. This typically requires the use of customer relationship management software or a database of some kind. Profiles of existing customers are created and analysed. Various demographic, behavioural, and psychographic patterns are built up using techniques such as cluster analysis. This process is sometimes called database marketing or micro-marketing. Its use is most appropriate in highly fragmented markets. McKenna (1988) claims that this approach treats every customer as a "micromajority". Pine (1993) used the bottom-up approach in what he called "segment of one marketing". Through this process mass customization is possible.

Creating a market segment will allow you to set yourself apart from other competitors.

Using Segmentation in Customer Retention

Segmentation is commonly used by organizations to improve their customer retention programs and help ensure that they are.

- Focused on retaining their most profitable customers
- Employing those tactics most likely to retain these customers

The basic approach to retention-based segmentation is that a company tags each of its active customers with 3 values:

Tag #1: Is this Customer at high risk of Canceling the Company's Service? (Or Becoming a non-user)

One of the most common indicators of high-risk customers is a drop off in usage of the company's service. For example, in the credit card industry this could be signaled through a customer's decline in spending on his card.

Tag #2: Is this Customer worth Retaining?

This determination boils down to whether the post-retention profit generated from the customer is predicted to be greater than the cost incurred to retain the customer.

Tag #3: What Retention Tactics Should be used to retain this Customer?

For customers who are deemed "save-worthy", it's essential for the company to know which save tactics are most likely to be successful. Tactics commonly used range from providing "special" customer discounts to sending customers communications that reinforce the value proposition of the given service.

Process for Tagging Customers

The basic approach to tagging customers is to utilize historical retention data to make predictions about active customers regarding:

- Whether they are at high risk of canceling their service.
- Whether they are profitable to retain.
- What retention tactics are likely to be most effective.

The idea is to match up active customers with customers from historic retention data who share similar attributes. Using the theory that "birds of a feather flock together", the approach is based on the assumption that active customers will have similar retention outcomes as those of their comparable predecessors.

From a technical perspective, the segmentation process is commonly performed using a combination of predictive analytics and cluster analysis.

Product Management

Product management is an organizational lifecycle function within a company dealing with the planning or marketing of a product or products at all stages of the product lifecycle.

Product management (inbound focused) and product marketing (outbound focused) are different yet complementary efforts with the objective of maximizing sales revenues, market share, and profit margins. The role of product management spans many activities from strategic to tactical and varies based on the organizational structure of the company. Product management can be a function separate on its own or a member of marketing or engineering. While involved with the entire product lifecycle, product management's main focus is on driving new product development. According to the Product Development and Management Association (PDMA), superior and differentiated new products-ones that deliver unique benefits and superior value to the customer-is the number one driver of success and product profitability.

Aspects of Product Management

Depending on the company size and history, product management has a variety of functions and roles. Sometimes there is a product manager, and sometimes the role of product manager is held by others. Frequently there is Profit and Loss (P&L) responsibility as a key metric for evaluating product manager performance. In some companies, the product management function is the hub of many other activities around the product. In others, it is one of many things that need to happen to bring a product to market. Product management often serves an inter-disciplinary role, bridging gaps within the company between teams of different expertise, most notably between engineering-oriented teams and business-oriented teams. For example product managers often translate business objectives set for a product by Marketing or Sales into engineering requirements. Conversely they may work to explain the capabilities and limitations of the finished product back to Marketing and Sales.

Product Planning

- Identifying new product candidates.
- Gathering market requirements.
- Determine business-case and feasibility.
- Scooping and defining new products at high level.
- Evangelizing new products within the company.
- Building product roadmaps, particularly Technology roadmaps.
- Product Life Cycle considerations.
- Product differentiation.
- Detailed Product planning.

Product Marketing

- Product positioning and outbound messaging.
- Promoting the product externally with press, customers, and partners.

- Bringing new products to market.
- Monitoring the competition.
- more detail on Product marketing.

Brand

A brand is a name or trademark connected with a product or producer. Brands have become increasingly important components of culture and the economy, now being described as "cultural accessories and personal philosophies".

Concepts

Some people distinguish the psychological aspect of a brand from the experiential aspect. The experiential aspect consists of the sum of all points of contact with the brand and is known as the brand experience. The psychological aspect, sometimes referred to as the brand image, is a symbolic construct created within the minds of people and consists of all the information and expectations associated with a product or service.

People engaged in branding seek to develop or align the expectations behind the brand experience, creating the impression that a brand associated with a product or service has certain qualities or characteristics that make it special or unique. A brand is therefore one of the most valuable elements in an advertising theme, as it demonstrates what the brand owner is able to offer in the marketplace. The art of creating and maintaining a brand is called brand management. Orientation of the whole organisation towards its brand is called integrated marketing.

Careful brand management, supported by a cleverly crafted advertising campaign, can be highly successful in convincing consumers to pay remarkably high prices for products which are inherently extremely cheap to make. This concept, known as creating value, essentially consists of manipulating the projected image of the product so that the consumer sees the product as being worth the amount that the advertiser wants him/her to see, rather than a more logical valuation that comprises an aggregate of the cost of raw materials, plus the cost of manufacture, plus the cost of distribution. Modern value-creation branding-and-advertising campaigns are highly successful at inducing consumers to pay, for example, 50 dollars for a T-shirt that cost a mere 50 cents to make, or 5 dollars for a box of breakfast cereal that contains a few cents' worth of wheat. Brands should be seen as more than the difference between the actual cost of a product and its selling price-they represent the sum of all valuable qualities of a product to the consumer. There are many intangibles involved in business, intangibles left wholly from the income statement and balance sheet which determine how a business is perceived. The learned skill of a knowledge worker, the type of metal working, the type of stitch: all may be without an 'accounting cost' but for those who truly know the product, for it is these people the company should wish to find and keep, the difference is incomparable. Failing to recognize these assets that a business, any business, can create and maintain will set an enterprise at a serious disadvantage.

A brand which is widely known in the marketplace acquires brand recognition. When brand recognition builds up to a point where a brand enjoys a critical mass of positive sentiment in the marketplace, it is said to have achieved brand franchise. One goal in brand recognition is the identification of a brand without the name of the company present. For example, Disney has been successful at branding with their particular script font (originally created for Walt Disney's "signature" logo), which it used in the logo for go.com.

Consumers may look on branding as an important value added aspect of products or services, as it often serves to denote a certain attractive quality or characteristic. From the perspective of brand owners, branded products or services also command higher prices. Where two products resemble each other, but one of the products has no associated branding (such as a generic, store-branded product), people may often select the more expensive branded product on the basis of the quality of the brand or the reputation of the brand owner.

Brand Name

The brand name is quite often used interchangeably within "brand", although it is more correctly used to specifically denote written or spoken linguistic elements of any product. In this context a "brand name" constitutes a type of trademark, if the brand name exclusively identifies the brand owner as the commercial source of products or services. A brand owner may seek to protect proprietary rights in relation to a brand name through trademark registration. Advertising spokespersons have also become part of some brands, for example: Mr. Whipple of Charmin toilet tissue and Tony the Tiger of Kellogg's.

Brand names will fall into one of three spectrums of use-Descriptive, Associative or Freestanding.

Descriptive brand names assist in describing the distinguishable selling point(s) of the product to the customer (eg Snap, Crackle and Pop or Bitter Lemon).

Associative brand names provide the customer with an associated word for what the product promises to do or be (e.g. Walkman, Sensodyne or Natrel)

Finally, Freestanding brand names have no links or ties to either descriptions or associations of use. (eg Mars Bar or Pantene)

The act of associating a product or service with a brand has become part of pop culture. Most products have some kind of brand identity, from common table salt to designer jeans. A brandnomer is a brand name that has colloquially become a generic term for a product or service, such as Band-Aid or Kleenex, which are often used to describe any kind of adhesive bandage or any kind of facial tissue respectively.

Brand Identity

A product identity, or brand image are typically the attributes one associates with a brand, how the brand owner wants the consumer to perceive the brand-and by extension the branded company, organization, product or service. The brand owner will seek to bridge the gap between the brand image and the brand identity. Effective brand names build a connection between the brand personality as it is perceived by the target audience and the actual product/service. The brand name should be conceptually on target with the product/service (what the company stands for). Furthermore, the brand name should be on target with the brand demographic. Typically, sustainable brand names are easy to remember, transcend trends and have positive connotations. Brand identity is fundamental to consumer recognition and symbolizes the brand's differentiation from competitors.

Brand identity is what the owner wants to communicate to its potential consumers. However, over time, a products brand identity may acquire (evolve), gaining new attributes from consumer perspective but not necessarily from the marketing communications an owner percolates to targeted consumers. Therefore, brand associations become handy to check the consumer's perception of the brand.

Brand identity needs to focus on authentic qualities-real characteristics of the value and brand promise being provided and sustained by organisational and/or production characteristics.

Brand Parity

Brand parity is the perception of the customers that all brands are equivalent.

Branding Approaches

Company Name

Often, especially in the industrial sector, it is just the company's name which is promoted (leading to one of the most powerful statements of "branding"; the saying, before the company's downgrading, "No one ever got fired for buying IBM").

In this case a very strong brand name (or company name) is made the vehicle for a range of products (for example, Mercedes-Benz or Black & Decker) or even a range of subsidiary brands (such as Cadbury Dairy Milk, Cadbury Flake or Cadbury Fingers in the United States).

Individual Branding

Each brand has a separate name (such as Seven-Up, Kool-Aid or Nivea Sun (Beiersdorf)), which may even compete against other brands from the same company (for example, Persil, Omo, Surf and Lynx are all owned by Unilever).

Attitude Branding and Iconic Brands

Attitude branding is the choice to represent a larger feeling, which is not necessarily connected with the product or consumption of the product at all. Marketing labelled as attitude branding include that of Nike, Starbucks, The Body Shop, Safeway, and Apple Inc.. In the 2000 book *No Logo*, Naomi Klein describes attitude branding as a "fetish strategy".

"A great brand raises the bar — it adds a greater sense of purpose to the experience, whether it's the challenge to do your best in sports and fitness, or the affirmation that the cup of coffee you're drinking really matters."-Howard Schultz (president, CEO, and chairman of Starbucks)

Iconic brands are defined as having aspects that contribute to consumer's self-expression and personal identity. Brands whose value to consumers comes primarily from having identity value comes are said to be "identity brands". Some of these brands have such a strong identity that they become more or less "cultural icons" which makes them iconic brands. Examples of iconic brands are: Apple Inc., Nike and Harley Davidson. Many iconic brands include almost ritual-like behaviour when buying and consuming the products.

There are four key elements to creating iconic brands (Holt 2004):

1. "Necessary conditions"-The performance of the product must at least be ok preferably with a reputation of having good quality.
2. "Myth-making"-A meaningful story-telling fabricated by cultural "insiders". These must be seen as legitimate and respected by consumers for stories to be accepted.
3. "Cultural contradictions"-Some kind of mismatch between prevailing ideology and emergent undercurrents in society. In other words a difference with the way consumers are and how they some times wish they were.
4. "The cultural brand management process"-Actively engaging in the myth-making process making sure the brand maintains its position as an icon.

"No-brand" Branding

Recently a number of companies have successfully pursued "No-Brand" strategies, examples include the Japanese company Muji, which means "No label" in English (from !qpSo,ÁT – "Mujirushi Ryohin" – literally, "No brand quality goods"). Although there is a distinct Muji brand, Muji products are not branded. This no-brand strategy means that little is spent on advertisement or classical marketing and Muji's success is attributed to the word-of-mouth, a simple shopping experience and the anti-brand movement. "No brand" branding is actually branding as the brand is made conspicous through its absence.

Derived Brands

In this case the supplier of a key component, used by a number of suppliers of the end-product, may wish to guarantee its own position by promoting that component as a brand in its own right. The most frequently quoted example is Intel, which secures its position in the PC market with the slogan "Intel Inside".

Brand Extension

The existing strong brand name can be used as a vehicle for new or modified products; for example, many fashion and designer companies extended brands into fragrances, shoes and accessories, home textile, home decor, luggage, (sun-) glasses, furniture, hotels, etc.

Mars extended its brand to ice cream, Caterpillar to shoes and watches, Michelin to a restaurant guide, Adidas and Puma to personal hygiene. Dunlop extended its brand from tires to other rubber products such as shoes, golf balls, tennis racquets and adhesives.

There is a difference between brand extension and line extension. When Coca-Cola launched "Diet Coke" and "Cherry Coke" they stayed within the originating product category: non-alcoholic carbonated beverages. Procter & Gamble (P&G) did likewise extending its strong lines (such as Fairy Soap) into neighbouring products (Fairy Liquid and Fairy Automatic) within the same category, dish washing detergents.

Multi-brands

Alternatively, in a market that is fragmented amongst a number of brands a supplier can choose deliberately to launch totally new brands in apparent competition with its own existing strong brand (and often with identical product characteristics); simply to soak up some of the share of the market which will in any case go to minor brands. The rationale is that having 3 out of 12 brands in such a market will give a greater overall share than having 1 out of 10 (even if much of the share of these new brands is taken from the existing one). In its most extreme manifestation, a supplier pioneering a new market which it believes will be particularly attractive may choose immediately to launch a second brand in competition with its first, in order to pre-empt others entering the market.

Individual brand names naturally allow greater flexibility by permitting a variety of different products, of differing quality, to be sold without confusing the consumer's perception of what business the company is in or diluting higher quality products.

Once again, Procter & Gamble is a leading exponent of this philosophy, running as many as ten detergent brands in the US market. This also increases the total number of "facings" it receives on supermarket shelves. Sara Lee, on the other hand, uses it to keep the very different parts of the business separate — from Sara Lee cakes through Kiwi polishes to L'Eggs pantyhose. In the hotel business, Marriott uses the name Fairfield Inns for its budget chain (and Ramada uses Rodeway for its own cheaper hotels).

Cannibalization is a particular problem of a "multibrand" approach, in which the new brand takes business away from an established one which the organization also owns. This may be acceptable (indeed to be expected) if there is a net gain overall. Alternatively, it may be the price the organization is willing to pay for shifting its position in the market; the new product being one stage in this process.

Own Brands and Generics

With the emergence of strong retailers the "own brand", a retailer's own branded product (or service), also emerged as a major factor in the marketplace. Where the retailer has a particularly strong identity (such as Marks & Spencer in the UK clothing sector) this "own brand" may be able to compete against even the strongest brand leaders, and may outperform those products that are not otherwise strongly branded.

Concerns were raised that such "own brands" might displace all other brands (as they have done in Marks & Spencer outlets), but the evidence is that — at least in supermarkets and department stores — consumers generally expect to see on display something over 50 percent (and preferably over 60 percent) of brands other than those of the retailer. Indeed, even the strongest own brands in the UK rarely achieve better than third place in the overall market.

This means that strong independent brands (such as Kellogg's and Heinz), which have maintained their marketing investments, are likely to continue their strong performance. More than 50 per cent of UK FMCG brand leaders have held their position for more than two decades, although it is arguable that those which have switched their budgets to "buy space" in the retailers may be more exposed.

The strength of the retailers has, perhaps, been seen more in the pressure they have been able to exert on the owners of even the strongest brands (and in particular on the owners of the weaker third and fourth brands). Relationship marketing has been applied most often to meet the wishes of such large customers (and indeed has been demanded by them as recognition of their buying power). Some of the more active marketers have now also switched to 'category marketing'- in which they take into account all the needs of a retailer in a product category rather than more narrowly focusing on their own brand. At the same time, probably as an outgrowth of consumerism, "generic" (that is, effectively unbranded) goods have also emerged. These made a positive virtue of saving the cost of almost all marketing activities; emphasizing the lack of advertising and, especially, the plain packaging (which was, however, often simply a vehicle for a different kind of image). It would appear that the penetration of such generic products peaked in the early 1980s, and most consumers still appear to be looking for the qualities that the conventional brand provides.

History

Although connected with the history of trademarks and including earlier examples which could be deemed "protobrands" (such as the marketing puns of the "Vesuvinum" wine jars found at Pompeii), brands in the field of mass-marketing originated in the 19th century with the advent of packaged goods. Industrialization moved the production of many household items, such as soap, from local communities to centralized factories. When shipping their items, the factories would literally brand their logo or insignia on the barrels used, extending the meaning of "brand" to that of trademark.

Bass & Company, the British brewery, claims their red triangle brand was the world's first trademark. Lyle's Golden Syrup makes a similar claim, having been named as Britain's oldest brand, with its green and gold packaging having remained almost unchanged since 1885.

Cattle were branded long before this; the term "maverick", originally meaning an unbranded calf, comes from Texas rancher Samuel Augustus Maverick who, following the American Civil War, decided that since all other cattle were branded, his would be identified by having no markings at all.

Factories established during the Industrial Revolution, generating mass-produced goods and needed to sell their products to a wider market, to a customer base familiar only with local goods. It quickly became apparent that a generic package of soap had difficulty competing with familiar, local products. The packaged goods manufacturers needed to convince the market that the public could place just as much trust in the non-local product. Campbell soup, Coca-Cola, Juicy Fruit gum, Aunt Jemima, and Quaker Oats were among the first products to be 'branded', in an effort to increase the consumer's familiarity with their products. Many brands of that era, such as Uncle Ben's rice and Kellogg's breakfast cereal furnish illustrations of the problem.

Around 1900, James Walter Thompson published a house ad explaining trademark advertising. This was an early commercial explanation of what we now know as branding. Companies soon adopted slogans, mascots, and jingles which began to appear on radio and early television. By the 1940s, manufacturers began to recognize the way in which consumers were developing relationships with their brands in a social/psychological/anthropological sense.

From there, manufacturers quickly learned to build their brand's identity and personality, such as youthfulness, fun or luxury. This began the practice we now know as "branding" today, where the consumers buy "the brand" instead of the product. This trend continued to the 1980s, and is now quantified in concepts such as brand value and brand equity. Naomi Klein has described this development as "brand equity mania". In 1988, for example, Philip Morris purchased Kraft for six times what the company was worth on paper; it was felt that what they really purchased was its brand name.

Marlboro Friday: April 2, 1993-marked by some as the death of the brand-the day Philip Morris declared that they were to cut the price of Marlboro cigarettes by 20%, in order to compete with bargain cigarettes. Marlboro cigarettes were notorious at the time for their heavy advertising campaigns, and well-nuanced brand image. In response to the announcement Wall street stocks nose-dived for a large number of 'branded' companies: Heinz, Coca Cola, Quaker Oats, PepsiCo. Many thought the event signalled the beginning of a trend towards "brand blindness" (Klein 13), questioning the power of "brand value".

Country of Origin

Country of origin (often abbreviated to COO), is the country of manufacture, production, or growth where an article or product comes from. There are differing rules of origin under various national laws and international treaties.

Country of Origin as a Marketing Strategy

From a marketing perspective, "country of origin" gives a way to differentiate the product from the competitors. Research shows (Josiassen and Harzing, 2008, European Management Review) that the country of origin has an impact on the willingness to buy a product, and studies (Shimp and Sharma, 1987, Journal of International Business Studies) have shown that consumers may tend to have a relative preference to products from their own country or may tend to have a relative preference for or aversion to certain products that originate from certain countries. The effect of country of origin is however debated (Usunier, 2006, European Management Review) as studies (e.g. Chao, 2001, Journal of Advertising) have shown that the origin of design (for instance Apple computers or Nike shoes) can be more important than the country of origin.

Non-specific Country of Origin Labeling

While many products made within the European Union carry the country of origin label or marking "Made in EU" or "Made in EC", some non-EU manufacturers in Europe and some others outside the continent of Europe use vaguer markings, such as "Made in Europe" (made anywhere else in Europe, but not in the EU or EC; this may constitute any country geographically close to Europe or the EU that also wishes to be in) or "Made for Europe" (made anywhere else in the world, but not in Europe or the European Union). These practices could lead to consumer deception, whereby a buyer not proficient in English may come to believe from looking at the label that the non-EU product he is interested in is made in the EU.

Country of Origin Contextual Importance for Consumer Choice

Consumers tend to utilize the country of origin more when they are less involved and less familiar (Josiassen et al., 2008, International Marketing Review). Consumers further tend to use country of origin more as a decision tool when they consider luxury products (Piron, 2000, Journal of Consumer Marketing).

Country of Origin in International Trade

When shipping products from one country to another, the products may have to be marked with country of origin, and the country of origin will generally be required to be indicated in the export/import documents and governmental submissions. Country of origin will affect its admissibility, the rate of duty, its entitlement to special duty or trade preference programs, antidumping, and government procurement.

Today, many products are an outcome of a large number of parts and pieces that come from many different countries, and that may then be assembled together in a third country. In these cases, it's hard to know exactly what is the country of origin, and different rules apply as to how to determine their "correct" country of origin. Generally, articles only change their country of origin if the work or material added to an article in the second country constitutes a substantial transformation, or, the article changes its name, tariff code, character or use (for instance from wheel to car). Value added in the second country may also be an issue.

Country of Origin in Movie and Television Production

The International Federation of Film Archives defines the country of origin as the country of the principal offices of the production company or individual by whom the moving image work was made. No consistent reference or definition exists. Sources include the item itself, accompanying material (e.g. scripts, shot lists, production records, publicity material, inventory lists, synopses etc.), the container (if not an integral part of the piece), or other sources (standard and special moving image reference tools). In law, definitions of "country of origin" and related terms are defined differently in different jurisdictions. Europe, Canada, and the United States have different definitions for a variety of reasons, including tax treatment, advertising regulations, distribution; even within the European Union, different member states have different legislation. As a result, an individual work can have multiple countries as its "country of origin", and may even have different countries recognized as originating places for the purpose of different legal jurisdictions. Under copyright law in the United States and other signatories of the Berne Convention, "country of origin" is defined in an inclusive way to ensure the protection of intellectual rights of writers and creators.

Marketing Plan

A marketing plan is a written document that details the necessary actions to achieve one or more marketing objectives. It can be for a product or service, a brand, or a product line. Marketing plans cover between one and five years. A marketing plan may be part of an overall business plan. Solid marketing strategy is the foundation of a well-written marketing plan. While a marketing plan contains a list of actions, a marketing plan without a sound strategic foundation is of little use.

The Marketing Planning Process

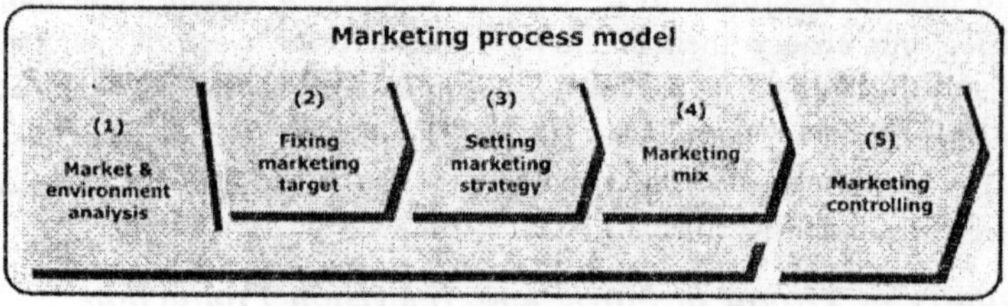

The marketing process model based on the publications of Philip Kotler. It consists of 5 steps, beginning with the market & environment research. After fixing the targets and setting the strategies, they will be realised by the marketing mix in step 4. The last step in the process is the marketing controlling.

In most organizations, "strategic planning" is an annual process, typically covering just the year ahead. Occasionally, a few organizations may look at a practical plan which stretches three or more years ahead.

To be most effective, the plan has to be formalized, usually in written form, as a formal "marketing plan." The essence of the process is that it moves from the general to the specific; from the overall objectives of the organization down to the individual action plan for a part of one marketing program. It is also an interactive process, so that the draft output of each stage is checked to see what impact it has on the earlier stages-and is amended..

Marketing Planning Aims and Objectives

Behind the corporate objectives, which in themselves offer the main context for the marketing plan, will lay the "corporate mission"; which in turn provides the context for these corporate objectives. In a sales-oriented organization, marketing planning function designs incentive pay plans to not only motivate and reward frontline staff fairly but also to align marketing activities with corporate mission.

This "corporate mission" can be thought of as a definition of what the organization is; of what it does: "Our business is ...". This definition should not be too narrow, or it will constrict the development of the organization; a too rigorous concentration on the view that "We are in the business of making meat-scales," as IBM was during the early 1900s, might have limited its subsequent development into other areas.

On the other hand, it should not be too wide or it will become meaningless; "We want to make a profit" is not too helpful in developing specific plans.

Abell suggested that the definition should cover three dimensions: "customer groups" to be served, "customer needs" to be served, and "technologies" to be utilized. Thus, the definition of IBM's "corporate mission" in the 1990s. might well have been: "We are in the business of handling accounting information for the larger US organizations [customer group] by means of punched cards [technology]."

Perhaps the most important factor in successful marketing is the "corporate vision." Surprisingly, it is largely neglected by marketing textbooks; although not by the popular exponents of corporate strategy-indeed, it was perhaps the main theme of the book by Peters and Waterman, in the form of their "Superordinate Goals." "In Search of Excellence" said: "Nothing drives progress like the imagination. The idea precedes the deed." If the organization in general, and its chief executive in particular, has a strong vision of where its future lies, then there is a good chance that the organization will achieve a strong position in its markets (and attain that future). This will be not least because its strategies will be consistent; and will be supported by its staff at all levels. In this context, all of IBM's marketing activities were underpinned by its philosophy of "customer service"; a vision originally promoted by the charismatic Watson dynasty. The emphasis at this stage is on obtaining a complete and accurate picture.

A "traditional"-albeit product-based-format for a "brand reference book" (or, indeed, a "marketing facts book") was suggested by Godley more than three decades ago:

1. Financial data—Facts for this section will come from management accounting, costing and finance sections.
2. Product data—From production, research and development.
3. Sales and distribution data-Sales, packaging, distribution sections.
4. Advertising, sales promotion, merchandising data-Information from these departments.
5. Market data and miscellany-From market research, who would in most cases act as a source for this information. His sources of data, however, assume the resources of a very large organization. In most organizations they would be obtained

from a much smaller set of people (and not a few of them would be generated by the marketing manager alone).

It is apparent that a marketing audit can be a complex process, but the aim is simple: *"it is only to identify those existing (external and internal) factors which will have a significant impact on the future plans of the company."* It is clear that the basic material to be input to the marketing audit should be comprehensive.

Accordingly, the best approach is to accumulate this material continuously, as and when it becomes available; since this avoids the otherwise heavy workload involved in collecting it as part of the regular, typically annual, planning process itself-when time is usually at a premium.

Even so, the first task of this *annual* process should be to check that the material held in the current *facts book* or *facts files* actually *is* comprehensive and accurate, and can form a sound basis for the marketing audit itself.

The structure of the facts book will be designed to match the specific needs of the organization, but one simple format-suggested by Malcolm McDonald-may be applicable in many cases. This splits the material into three groups:

1. Review of the marketing environment. A study of the organization's markets, customers, competitors and the overall economic, political, cultural and technical environment; covering developing trends, as well as the current situation.
2. Review of the detailed marketing activity. A study of the company's marketing mix; in terms of the 7 Ps.
3. Review of the marketing system. A study of the marketing organization, marketing research systems and the current marketing objectives and strategies. The last of these is too frequently ignored. The marketing system itself needs to be regularly questioned, because the validity of the whole marketing plan is reliant upon the accuracy of the input from this system, and 'garbage in, garbage out' applies with a vengeance.

- Portfolio planning. In addition, the coordinated planning of the individual products and services can contribute towards the balanced portfolio.
- 80:20 rule. To achieve the maximum impact, the marketing plan must be clear, concise and simple. It needs to concentrate

on the 20 percent of products or services, and on the 20 percent of customers, which will account for 80 percent of the volume and 80 percent of the profit.

- 7 P's: Product, Place, Price and Promotion, Physical Environment, People, Process. The 7 P's can sometimes divert attention from the customer, but the framework they offer can be very useful in building the action plans.

It is only at this stage (of deciding the marketing objectives) that the active part of the marketing planning process begins'. This next stage in marketing planning is indeed the key to the whole marketing process.

The "marketing objectives" state just where the company intends to be; at some specific time in the future.

James Quinn succinctly defined objectives in general as: *Goals (or objectives) state what is to be achieved and when results are to be accomplished, but they do not state 'how' the results are to be achieved.* They typically relate to what products (or services) will be where in what markets (and must be realistically based on customer behaviour in those markets). They are essentially about the match between those "products" and "markets." Objectives for pricing, distribution, advertising and so on are at a lower level, and should not be confused with marketing objectives. They are part of the marketing strategy needed to achieve marketing objectives. To be most effective, objectives should be capable of measurement and therefore "quantifiable." This measurement may be in terms of sales volume, money value, market share, percentage penetration of distribution outlets and so on. An example of such a measurable marketing objective might be "to enter the market with product Y and capture 10 percent of the market by value within one year." As it is quantified it can, within limits, be unequivocally monitored; and corrective action taken as necessary.

The marketing objectives must usually be based, above all, on the organization's financial objectives; converting these financial measurements into the related marketing measurements. He went on to explain his view of the role of "policies," with which strategy is most often confused: "Policies are rules or guidelines that express the 'limits' within which action should occur." Simplifying somewhat, marketing strategies can be seen as the means, or "game plan," by which marketing objectives will be achieved and, in the framework that we have chosen to use, are generally concerned with the 8 P's. Examples are:

1. Price-The amount of money needed to buy products
2. Product-The actual product
3. Promotion (advertising)-Getting the product known
4. Placement-Where the product is located
5. People-Represent the business
6. Physical environment-The ambiance, mood, or tone of the environment
7. Process-How do people obtain your product
8. Packaging-How the product will be protected.

(Note: At GCSE the 4 P's are Place, Promotion, Product and Price and the "secret" 5th P is Packaging, but which applies only to physical products, not services usually, and mostly those sold to individual consumers)

In principle, these strategies describe how the objectives will be achieved. The 7 P's are a useful framework for deciding how the company's resources will be manipulated (strategically) to achieve the objectives. It should be noted, however, that they are not the only framework, and may divert attention from the real issues. The focus of the strategies must be the objectives to be achieved-not the process of planning itself. Only if it fits the needs of these objectives should you choose, as we have done, to use the framework of the 7 P's. The strategy statement can take the form of a purely verbal description of the strategic options which have been chosen. Alternatively, and perhaps more positively, it might include a structured list of the major options chosen.

One aspect of strategy which is often overlooked is that of "timing." Exactly when it is the best time for each element of the strategy to be implemented is often critical. Taking the right action at the wrong time can sometimes be almost as bad as taking the wrong action at the right time. Timing is, therefore, an essential part of any plan; and should normally appear as a schedule of planned activities. Having completed this crucial stage of the planning process, you will need to re-check the feasibility of your objectives and strategies in terms of the market share, sales, costs, profits and so on which these demand in practice. As in the rest of the marketing discipline, you will need to employ judgment, experience, market research or anything else which helps you to look at your conclusions from all possible angles.

Detailed Plans and Programs

At this stage, you will need to develop your overall marketing strategies into detailed plans and program. Although these detailed plans may cover each of the 7 P's, the focus will vary, depending upon your organization's specific strategies. A product-oriented company will focus its plans for the 7 P's around each of its products. A market or geographically oriented company will concentrate on each market or geographical area. Each will base its plans upon the detailed needs of its customers, and on the strategies chosen to satisfy these needs.

Again, the most important element is, indeed, that of the detailed plans; which spell out exactly what programs and individual activities will take place over the period of the plan (usually over the next year). Without these specified-and preferably quantified-activities the plan cannot be monitored, even in terms of success in meeting its objectives. It is these programs and activities which will then constitute the "marketing" of the organization over the period. As a result, these detailed marketing programs are the most important, practical outcome of the whole planning process. These plans therefore be:

- Clear-They should be an unambiguous statement of 'exactly' what is to be done.
- Quantified-The predicted outcome of each activity should be, as far as possible, quantified; so that its performance can be monitored.
- Focused-The temptation to proliferate activities beyond the numbers which can be realistically controlled should be avoided. The 80:20 Rule applies in this context too.
- Realistic-They should be achievable.
- Agreed-Those who are to implement them should be committed to them, and agree that they are achievable. The resulting plans should become a working document which will guide the campaigns taking place throughout the organization over the period of the plan. If the marketing plan is to work, every exception to it (throughout the year) must be questioned; and the lessons learned, to be incorporated in the next year's planning.

Content of the Marketing Plan

A marketing plan for a small business typically includes Small Business Administration Description of competitors, including the level of demand for the product or service and the strengths and weaknesses of competitors

1. Description of the product or service, including special features
2. Marketing budget, including the advertising and promotional plan
3. Description of the business location, including advantages and disadvantages for marketing
4. Pricing strategy
5. Market Segmentation.

Medium-sized and Large Organizations

The main contents of a marketing plan are.

1. Executive Summary.
2. Situational Analysis.
3. Opportunities/Issue Analysis-SWOT Analysis.
4. Objectives.
5. Strategy.
6. Action Program (the operational marketing plan itself for the period under review).
7. Financial Forecast.
8. Controls.

In detail, a Complete Marketing plan Typically Includes:

1. Title page.
2. Executive Summary.
3. Current Situation-Macroenvironment.
   - economy.
   - legal.
   - government.
   - technology.
   - ecological.
   - sociocultural.

- supply chain.

4. Current Situation-Market Analysis.
    - market definition.
    - market size.
    - market segmentation.
    - industry structure and strategic groupings.
    - Porter 5 forces analysis.
    - competition and market share.
    - competitors' strengths and weaknesses.
    - market trends.
5. Current Situation-Consumer Analysis
    - nature of the buying decision.
    - participants.
    - demographics.
    - psychographics.
    - buyer motivation and expectations.
    - loyalty segments.
6. Current Situation-Internal.
    - company resources.
        - financial.
        - people.
        - time.
        - skills.
    - objectives.
        - mission statement and vision statement.
        - corporate objectives.
        - financial objective.
        - marketing objectives.
        - long term objectives.
        - description of the basic business philosophy.
    - corporate culture.
7. Summary of Situation Analysis.
    - external threats.

- external opportunities.
- internal strengths.
- internal weaknesses.
- Critical success factors in the industry.
- our sustainable competitive advantage.

8. Marketing research.
    - information requirements.
    - research methodology.
    - research results.
9. Marketing Strategy-Product.
    - product mix.
    - product strengths and weaknesses.
        - perceptual mapping.
    - product life cycle management and new product development.
    - Brand name, brand image, and brand equity.
    - the augmented product.
    - product portfolio analysis.
        - B.C.G. Analysis.
        - contribution margin analysis.
        - G.E. Multi Factoral analysis.
        - Quality Function Deployment.
10. Marketing Strategy-segmented marketing actions and market share objectives.
    - by product,
    - by customer segment,
    - by geographical market,
    - by distribution channel.
11. Marketing Strategy-Price.
    - pricing objectives.
    - pricing method (eg.: cost plus, demand based, or competitor indexing).
    - pricing strategy (eg.: skimming, or penetration).

- discounts and allowances.
- price elasticity and customer sensitivity.
- price zoning.
- break even analysis at various prices.

12. Marketing Strategy-promotion.
    - promotional goals.
    - promotional mix.
    - advertising reach, frequency, flights, theme, and media.
    - sales force requirements, techniques, and management.
    - sales promotion.
    - publicity and public relations.
    - electronic promotion (eg.: Web, or telephone).
    - word of mouth marketing (buzz).
    - viral marketing.
13. Marketing Strategy-Distribution.
    - geographical coverage.
    - distribution channels.
    - physical distribution and logistics.
    - electronic distribution.
14. Implementation.
    - personnel requirements.
        - assign responsibilities.
        - give incentives.
        - training on selling methods.
    - financial requirements.
    - management information systems requirements.
    - month-by-month agenda.
    - PERT or critical path analysis.
    - monitoring results and benchmarks.
    - adjustment mechanism.
    - contingencies (What if's).
15. Financial Summary.
    - assumptions.

- pro-forma monthly income statement.
- contribution margin analysis.
- breakeven analysis.
- Monte Carlo method.
- ISI: Internet Strategic Intelligence.

16. Scenarios.
    - Prediction of Future Scenarios.
    - Plan of Action for each Scenario.
17. Appendix.
    - pictures and specifications of the new product.
    - results from research already completed.

Measurement of Progress

The final stage of any marketing planning process is to establish targets (or standards) so that progress can be monitored.

Accordingly, it is important to put both quantities and timescales into the marketing objectives (for example, to capture 20 percent by value of the market within two years) and into the corresponding strategies.

Changes in the environment mean that the forecasts often have to be changed. Along with these, the related plans may well also need to be changed.

Continuous monitoring of performance, against predetermined targets, represents a most important aspect of this. However, perhaps even more important is the enforced discipline of a regular formal review. Again, as with forecasts, in many cases the best (most realistic) planning cycle will revolve around a quarterly review. Best of all, at least in terms of the quantifiable aspects of the plans, if not the wealth of backing detail, is probably a quarterly rolling review-planning one full year ahead each new quarter. Of course, this does absorb more planning resource; but it also ensures that the plans embody the latest information, and-with attention focused on them so regularly-forces both the plans and their implementation to be realistic.

Plans only have validity if they are actually used to control the progress of a company: their success lies in their implementation, not in the writing'.

Performance Analysis

The most important elements of marketing performance, which are normally tracked, are:

Sales Analysis

Most organizations track their sales results; or, in non-profit organizations for example, the number of clients. The more sophisticated track them in terms of 'sales variance'-the deviation from the target figures-which allows a more immediate picture of deviations to become evident.

'Micro-analysis', which is a nicely pseudo-scientific term for the normal management process of investigating detailed problems, then investigates the individual elements (individual products, sales territories, customers and so on) which are failing to meet targets.

Market share Analysis

Few organizations track market share though it is often an important metric. Though absolute sales might grow in an expanding market, a firm's share of the market can decrease which bodes ill for future sales when the market starts to drop. Where such market share is tracked, there may be a number of aspects which will be followed:

- overall market share
- segment share-that in the specific, targeted segment
- relative share-in relation to the market leaders
- annual fluctuation rate of market share

Expense Analysis

The key ratio to watch in this area is usually the 'marketing expense to sales ratio'; although this may be broken down into other elements (advertising to sales, administration to sales, and so on).

Financial Analysis

The "bottom line" of marketing activities should at least in theory, be the net profit (for all except non-profit organizations, where the comparable emphasis may be on remaining within budgeted costs). There are a number of separate performance figures and key ratios which need to be tracked:

- gross contribution<>net profit.

- gross profit<>return on investment.
- net contribution<>profit on sales.

There can be considerable benefit in comparing these figures with those achieved by other organizations (especially those in the same industry); using, for instance, the figures which can be obtained (in the UK) from 'The Centre for Interfirm Comparison'. The most sophisticated use of this approach, however, is typically by those making use of PIMS (Profit Impact of Management Strategies), initiated by the General Electric Company and then developed by Harvard Business School, but now run by the Strategic Planning Institute.

The above performance analyses concentrate on the quantitative measures which are directly related to short-term performance. But there are a number of indirect measures, essentially tracking customer attitudes, which can also indicate the organization's performance in terms of its longer-term marketing strengths and may accordingly be even more important indicators. Some useful measures are:

- market research-including customer panels (which are used to track changes over time)
- lost business-the orders which were lost because, for example, the stock was not available or the product did not meet the customer's exact requirements
- customer complaints-how many customers complain about the products or services, or the organization itself, and about what.

Use of Marketing Plans

A formal, written marketing plan is essential; in that it provides an unambiguous reference point for activities throughout the planning period. However, perhaps the most important benefit of these plans is the planning process itself. This typically offers a unique opportunity, a forum, for information-rich and productively focused discussions between the various managers involved. The plan, together with the associated discussions, then provides an agreed context for their subsequent management activities, even for those not described in the plan itself.

Budgets as Managerial Tools

The classic quantification of a marketing plan appears in the form of budgets. Because these are so rigorously quantified, they are particularly important. They should, thus, represent an unequivocal projection of actions and expected results. What is more, they should be capable of being monitored accurately; and, indeed, performance against budget is the main (regular) management review process.

The purpose of a marketing budget is, thus, to pull together all the revenues and costs involved in marketing into one comprehensive document. It is a managerial tool that balances what is needed to be spent against what can be afforded, and helps make choices about priorities. It is then used in monitoring performance in practice.

The marketing budget is usually the most powerful tool by which you think through the relationship between desired results and available means. Its starting point should be the marketing strategies and plans, which have already been formulated in the marketing plan itself; although, in practice, the two will run in parallel and will interact. At the very least, the rigorous, highly quantified, budgets may cause a rethink of some of the more optimistic elements of the plans.

Mass Customization

Mass customization, in marketing, manufacturing, call centres and management, is the use of flexible computer-aided manufacturing systems to produce custom output. Those systems combine the low unit costs of mass production processes with the flexibility of individual customization.

"Mass Customization" is the new frontier in business competition for both manufacturing and service industries. At its core is a tremendous increase in variety and customization without a corresponding increase in costs. At its limit, it is the mass production of individually customized goods and services. At its best, it provides strategic advantage and economic value.

Mass Customization is the method of "effectively postponing the task of differentiating a product for a specific customer until the latest possible point in the supply network."

The concept of mass customization is attributed to Stan Davis in *Future Perfect* and was defined by Tseng & Jiao (2001, p. 685) as "producing goods and services to meet individual customer's needs with near mass production efficiency". Kaplan & Haenlein (2006) concurred, calling it "a strategy that creates value by some form of company-customer interaction at the fabrication and assembly stage of the operations level to create customized products with production cost and monetary price similar to those of mass-produced products".

Implementation

Many implementations of mass customization are operational today, such as software-based product configurators which make it possible to add and/or change functionalities of a core product or to build fully custom enclosures from scratch. This degree of mass customization has only seen limited adoption, however. If an enterprise's marketing department offers individual products (atomic market fragmentation) it doesn't often mean that a product is produced individually, but rather that similar variants of the same mass-produced item are available.

Companies which have succeeded with mass-customization business models tend to supply purely electronic products. However, these are not true "mass customizers" in the original sense, since they do not offer an alternative to mass production of material goods.

Service industries are also waking up to the power of a mass customization orientation. Call centres are leveraging agent-assisted voice technology to build pre-programmed, pre-recorded call flows to handle customers' inquiries. The agent executes the process, varying it only as they need to because of something the customer says or needs, as opposed to varying everything, every time.

Variants

Pine II (1992) described four types of mass customization.

- Collaborative customization-firms talk to individual customers to determine the precise product offering that best serves the customer's needs. This information is then used to specify and manufacture a product that suits that specific customer. For example, some clothing companies will manufacture blue jeans to fit an individual customer.
- Adaptive customization-firms produce a standardized product, but this product is customizable in the hands of the end-user (the customers alter the product themselves)
- Transparent customization-firms provide individual customers with unique products, without explicitly telling them that the

products are customized. In this case there is a need to accurately assess customer needs.

- Cosmetic customization-firms produce a standardized physical product, but market it to different customers in unique ways.

He suggested a business model, "the 8.5-figure-path", a process going from invention to mass production to continuous improvement to mass customization and back to invention.

Positioning (Marketing)

In marketing, positioning has come to mean the process by which marketers try to create an image or identity in the minds of their target market for its product, brand, or organization. It is the 'relative competitive comparison' their product occupies in a given market as perceived by the target market.

Re-positioning involves changing the identity of a product, relative to the identity of competing products, in the collective minds of the target market.

De-positioning involves attempting to change the identity of competing products, relative to the identity of your own product, in the collective minds of the target market.

The original work on Positioning was consumer marketing oriented, and was not as much focused on the question relative to competitive products as much as it was focused on cutting through the ambient "noise" and establishing a moment of real contact with the intended recipient. In the classic example of Avis claiming "No.2, We Try Harder", the point was to say something so shocking (it was by the standards of the day) that it cleared space in your brain and made you forget all about who was #1, and not to make some philosophical point about being "hungry" for business.

The growth of high-tech marketing may have had much to do with the shift in definition towards competitive positioning.

Definitions

Although there are different definitions of Positioning, probably the most common is: "A product's position is how potential buyers see the product", and is expressed relative to the position of competitors.

Positioning is a concept in marketing which was first popularized by Al Ries and Jack Trout in their bestseller book " Positioning-a battle for your mind".

This differs slightly from the context in which the term was first published in 1969 by Jack Trout in the paper *"Positioning" is a game people play in today's me-too market place"* in the publication *Industrial Marketing*, in which the case is made that the typical consumer is overwhelmed with unwanted advertising, and has a natural tendency to discard all information that does not immediately find a comfortable (and empty) slot in the consumers mind. It was then expanded into their ground-breaking first book, *"Positioning: The Battle for Your Mind"*, in which they define Positioning as "an organized system for finding a window in the mind. It is based on the concept that communication can only take place at the right time and under the right circumstances." (p. 19 of 2001 paperback edition).

What most will agree on is that Positioning is something (perception) that happens in the minds of the target market. It is the aggregate perception the market has of a particular company, product or service in relation to their perceptions of the competitors in the same category. It will happen whether or not a company's management is proactive, reactive or passive about the on-going process of evolving a position. But a company can positively influence the perceptions through enlightened strategic actions.

Product Positioning Process

Generally, the product positioning process involves.

1. Defining the market in which the product or brand will compete (who the relevant buyers are).
2. Identifying the attributes (also called dimensions) that define the product 'space'.
3. Collecting information from a sample of customers about their perceptions of each product on the relevant attributes.
4. Determine each product's share of mind.
5. Determine each product's current location in the product space.
6. Determine the target market's preferred combination of attributes (referred to as an *ideal vector*).
7. Examine the fit between.
    - The position of your product.

- The position of the ideal vector.

8. Position.

The process is similar for positioning your company's services. Services, however, don't have the physical attributes of products-that is, we can't feel them or touch them or show nice product pictures. So you need to ask first your customers and then yourself, what value do clients get from my services? How are they better off from doing business with me? Also ask: is there a characteristic that makes my services different?

Write out the value customers derive and the attributes your services offer to create the first draft of your positioning. Test it on people who don't really know what you do or what you sell, watch their facial expressions and listen for their response. When they want to know more because you've piqued their interest and started a conversation, you'll know you're on the right track.

Positioning Concepts

More generally, there are three types of positioning concepts.

1. Functional positions.
   - Solve problems.
   - Provide benefits to customers.
   - Get favourable perception by investors (stock profile) and lenders.
2. Symbolic positions.
   - Self-image enhancement.
   - Ego identification.
   - Belongingness and social meaningfulness.
   - Affective fulfilment.
3. Experiential positions.
   - Provide sensory stimulation.
   - Provide cognitive stimulation.

Measuring the Positioning

Positioning is facilitated by a graphical technique called perceptual mapping, various survey techniques, and statistical techniques like multi dimensional scaling, factor analysis, conjoint analysis, and logit analysis.

Repositioning a Company

In volatile markets, it can be necessary-even urgent-to reposition an entire company, rather than just a product line or brand. Take, for example, when Goldman Sachs and Morgan Stanley suddenly shifted from investment to commercial banks. The expectations of investors, employees, clients and regulators all need to shift, and each company will need to influence how these perceptions change. Doing so involves repositioning the entire firm.

This is especially true of small and medium-sized firms, many of which often lack strong brands for individual product lines. In a prolonged recession, business approaches that were effective during healthy economies often become ineffective and it becomes necessary to change a firm's positioning. Upscale restaurants, for example, which previously flourished on expense account dinners and corporate events, may for the first time need to stress value as a sale tool.

Repositioning a company involves more than a marketing challenge. It involves making hard decisions about how a market is shifting and how a firm's competitors will react. Often these decisions must be made without the benefit of sufficient information, simply because the definition of "volatility" is that change becomes difficult or impossible to predict.

Product Life Cycle Management

Product life cycle management is the succession of strategies used by management as a product goes through its product life cycle. The conditions in which a product is sold changes over time and must be managed as it moves through its succession of stages.

Product Life Cycle

The product life cycle goes through many phases, involves many professional disciplines, and requires many skills, tools and processes. Product life cycle (PLC) has to do with the life of a product in the market with respect to business/commercial costs and sales measures; whereas product life cycle management (PLM) has more to do with managing descriptions and properties of a product through its development and useful life, mainly from a business/engineering point of view. To say that a product has a life cycle is to assert four things:

- that products have a limited life.

- product sales pass through distinct stages, each posing different challenges, opportunities, and problems to the seller.
- profits rise and fall at different stages of product life cycle, and.
- products require different marketing, financial, manufacturing, purchasing, and human resource strategies in each life cycle stage.

Request for Deviation

In the process of building a product following defined procedure, an RFD is a request for authorization, granted prior to the manufacture of an item, to depart from a particular performance or design requirement of a specification, drawing or other document, for a specific number of units or a specific period of time.....

Market Identification

A "micro-market" can be used to describe a Walkman, more portable, as well as individually and privately recordable; and then Compact Discs ("CDS") brought increased capacity and CD-R offered individual private recording...and so the process goes. The below section on the "technology lifecycle" is a most appropriate concept in this context. Most of the context is not in English so you may need a translator.

In short, termination is not always the end of the cycle; it can be the end of a micro-entrant within the grander scope of a macro-environment. The auto industry, fast-food industry, petro-chemical industry, are just a few that demonstrate a macro-environment that overall has not terminated even while micro-entrants over time have come and gone.

Lessons of the Product Life Cycle (PLC)

It is claimed that every product has a life period, It is launched, it grows, and at some point, may die. A fair comment is that-at least in the short term-not all products or services die. Jeans may die, but clothes probably will not. Legal services or medical services may die, but depending on the social and political climate, probably will not.

Even though its validity is questionable, it can offer a useful 'model' for managers to keep at the back of their mind. Indeed, if their products are in the introductory or growth phases, or in that of decline, it perhaps should be at the front of their mind; for the predominant features of these phases may be those revolving around such life and death. Between these two extremes, it is salutary for them to have that vision of mortality in front of them.

However, the most important aspect of product life-cycles is that, even under normal conditions, to all practical intents and purposes they often do not exist (hence, there needs to be more emphasis on model/reality mappings). In most markets the majority of the major brands have held their position for at least two decades. The dominant product life-cycle, that of the brand leaders which almost monopolize many markets, is therefore one of continuity.

In the Criticism of the Product Life Cycle, Dhalla & Yuspeh State

The PLC is a dependent variable which is determined by market actions; it is not an independent variable to which companies should adapt their marketing programs. Marketing management itself can alter the shape and duration of a brand's life cycle. Thus, the life cycle may be useful as a description, but not as a predictor; and usually should be firmly under the control of the marketer. The important point is that in many markets the product or brand life cycle is significantly longer than the planning cycle of the organisations involved. Thus, it offers little practical value for most marketers. Even if the PLC (and the related PLM support) exists for them, their plans will be based just upon that piece of the curve where they currently reside (most probably in the 'mature' stage); and their view of that part of it will almost certainly be 'linear' (and limited), and will not encompass the whole range from growth to decline.

Limitations

The PLC model is of some degree of usefulness to marketing managers, in that it is based on factual assumptions. Nevertheless, it is difficult for marketing management to gauge accurately where a product is on its PLC graph. A rise in sales *per se* is not necessarily evidence of growth. A fall in sales *per se* does not typify decline. Furthermore, some products do not (and to date, at the least, have not) experienced a decline. Coca Cola and Pepsi are examples of two products that have existed for many decades, but are still popular products all over the world. Both modes of cola have been in maturity for some years. Another factor is that differing products would possess different PLC "shapes". A fad product would hold a steep sloped growth stage, a short maturity stage, and a steep sloped decline stage. A product such as Coca Cola and Pepsi would experience growth, but also a constant level of sales over a number of decades. It can probably be said that a given product (or products collectively within an industry) may hold a unique PLC shape, and the typical PLC model can only be used as a rough guide for marketing management.

The Product Life Cycle (PLC) is based upon the biological life cycle. For example, a seed is planted (introduction); it begins to sprout (growth); it shoots out leaves and puts down roots as it becomes an adult (maturity); after a long period as an adult the plant begins to shrink and die out (decline). In theory it's the same for a product. After a period of development it is introduced or launched into the market; it gains more and more customers as it grows; eventually the market stabilises and the product becomes mature; then after a period of time the product is overtaken by development and the introduction of superior competitors, it goes into decline and is eventually withdrawn.

Strategies for the Differing Stages of the Product Life Cycle

The need for immediate profit is not a pressure. The product is promoted to create awareness. If the product has no or few competitors, a skimming price strategy is employed. Limited numbers of product are available in few channels of distribution.

Growth

Competitors are attracted into the market with very similar offerings. Products become more profitable and companies form alliances, joint ventures and take each other over. Advertising spend is high and focuses upon building brand. Market share tends to stabilise.

Maturity

Those products that survive the earlier stages tend to spend longest in this phase. Sales grow at a decreasing rate and then stabilise. Producers attempt to differentiate products and brands are key to this. Price wars and intense competition occur. At this point the market reaches saturation. Producers begin to leave the market due to poor margins. Promotion becomes more widespread and use a greater variety of media.

Decline

At this point there is a downturn in the market. For example more innovative products are introduced or consumer tastes have changed.

There is intense price-cutting and many more products are withdrawn from the market. Profits can be improved by reducing marketing spend and cost cutting.

Problems with Product Life Cycle

In reality very few products follow such a prescriptive cycle. The length of each stage varies enormously. The decisions of marketers can change the stage, for example from maturity to decline by price-cutting. Not all products go through each stage. Some go from introduction to decline. It is not easy to tell which stage the product is in. Remember that PLC is like all other tools. Use it to inform your gut feeling. Another marketing tool for evaluating PRODUCT is the Three Levels of a Product.

Research and Development

The phrase research and development (also R and D or, more often, R&D), according to the Organization for Economic Co-operation and Development, refers to "creative work undertaken on a systematic basis in order to increase the stock of knowledge, including knowledge of man, culture and society, and the use of this stock of knowledge to devise new applications"

R&D

New product design and development is more often than not a crucial factor in the survival of a company. In an industry that is fast changing, firms must continually revise their design and range of products. This is necessary due to continuous technology change and development as well as other competitors and the changing preference of customers. A system driven by marketing is one that puts the customer needs first, and only produces goods that are known to sell. Market research is carried out, which establishes what is needed. If the development is technology driven then it is a matter of selling what it is possible to make. The product range is developed so that production processes are as efficient as possible and the products are technically superior, hence possessing a natural advantage in the market place.

R&D has a special economic significance apart from its conventional association with scientific and technological development. R&D investment generally reflects a government's or organization's willingness to forgo current operations or profit to improve future performance or returns, and its abilities to conduct research and development. In 2006, the world's four largest spenders of R&D were the United States (US$343 billion), the EU (US$231 billion), China (US$136 billion), and Japan (US$130 billion). In terms of percentage of GDP, the order of these spenders for 2006 was China (US$115 billion of US$2,668 billion GDP), Japan, United States, EU with approximate percentages of 4.3, 3.2, 2.6, and 1.8 respectively. The top 10 spenders in terms of percentage of GDP were Israel (4.53%), Sweden (3.73%), Finland (3.45%), Japan (3.39%), South Korea (3.23%), Switzerland (2.9%), Iceland (2.78%), United States (2.62%), Germany (2.53%) and Austria (2.45%).

In general, R&D activities are conducted by specialized units or centres belonging to companies, universities and state agencies. In the context of commerce, "research and development" normally refers to future-oriented, longer-term activities in science or technology, using similar techniques to scientific research without predetermined outcomes and with broad forecasts of commercial yield. Statistics on organizations devoted to "R&D" may express the state of an industry, the degree of competition or the lure of progress. Some common measures include: budgets, numbers of patents or on rates of peer-reviewed publications. Bank ratios are one of the best measures, because they are continuously maintained, public and reflect risk.

In the U.S., a typical ratio of research and development for an industrial company is about 3.5% of revenues. A high technology company such as a computer manufacturer might spend 7%. Although Allergan (a biotech company) tops the spending table 43.4% investment, anything over 15% is remarkable and usually gains a reputation for being a high technology company. Companies in this category include pharmaceutical companies such as Merck & Co. (14.1%) or Novartis (15.1%), and engineering companies like Ericsson (24.9%).

Such companies are often seen as poor credit risks because their spending ratios are so unusual.

Generally such firms prosper only in markets whose customers have extreme needs, such as medicine, scientific instruments, safety-critical mechanisms (aircraft) or high technology military armaments. The extreme needs justify the high risk of failure and consequently high gross margins from 60% to 90% of revenues. That is, gross profits will be as much as 90% of the sales cost, with manufacturing costing only 10% of the product price, because so many individual projects yield no exploitable product. Most industrial companies get only 40% revenues. On a technical level, high tech organisations explore ways to re-purpose and repackage advanced technologies as a way of amortizing the high overhead. They often reuse advanced manufacturing processes, expensive safety certifications, specialized embedded software, computer-aided design software, electronic designs and mechanical subsystems. Research has shown that firms with a persistent R&D strategy outperform those with an irregular or no R&D investment programme.

Pharmaceuticals

Research often refers to basic experimental research; development refers to the exploitation of discoveries. Research involves the identification of possible chemical compounds or theoretical mechanisms. In the United States, universities are the main provider of research level products. In the United States, corporations buy licences from universities or hire scientists directly when economically solid research level products emerge and the development phase of drug delivery is almost entirely managed by private enterprise. Development is concerned with proof of concept, safety testing, and determining ideal levels and delivery mechanisms. Development often occurs in phases that are defined by drug safety regulators in the country of interest. In the United States, the development phase can cost between $10 to $200 million and approximately one in ten compounds identified by basic research pass all development phases and reach market.

Business

Research and development is nowadays of great importance in business as the level of competition, production processes and methods are rapidly increasing. It is of special importance in the field of marketing where companies keep an eagle eye on competitors and customers in order to keep pace with modern trends and analyse the needs, demands and desires of their customers. Unfortunately, research and development are very difficult to manage, since the defining feature of research is that the researchers do not know in advance exactly how to accomplish the desired result. As a result, higher R&D spending does not guarantee "more creativity, higher profit or a greater market share."

R&D Alliance

An R&D alliance is a mutually beneficial formal relationship formed between two or more parties to pursue a set of agreed upon goals while remaining independent organisations, where acquiring new knowledge is a goal by itself. The different parties agree to combine their knowledge to create new innovative products. Thanks to funding from government organizations, like the European Union's Seventh Framework Programme (FP7), and modern advances in technology, such as Eures Tools, R&D alliances have now become more efficient. Research and development is nowadays of great importance in business as the level of competition, production processes and methods are rapidly increasing. It is of special importance in the field of marketing where companies keep an eagle eye on competitors and customers in order to keep pace with modern trends and analyse the needs, demands and desires of their customers.

Unfortunately, research and development are very difficult to manage, since the defining feature of research is that the researchers do not know in advance exactly how to accomplish the desired result. As a result, higher R&D spending and does not guarantee "more creativity, higher profit or a greater market share."

Basic Research

Basic research or fundamental research (sometimes pure research) is research carried out to increase understanding of fundamental principles. Many times the end results have no direct or immediate commercial benefits: basic research can be thought of as arising out of curiosity. However, in the long term it is the basis for many commercial products and applied research. Basic research is mainly carried out by universities

Office of Scientific Research and Development

The Office of Scientific Research and Development (OSRD) was an agency of the United States federal government created to coordinate scientific research for military purposes during World War II. Arrangements were made for its creation during May 1941, and it was created formally by Executive Order 8807 on June 28, 1941. It superseded the work of the National Defence Research Committee (NDRC), was given almost unlimited access to funding and resources, and was directed by Vannevar Bush, who reported only to President Franklin Delano Roosevelt.

The research was widely varied, and included projects devoted to new and more accurate bombs, reliable detonators, work on the proximity fuze, radar and early-warning systems, lighter and more accurate hand weapons, more effective medical treatments, more versatile vehicles, and, most secret of all, the "S-1 Section", which later became the Manhattan Project and developed the first nuclear weapons.

From October 1943 to October 1946, OSRD used conscientious objectors from Civilian Public Service as subjects for research of malaria, altitude pressure, life raft rations, high altitude, frost bite, psycho-acoustics, poison gas, ingestion of and exposure to sea water, temperature extremes, climate, physiological hygiene, thiamine, bed rest and aero medicine.

To study the effects of diet and nutrition, Dr. Ancel Keys of the University of Minnesota Laboratory of Physiological Hygiene placed 32 conscientious objectors on a controlled diet. For three months they were given a normal 3200 calorie diet. This was followed by six months of an 1800 calorie diet, fewer calories than provided by the famine diet experienced by the civilian population in wartime Europe. The research documented the men's ability to maintain physical output and the psychological effects such as introversion, lethargy, irritability and severe depression. The study then studied the men's recovery as they returned to a normal diet and regained the weight lost during the experimentation. The men indicated later they would not have volunteered for this project had they known how rigorous it would be.

The OSRD was discontinued during December 1947.

Research & Development

Syngenta has a deep understanding of plants, based on many decades of research and development. Around 4,000 employees at five main R&D centres and numerous field stations around the world are dedicated to raising crop yields and improving quality.

In 2008, the Company invested $969 million in R&D, again placing us among the industry leaders. With projects spanning crop protection, seeds and biotechnology, Syngenta has a uniquely diverse platform. This enables us to co-operate across traditional business lines and provide ideal combinations of genetic and chemical solutions to meet the challenge of raising growers' productivity.

One of the best examples of successful crossbusiness collaboration is Seed Care. We create maximum value for growers by combining selected seed traits with chemical treatments that protect the seed from the day it is sown. Our Crop Protection and Seeds pipelines provide clear evidence of the common direction and interlinkage of our research. Both pipelines are targeting drought tolerance technologies ranging from chemical treatment to drought tolerant corn seeds which can improve yield in conditions of limited water availability. We also see potential synergies between our second generation trait technology and our crop protection portfolio..

Innovation, life Cycle Management

International co-operation between R&D teams accelerates the pace of innovation, bringing new products to market more quickly and increasing the return on investment. Recent changes in our processes include simultaneous management of previously sequential development phases. This has enabled us to reduce the average time from a compound's discovery to its market introduction by about two years. Syngenta now has an overall R&D process that is among the fastest in the crop protection industry. In Seeds, we have brought traits such as AGRISURE® RW to market with record speed.

The R&D process for chemicals is still a lengthy one-around eight years-with environmental testing a key element throughout. Respect for the environment is inherent in the development of our products, and is a cornerstone of our commitment to make agriculture more sustainable.

Life cycle management is also an integral part of our R&D investment. It enables us to maximize the value of our compounds and to meet the challenge of dealing with living organisms-weeds, diseases and insects-that can frequently develop resistance to existing solutions. The significantly increased sales potential for our fungicide AMISTAR®, for example, reflects our ability to combine it with other products to achieve new effects and solutions. Life cycles in Seeds are continuously extended through the use of molecular-assisted breeding to bring new varieties to market.

New Facilities, Additional Partners

Following on from the opening of our chemical R&D centre in Goa, India, in 2007, Syngenta took significant steps to strengthen further its global R&D capacity. In April, we officially opened the Chemistry Research laboratories and Seed Care Institute at our existing site in Stein, Switzerland. At the same time we announced the opening of a new biotechnology centre in Beijing, China. This facility will concentrate on early-stage evaluation of GM traits for key crops such as corn and soybean, in the areas of yield improvement, drought resistance, disease control and biomass conversion for biofuels.

We are also investing £35 million at our R&D centre at Jealott's Hill in the UK, which focuses on the development of new herbicides. The investment will enhance the centre's industry-leading technological capability and will accelerate further the delivery of new products to market.

Reseach at Jealott's Hill is complemented by the work of Syngenta Biotechnology Inc (SBI), based at Research Triangle Park in North Carolina, USA, which focuses on biotechnology solutions including herbicide tolerant crops.

As well as the extension of our own global R&D organization, we continue to partner with numerous other companies and institutions. Additions to our network of collaborations around the world in 2008 included agreements with Athenix Corporation for the discovery of novel corn insect and soybean cyst nematode resistance genes, and with Dow Agro Sciences® to evaluate compounds for our Seed Care portfolio. In total, Syngenta is involved in over 400 scientific collaborations worldwide.

Our venture capital fund LSPB announced two additional minority equity investments last year. One is in Asoyia, a seed company developing soybean with low linolenic acid oil; the other is in IBI, which develops and manufactures portable testing systems for micro-organisms, proteins and small molecules. These investments increase the fund's portfolio to six companies.

4

Basic Concepts in Noncooperative Game Theory

Game theory is a branch of applied mathematics that is used in the social sciences, most notably in economics, as well as in biology, engineering, political science, international relations, computer science, and philosophy. Game theory attempts to mathematically capture behaviour in *strategic situations*, in which an individual's success in making choices depends on the choices of others. While initially developed to analyse competitions in which one individual does better at another's expense (zero sum games), it has been expanded to treat a wide class of interactions, which are classified according to several criteria. Today, "game theory is a sort of umbrella or 'unified field' theory for the rational side of social science, where 'social' is interpreted broadly, to include human as well as non-human players (computers, animals, plants)" (Aumann 1987).

Traditional applications of game theory attempt to find equilibria in these games. In an equilibrium, each player of the game has adopted a strategy that they are unlikely to change. Many equilibrium concepts have been developed (most famously the Nash equilibrium) in an attempt to capture this idea. These equilibrium concepts are motivated differently depending on the field of application, although they often overlap or coincide. This methodology is not without criticism, and debates continue over the appropriateness of particular equilibrium concepts, the appropriateness of equilibria altogether, and the usefulness of mathematical models more generally.

Although some developments occurred before it, the field of game theory came into being with the 1944 book *Theory of Games and Economic*

Behaviour by John von Neumann and Oskar Morgenstern. This theory was developed extensively in the 1990s. by many scholars. Game theory was later explicitly applied to biology in the 1970s, although similar developments go back at least as far as the 1990s. Game theory has been widely recognized as an important tool in many fields. Eight game theorists have won Nobel prizes in economics, and John Maynard Smith was awarded the Crafoord Prize for his application of game theory to biology.

Representation of Games

The games studied in game theory are well-defined mathematical objects. A game consists of a set of players, a set of moves (or strategies) available to those players, and a specification of payoffs for each combination of strategies. Most cooperative games are presented in the characteristic function form, while the extensive and the normal forms are used to define noncooperative games.

The extensive form can be used to formalize games with some important order. Games here are often presented as trees (as pictured to the left). Here each vertex (or node) represents a point of choice for a player. The player is specified by a number listed by the vertex. The lines out of the vertex represent a possible action for that player. The payoffs are specified at the bottom of the tree.

In the game pictured here, there are two players. *Player 1* moves first and chooses either *F* or *U*. *Player 2* sees *Player 1*'s move and then chooses *A* or *R*. Suppose that *Player 1* chooses *U* and then *Player 2* chooses *A*, then *Player 1* gets 8 and *Player 2* gets 2.

The extensive form can also capture simultaneous-move games and games with imperfect information. To represent it, either a dotted line connects different vertices to represent them as being part of the same information set (i.e., the players do not know at which point they are), or a closed line is drawn around them.

Normal Form

The normal (or strategic form) game is usually represented by a matrix which shows the players, strategies, and payoffs. More generally it can be represented by any function that associates a payoff for each player with every possible combination of actions. In the accompanying example there are two players; one chooses the row and the other chooses the column. Each player has two strategies, which are specified by the number of rows and the number of columns. The payoffs are provided in the interior. The first number is the payoff received by the row player (Player 1 in our example); the second is the payoff for the column player (Player 2 in our example). Suppose that Player 1 plays *Up* and that Player 2 plays *Left*. Then Player 1 gets a payoff of 4, and Player 2 gets 3.

When a game is presented in normal form, it is presumed that each player acts simultaneously or, at least, without knowing the actions of the other. If players have some information about the choices of other players, the game is usually presented in extensive form.

Characteristic Function Form

In cooperative games with transferable utility no individual payoffs are given. Instead, the characteristic function determines the payoff of each coalition. The standard assumption is that the empty coalition obtains a payoff of 0.

The origin of this form is to be found in the seminal book of von Neumann and Morgenstern who, when studying coalitional normal form games, assumed that when a coalition C forms, it plays against the complementary coalition () as if they were playing a 2-player game. The equilibrium payoff of C is *characteristic*. Now there are different models to derive coalitional values from normal form games, but not all games in characteristic function form can be derived from normal form games.

Formally, a characteristic function form game (also known as a TU-game) is given as a pair (N,v), where N denotes a set of players and is a characteristic function.

The characteristic function form has been generalised to games without the assumption of transferable utility.

Partition Function Form

The characteristic function form ignores the possible externalities of coalition formation. In the partition function form the payoff of a coalition depends not only on its members, but also on the way the rest of the players are partitioned (Thrall & Lucas 1963).

Application and Challenges

Game theory has been used to study a wide variety of human and animal behaviours. It was initially developed in economics to understand a large collection of economic behaviours, including behaviours of firms, markets, and consumers. The use of game theory in the social sciences has expanded, and game theory has been applied to political, sociological, and psychological behaviours as well.

Game theoretic analysis was initially used to study animal behaviour by Ronald Fisher in the 1990s. (although even Charles Darwin makes a few informal game theoretic statements). This work predates the name "game theory", but it shares many important features with this field. The developments in economics were later applied to biology largely by John Maynard Smith in his book *Evolution and the Theory of Games.*

In addition to being used to predict and explain behaviour, game theory has also been used to attempt to develop theories of ethical or normative behaviour. In economics and philosophy, scholars have applied game theory to help in the understanding of good or proper behaviour. Game theoretic arguments of this type can be found as far back as Plato.

Political Science

The application of game theory to political science is focused in the overlapping areas of fair division, political economy, public choice, war bargaining, positive political theory, and social choice theory. In each of these areas, researchers have developed game theoretic models in which the players are often voters, states, special interest groups, and politicians.

For early examples of game theory applied to political science, see the work of Anthony Downs. In his book An Economic Theory of Democracy (Downs 1957), he applies the Hotelling firm location model to the political process. In the Downsian model, political candidates commit to ideologies on a one-dimensional policy space. The theorist shows how the political candidates will converge to the ideology preferred by the median voter. For more recent examples, see the books by Steven Brams, George Tsebelis, Gene M. Grossman and Elhanan Helpman, or David Austen-Smith and Jeffrey S. Banks.

A game-theoretic explanation for democratic peace is that public and open debate in democracies send clear and reliable information regarding their intentions to other states. In contrast, it is difficult to know the intentions of nondemocratic leaders, what effect concessions will have, and if promises will be kept. Thus there will be mistrust and unwillingness to make concessions if at least one of the parties in a dispute is a nondemocracy (Levy & Razin 2003).

Economics and Business

Economists have long used game theory to analyse a wide array of economic phenomena, including auctions, bargaining, duopolies, fair division, oligopolies, social network formation, and voting systems. This research usually focuses on particular sets of strategies known as equilibria in games. These "solution concepts" are usually based on what is required by norms of rationality. In non-cooperative games, the most famous of these is the Nash equilibrium. A set of strategies is a Nash equilibrium if each represents a best response to the other strategies. So, if all the players are playing the strategies in a Nash equilibrium, they have no unilateral incentive to deviate, since their strategy is the best they can do given what others are doing.

The payoffs of the game are generally taken to represent the utility of individual players. Often in modelling situations the payoffs represent money, which presumably corresponds to an individual's utility. This assumption, however, can be faulty.

A prototypical paper on game theory in economics begins by presenting a game that is an abstraction of some particular economic situation. One or more solution concepts are chosen, and the author demonstrates which strategy sets in the presented game are equilibria of the appropriate type. Naturally one might wonder to what use should this information be put. Economists and business professors suggest two primary uses: *descriptive* and *prescriptive.*

Descriptive

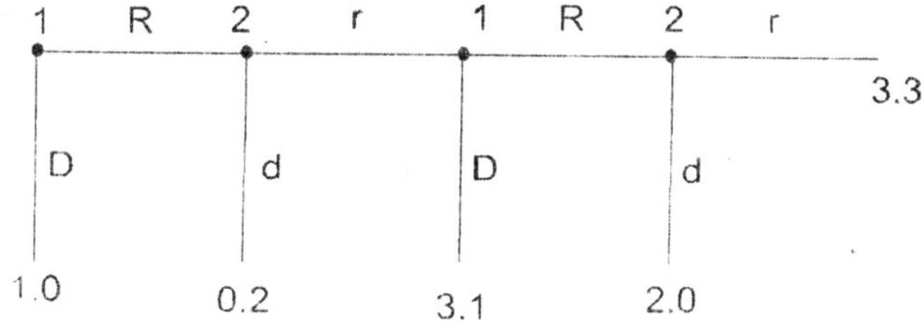

A three stage Centipede Game

The first known use is to inform us about how actual human populations behave. Some scholars believe that by finding the equilibria of games they can predict how actual human populations will behave when confronted with situations analogous to the game being studied. This particular view of game theory has come under recent criticism. First, it is criticized because the assumptions made by game theorists are often violated. Game theorists may assume players always act in a way to directly maximize their wins (the Homo economicus model), but in practice, human behaviour often deviates from this model. Explanations of this phenomenon are many; irrationality, new models of deliberation, or even different motives (like that of altruism). Game theorists respond by comparing their assumptions to those used in physics. Thus while their assumptions do not always hold, they can treat game theory as a reasonable scientific ideal akin to the models used by physicists. However, additional criticism of this use of game theory has been levied because some experiments have demonstrated that individuals do not play equilibrium strategies. For instance, in the centipede game, guess 2/3 of the average game, and the dictator game, people regularly do not play Nash equilibria. There is an ongoing debate regarding the importance of these experiments.

Alternatively, some authors claim that Nash equilibria do not provide predictions for human populations, but rather provide an explanation for why populations that play Nash equilibria remain in that state. However, the question of how populations reach those points remains open.

Some game theorists have turned to evolutionary game theory in order to resolve these worries. These models presume either no rationality or bounded rationality on the part of players. Despite the name, evolutionary game theory does not necessarily presume natural selection in the biological sense. Evolutionary game theory includes both biological as well as cultural evolution and also models of individual learning (for example, fictitious play dynamics).

Prescriptive or Normative Analysis

On the other hand, some scholars see game theory not as a predictive tool for the behaviour of human beings, but as a suggestion for how people ought to behave. Since a Nash equilibrium of a game constitutes one's best response to the actions of the other players, playing a strategy that is part of a Nash equilibrium seems appropriate. However, this use for game theory has also come under criticism. First, in some cases it is appropriate to play a non-equilibrium strategy if one expects others to play non-equilibrium strategies as well.

Second, the Prisoner's dilemma presents another potential counterexample. In the Prisoner's Dilemma, each player pursuing his own self-interest leads both players to be worse off than had they not pursued their own self-interests.

Biology

Unlike economics, the payoffs for games in biology are often interpreted as corresponding to fitness. In addition, the focus has been less on equilibria that correspond to a notion of rationality, but rather on ones that would be maintained by evolutionary forces. The best known equilibrium in biology is known as the *evolutionarily stable strategy* (or ESS), and was first introduced in (Smith & Price 1973). Although its initial motivation did not involve any of the mental requirements of the Nash equilibrium, every ESS is a Nash equilibrium.

In biology, game theory has been used to understand many different phenomena. It was first used to explain the evolution (and stability) of the approximate 1:1 sex ratios. (Fisher 1930) suggested that the 1:1 sex ratios are a result of evolutionary forces acting on individuals who could be seen as trying to maximize their number of grandchildren.

Additionally, biologists have used evolutionary game theory and the ESS to explain the emergence of animal communication (Harper & Maynard Smith 2003). The analysis of signaling games and other communication games has provided some insight into the evolution of communication among animals. For example, the mobbing behaviour of many species, in which a large number of prey animals attack a larger predator, seems to be an example of spontaneous emergent organization.

Biologists have used the game of chicken to analyse fighting behaviour and territoriality.

Maynard Smith, in the preface to *Evolution and the Theory of Games*, writes, "[p]aradoxically, it has turned out that game theory is more readily applied to biology than to the field of economic behaviour for which it was originally designed". Evolutionary game theory has been used to explain many seemingly incongruous phenomena in nature.

One such phenomenon is known as biological altruism. This is a situation in which an organism appears to act in a way that benefits other organisms and is detrimental to itself. This is distinct from traditional notions of altruism because such actions are not conscious, but appear to be evolutionary adaptations to increase overall fitness. Examples can be found in species ranging from vampire bats that regurgitate blood they have obtained from a night's hunting and give it to group members who have failed to feed, to worker bees that care for the queen bee for their entire lives and never mate, to Vervet monkeys that warn group members of a predator's approach, even when it endangers that individual's chance of survival. All of these actions increase the overall fitness of a group, but occur at a cost to the individual.

Evolutionary game theory explains this altruism with the idea of kin selection. Altruists discriminate between the individuals they help; and favour relatives. Hamilton's rule explains the evolutionary reasoning behind this selection with the equation c<b*r where the cost (c) to the altruist must be less than the benefit (b) to the recipient multiplied by the coefficient of relatedness (r). The more closely related two organisms are causes the incidence of altruism to increase because they share many of the same alleles. This means that the altruistic individual, by ensuring that the alleles of its close relative are passed on, (through survival of its offspring) can forgo the option of having offspring itself because the same number of alleles are passed on. Helping a sibling for example, has a coefficient of ½, because an individual shares ½ of the alleles in its sibling's offspring. Ensuring that enough of a sibling's offspring survive to adulthood precludes the necessity of the altruistic individual producing offspring. The coefficient values depend heavily on the scope of the playing field; for example if the choice of whom to favour includes all genetic living things, not just all relatives, we assume the discrepancy between all humans only accounts for approximately 1% of the diversity in the playing field, a co-efficient that was ½ in the smaller field becomes 0.995. Similarly if it is considered that information other than that of a genetic nature (e.g. epigenetics, religion, science, etc.) persisted through time the playing field becomes larger still, and the discrepancies smaller.

Computer Science and Logic

Game theory has come to play an increasingly important role in logic and in computer science. Several logical theories have a basis in game semantics. In addition, computer scientists have used games to model interactive computations. Also, game theory provides a theoretical basis to the field of multi-agent systems.

Separately, game theory has played a role in online algorithms. In particular, the k-server problem, which has in the past been referred to as *games with moving costs* and *request-answer games* (Ben David, Borodin & Karp et al. 1994). Yao's principle is a game-theoretic technique for proving lower bounds on the computational complexity of randomized algorithms, and especially of online algorithms.

The field of algorithmic game theory combines computer science concepts of complexity and algorithm design with game theory and economic theory. The emergence of the internet has motivated the development of algorithms for finding equilibria in games, markets, computational auctions, peer-to-peer systems, and security and information markets.

Philosophy

Game theory has been put to several uses in philosophy. Responding to two papers by W.V.O. Quine (1960, 1967), Lewis (1969) used game theory to develop a philosophical account of convention. In so doing, he provided the first analysis of common knowledge and employed it in analyzing play in coordination games. In addition, he first suggested that one can understand meaning in terms of signaling games. This later suggestion has been pursued by several philosophers since Lewis (Skyrms (1996), Grim, Kokalis, and Alai-Tafti et al. (2004)). Following Lewis (1969) game-theoretic account of conventions, Ullmann Margalit (1977) and Bicchieri (2006) have developed theories of social norms that define them as Nash equilibria that result from transforming a mixed-motive game into a coordination game.

Game theory has also challenged philosophers to think in terms of interactive epistemology: what it means for a collective to have common beliefs or knowledge, and what are the consequences of this knowledge for the social outcomes resulting from agents' interactions. Philosophers who have worked in this area include Bicchieri (1989, 1993), Skyrms (1990), and Stalnaker (1999).

In ethics, some authors have attempted to pursue the project, begun by Thomas Hobbes, of deriving morality from self-interest. Since games like the Prisoner's dilemma present an apparent conflict between morality and self-interest, explaining why cooperation is required by self-interest is an important component of this project. This general strategy is a component of the general social contract view in political philosophy.

Other authors have attempted to use evolutionary game theory in order to explain the emergence of human attitudes about morality and corresponding animal behaviours. These authors look at several games including the Prisoner's dilemma, Stag hunt, and the Nash bargaining game as providing an explanation for the emergence of attitudes about morality.

Some assumptions used in some parts of game theory have been challenged in philosophy; psychological egoism states that rationality reduces to self-interest—a claim debated among philosophers.

Types of Games

Cooperative or Non-cooperative

A game is *cooperative* if the players are able to form binding commitments. For instance the legal system requires them to adhere to their promises. In noncooperative games this is not possible.

Often it is assumed that *communication* among players is allowed in cooperative games, but not in noncooperative ones. This classification on two binary criteria has been rejected (Harsanyi 1974).

Of the two types of games, noncooperative games are able to model situations to the finest details, producing accurate results. Cooperative games focus on the game at large. Considerable efforts have been made to link the two approaches. The so-called Nash-programme has already established many of the cooperative solutions as noncooperative equilibria.

Hybrid games contain cooperative and non-cooperative elements. For instance, coalitions of players are formed in a cooperative game, but these play in a non-cooperative fashion.

Symmetric and Asymmetric

A symmetric game is a game where the payoffs for playing a particular strategy depend only on the other strategies employed, not on who is playing them. If the identities of the players can be changed without changing the payoff to the strategies, then a game is symmetric. Many of the commonly studied 2×2 games are symmetric. The standard representations of chicken, the prisoner's dilemma, and the stag hunt are all symmetric games. Some scholars would consider certain asymmetric games as examples of these games as well. However, the most common payoffs for each of these games are symmetric.

Most commonly studied asymmetric games are games where there are not identical strategy sets for both players. For instance, the ultimatum game and similarly the dictator game have different strategies for each player. It is possible, however, for a game to have identical strategies for both players, yet be asymmetric. For example, the game pictured to the right is asymmetric despite having identical strategy sets for both players.

Zero-sum and Non-zero-sum

Zero-sum games are a special case of constant-sum games, in which choices by players can neither increase nor decrease the available resources. In zero-sum games the total benefit to all players in the game, for every combination of strategies, always adds to zero (more informally, a player benefits only at the equal expense of others). Poker exemplifies a zero-sum game (ignoring the possibility of the house's cut), because one wins exactly the amount one's opponents lose. Other zero-sum games include matching pennies and most classical board games including Go and chess.

Many games studied by game theorists (including the famous prisoner's dilemma) are non-zero-sum games, because some outcomes have net results greater or less than zero. Informally, in non-zero-sum games, a gain by one player does not necessarily correspond with a loss by another.

Constant-sum games correspond to activities like theft and gambling, but not to the fundamental economic situation in which there are potential gains from trade. It is possible to transform any game into a (possibly asymmetric) zero-sum game by adding an additional dummy player (often called "the board"), whose losses compensate the players' net winnings.

Simultaneous and Sequential

Simultaneous games are games where both players move simultaneously, or if they do not move simultaneously, the later players are unaware of the earlier players' actions (making them *effectively* simultaneous). Sequential game (or dynamic games) are games where later players have some knowledge about earlier actions. This need not be perfect information about every action of earlier players; it might be very little knowledge. For instance, a player may know that an earlier player did not perform one particular action, while he does not know which of the other available actions the first player actually performed.

The difference between simultaneous and sequential games is captured in the different representations discussed above. Often, normal form is used to represent simultaneous games, and extensive form is used to represent sequential ones; although this isn't a strict rule in a technical sense.

Perfect Information and Imperfect Information

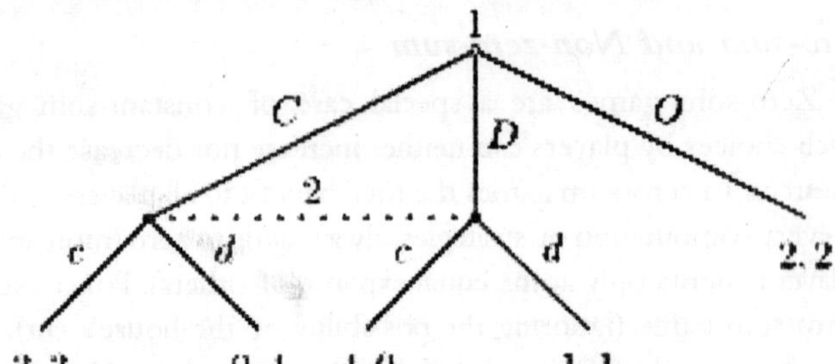

A game of imperfect information (the dotted line represents ignorance on the part of player 2)

An important subset of sequential games consists of games of perfect information. A game is one of perfect information if all players know the moves previously made by all other players. Thus, only sequential games can be games of perfect information, since in simultaneous games not every player knows the actions of the others. Most games studied in game theory are imperfect-information games, although there are some interesting examples of perfect-information games, including the ultimatum game and centipede game. Perfect-information games include also chess, go, mancala, and arimaa.

Perfect information is often confused with complete information, which is a similar concept. Complete information requires that every player know the strategies and payoffs of the other players but not necessarily the actions.

Infinitely Long Games

Games, as studied by economists and real-world game players, are generally finished in a finite number of moves. Pure mathematicians are not so constrained, and set theorists in particular study games that last for an infinite number of moves, with the winner (or other payoff) not known until *after* all those moves are completed.

The focus of attention is usually not so much on what is the best way to play such a game, but simply on whether one or the other player has a winning strategy. (It can be proven, using the axiom of choice, that there are games—even with perfect information, and where the only outcomes are "win" or "lose"—for which *neither* player has a winning strategy.) The existence of such strategies, for cleverly designed games, has important consequences in descriptive set theory.

Discrete and Continuous Games

Much of game theory is concerned with finite, discrete games, that have a finite number of players, moves, events, outcomes, etc. Many concepts can be extended, however. Continuous games allow players to choose a strategy from a continuous strategy set. For instance, Cournot competition is typically modelled with players' strategies being any non-negative quantities, including fractional quantities.

Differential games such as the continuous pursuit and evasion game are continuous games.

One-player and many-player Games

Individual decision problems are sometimes considered "one-player games". While these situations are not game theoretical, they are modelled using many of the same tools within the discipline of decision theory. It is only with two or more players that a problem becomes game theoretical. A randomly acting player who makes "chance moves", also known as "moves by nature", is often added (Osborne & Rubinstein 1994). This player is not typically considered a third player in what is otherwise a two-player game, but merely serves to provide a roll of the dice where required by the game. Games with an infinite number of players are often called n-person games (Luce & Raiffa 1957).

Metagames

These are games the play of which is the development of the rules for another game, the target or subject game. Metagames seek to maximize the utility value of the rule set developed. The theory of metagames is related to mechanism design theory.

Non-cooperative Game

In game theory, a non-cooperative game is a one in which players make decisions independently. Thus, while they may be able to cooperate, any cooperation must be self-enforcing.

A game in which players can enforce contracts through third parties is a cooperative game.

Nash Equilibrium

In game theory, Nash equilibrium (named after John Forbes Nash, who proposed it) is a solution concept of a game involving two or more players, in which each player is assumed to know the equilibrium strategies of the other players, and no player has anything to gain by changing only his or her own strategy unilaterally. If each player has chosen a strategy and no player can benefit by changing his or her strategy while the other players keep theirs unchanged, then the current set of strategy choices and the corresponding payoffs constitute a Nash equilibrium.

Stated simply, Amy and Bill are in Nash equilibrium if Amy is making the best decision she can, taking into account Bill's decision, and Bill is making the best decision he can, taking into account Amy's decision. Likewise, a group of players is in Nash equilibrium if each one is making the best decision that he or she can, taking into account the decisions of the others. However, Nash equilibrium does not necessarily mean the best cumulative payoff for all the players involved; in many cases all the players might improve their payoffs if they could somehow agree on strategies different from the Nash equilibrium (e.g. competing businesses forming a cartel in order to increase their profits).

Applications

The Nash equilibrium concept is used to analyse the outcome of the strategic interaction of several decision makers. In other words, it is a way of predicting what will happen if several people or several institutions are making decisions at the same time, and if the decision of each one depends on the decisions of the others. The simple insight underlying John Nash's idea is that we cannot predict the result of the choices of multiple decision makers if we analyse those decisions in isolation. Instead, we must ask what each player would do, *taking into account* the decision-making of the others.

Nash equilibrium has been used to analyse hostile situations like war and arms races, and also how conflict may be mitigated by repeated interaction. It has also been used to study to what extent people with different preferences can cooperate, and whether they will take risks to achieve a cooperative outcome. It has been used to study the adoption of technical standards, and also the occurrence of bank runs and currency crises. Other applications include traffic flow, how to organize auctions, and even penalty kicks in soccer.

History

A version of the Nash equilibrium concept was first used by Antoine Augustin Cournot in his theory of oligopoly (1838). In Cournot's theory, firms choose how much output to produce to maximize their own profit. However, the best output for one firm depends on the outputs of others. A Cournot equilibrium occurs when each firm's output maximizes its profits given the output of the other firms, which is a pure strategy Nash Equilibrium.

The modern game-theoretic concept of Nash Equilibrium is instead defined in terms of mixed strategies, where players choose a probability distribution over possible actions. The concept of the mixed strategy Nash Equilibrium was introduced by John von Neumann and Oskar Morgenstern in their 1944 book *The Theory of Games and Economic Behaviour*. However, their analysis was restricted to the special case of zero-sum games. They showed that a mixed-strategy Nash Equilibrium will exist for any zero-sum game with a finite set of actions. The contribution of John Forbes Nash in his 1951 article *Non-Cooperative Games* was to define a mixed strategy Nash Equilibrium for any game with a finite set of actions and prove that at least one (mixed strategy) Nash Equilibrium must exist.

Since the development of the Nash equilibrium concept, game theorists have discovered that it makes misleading predictions (or fails to make a unique prediction) in certain circumstances. Therefore they have proposed many related solution concepts (also called 'refinements' of Nash equilibrium) designed to overcome perceived flaws in the Nash concept. One particularly important issue is that some Nash equilibria may be based on threats that are not 'credible'. Therefore, in 1965 Reinhard Selten proposed subgame perfect equilibrium as a refinement that eliminates equilibria which depend on non-credible threats. Other extensions of the Nash equilibrium concept have addressed what happens if a game is repeated, or what happens if a game is played in the absence of perfect information. However, subsequent refinements and extensions of the Nash equilibrium concept share the main insight on which Nash's concept rests: all equilibrium concepts analyse what choices will be made when each player takes into account the decision-making of others.

Definitions

Informal Definition

Informally, a set of strategies is a Nash equilibrium if no player can do better by unilaterally changing his or her strategy. To see what this means, imagine that each player is told the strategies of the others. Suppose then that each player asks himself or herself: "Knowing the strategies of the other players, and treating the strategies of the other players as set in stone, can I benefit by changing my strategy?"

If any player would answer "Yes", then that set of strategies is not a Nash equilibrium. But if every player prefers not to switch (or is indifferent between switching and not) then the set of strategies is a Nash equilibrium. Thus, each strategy in a Nash equilibrium is a best response to all other strategies in that equilibrium.

The Nash equilibrium may sometimes appear non-rational in a third-person perspective. This is because it may happen that a Nash equilibrium is not Pareto optimal.

The Nash equilibrium may also have non-rational consequences in sequential games because players may "threaten" each other with non-rational moves. For such games the Subgame perfect Nash equilibrium may be more meaningful as a tool of analysis.

Formal Definition

Let (S, f) be a game with n players, where S_i is the strategy set for player i, $S=S_1 X S_2 ... X S_n$ is the set of strategy profiles and $f=(f_1(x),..., f_n(x))$ is the payoff function. Let x_{-i} be a strategy profile of all players except for player i. When each player i {1,..., n} chooses strategy x_i resulting in strategy profile $x = (x_1,..., x_n)$ then player i obtains payoff $f_i(x)$. Note that the payoff depends on the strategy profile chosen, i.e. on the strategy chosen by player i as well as the strategies chosen by all the other players. A strategy profile x^* S is a Nash equilibrium (NE) if no unilateral deviation in strategy by any single player is profitable for that player, that is

A game can have either a pure-strategy or a mixed Nash Equilibrium, (in the latter a pure strategy is chosen stochastically with a fixed frequency). Nash proved that if we allow mixed strategies, then every n-player game in which every player can choose from finitely many strategies admits at least one Nash equilibrium.

When the inequality above holds strictly (with > instead of) for all players and all feasible alternative strategies, then the equilibrium is classified as a strict Nash equilibrium. If instead, for some player, there is exact equality between and some other strategy in the set *S*, then the equilibrium is classified as a weak Nash equilibrium.

Assured Destruction

Assured destruction is a concept sometimes used in game theory and similar discussions to describe a condition where certain behaviours or choices are deterred because they will lead to the imposition by others of overwhelming punitive consequences.

The concept of assured destruction occasionally arises in the death penalty debate and biotechnology debate, though it is most well known in the context of nuclear strategy where it is most often discussed as mutually assured destruction — a deterrent strategy where both participants have the ability to respond overwhelmingly against whoever strikes first.

For an assured destruction strategy to be successful,

- the threat must be known in advance,
- the threat must be credible both in the opponent's ability and moral willingness to retaliate,
- the target of the strategy must behave based on rational self-interest to the extent that the threat will be effective in preventing the behaviour.

Other examples of attempts to establish the conditions for assured destruction include:

- Three-man cells in terrorist organizations, who establish interlocking treaties between each pair of the participants for the death of any party who refuses to cooperate.
- Poison pills in stockholder agreements.

- Highly punitive criminal and civil punishments for drug possession.

When the concept of assured destruction is applied in the doctrine of law, it is often criticized by proponents of the restorative justice and transformative justice movements, who point out that assured destruction doctrines are rarely implemented with rigor or integrity of due process. This is a major contributor to the controversy of the death penalty debate.

Psychologists, notably B. F. Skinner, are of the opinion that promises of punishment seem to play little or no role in deterrence of adult behaviour. Challengers of the general application of assured destruction tactics point to the failure of post-facto measures to end standoffs presumed to lead to mutually assured destruction, as well as the role of martyrs and the effectiveness of suicide attacks in breaking or destabilizing the status quo whose upholding is often the intent of assured destruction.

Assured destruction tactics are not to be confused with "insurance" tactics such as retaliatory trade tariffs that are merely intended to compensate the aggrieved or to return conditions to the preexisting "level playing field".

Grim Trigger

Grim trigger (also called the grim strategy or just grim) is a trigger strategy in game theory for a repeated game, such as an iterated prisoner's dilemma. Initially, a player using grim trigger will cooperate, but as soon as the opponent defects (thus satisfying the trigger condition), the player using grim trigger will defect for the remainder of the iterated game. Since a single defect by the opponent triggers defection forever, grim trigger is the most strictly unforgiving of strategies in an iterated game.

In iterated prisoner's dilemma strategy competitions, Grim Trigger performs poorly even without noise, and adding signal errors makes it even worse. It has many defects but it primarily suffers from the inability to threaten permanent defection.

In Robert Axelrod's book *The Evolution of Cooperation*, grim trigger is called "FRIEDMAN" (James Friedman uses the concept in the 1971 paper: *A Non-cooperative Equilibrium for Supergames*).

Proper Equilibrium

Proper equilibrium is a refinement of Nash Equilibrium due to Roger B. Myerson. Proper equilibrium further refines Reinhard Selten's notion of a trembling hand perfect equilibrium by assuming that more costly trembles are made with significantly smaller probability than less costly ones.

Definition

Given a normal form game and a parameter a > 0, a totally mixed strategy profile for the game is defined to be a-proper if the following holds: If, for two pure strategies s and s' for the same player it is the case that the expected payoff of playing s is smaller than the expected payoff of playing s' (against the mixed strategies of the other players in the profile), then the probability assigned to s is at most a times the probability assigned to s'.

A strategy profile of the game is then said to be a proper equilibrium if it is a limit point, as a approaches 0, of a sequence of a-proper totally mixed strategy profiles.

Example

The game to the right is a variant of Matching Pennies.

Player 1 (row player) hides a penny and if Player 2 (column player) guesses correctly whether it is heads up or tails up, he gets the penny. In this variant, Player 2 has a third option: Grabbing the penny without guessing. The Nash equilibria of the game are the strategy profiles where Player 2 grabs the penny with probability 1. Any mixed strategy of Player 1 is in (Nash) equilibrium with this pure strategy of Player 2. Any such pair is even trembling hand perfect. Intuitively, since Player 1 expects Player 2 to grab the penny, he is not concerned about leaving Player 2 uncertain about whether it is heads up or tails up. However, it can be seen that the unique proper equilibrium of this game is the one where Player 1 hides the penny heads up with probability 1/2 and tails up with probability 1/2 (and Player 2 grabs the penny). This unique proper equilibrium can be motivated intuitively as follows: Player 1 fully expects Player 2 to grab the penny. However, Player 1 still prepares for the unlikely event that Player 2 does not grab the penny and instead for some reason decides to make a guess. Player 1 prepares for this event by making sure that Player 2 has no information about whether the penny is heads up or tails up, exactly as in the original Matching Pennies game.

Proper Equilibria of Extensive Games

One may apply the properness notion to extensive form games in two different ways, completely analogous to the two different ways trembling hand perfection is applied to extensive games. This leads to the notions of normal form proper equilibrium and extensive form proper equilibrium of an extensive form game. It was shown by van Damme that a normal form proper equilibrium of an extensive form game is behaviorally equivalent to a quasi-perfect equilibrium of that game.

Tit for tat

Tit for tat is a highly effective strategy in game theory for the iterated prisoner's dilemma. It was first introduced by Anatol Rapoport in Robert Axelrod's two tournaments, held around 1980. Based on the English saying meaning "equivalent retaliation" ("tit for tat"), an agent using this strategy will initially cooperate, then respond in kind to an opponent's previous action. If the opponent previously was cooperative, the agent is cooperative. If not, the agent is not. This is similar to reciprocal altruism in biology.

Overview

This strategy is dependent on four conditions that has allowed it to become the most prevalent strategy for the prisoner's dilemma:

1. Unless provoked, the agent will always cooperate
2. If provoked, the agent will retaliate
3. The agent is quick to forgive
4. The agent must have a good chance of competing against the opponent more than once.

In the last condition, the definition of "good chance" depends on the payoff matrix of the prisoner's dilemma. The important thing is that the competition continues long enough for repeated punishment and forgiveness to generate a long-term payoff higher than the possible loss from cooperating initially.

A fifth condition applies to make the competition meaningful: if an agent knows that the next play will be the last, it should naturally defect for a higher score. Similarly if it knows that the next two plays will be the last, it should defect twice, and so on. Therefore the number of competitions must not be known in advance to the agents.

Against a variety of alternative strategies, tit for tat was the most effective, winning in several annual automated tournaments against (generally far more complex) strategies created by teams of computer scientists, economists, and psychologists. Game theorists informally believed the strategy to be optimal (although no proof was presented).

It is important to know that tit for tat still is the most effective strategy if the average performance of each competing team is compared. The team which recently won over a pure tit for tat team only outperformed it with some of their algorithms because they submitted multiple algorithms which would recognize each other and assume a master and slave relationship (one algorithm would "sacrifice" itself and obtain a very poor result for the other algorithm to be able to outperform Tit for Tat on an individual basis, but not as a pair or group). Still, this "group" victory illustrates an important limitation of the Prisoner's Dilemma in representing social reality, namely, that it does not include any natural equivalent for friendship or alliances. The advantage of "tit for tat" thus pertains only to a Hobbesian world of rational solutions, not to a world in which humans are inherently social. However, the fact that this solution does not work effectively against groups of agents running tit-for-tat does illustrate the strengths of tit-for-tat when employed in a team (that the team does better overall, and all the agents on the team do well individually, when every agent cooperates).

Example of Play

Assume there are four agents: two use the Tit for Tat strategy, and two are "defectors" who will simply try to maximize their own winnings by always giving evidence against the other. Assume that each player faces the other three over a series of six games. If one player gives evidence against a player who does not, the former gains 5 points and the latter nets 0. If both refrain from giving evidence, both gain 3 points. If both give evidence against each other, both gain 1 point.

When a tit-for-tat agent faces off against a defector, the former refrains from giving evidence in the first game while the defector does the opposite, gaining the control 5 points. In the remaining 5 games, both players give evidence against each other, netting 1 point each game.

The defector scores a total of 10, and the tit-for-tat agent scores. When the tit-for-tat agents face off against each other, each refrains from giving evidence in all six games. Both agents win 3 points per game, for a total of 18 points each.

When the defectors face off, each gives evidence against the other in all six games. Both defectors win 1 point per game, for a total of 6 points each.

Each tit-for-tat agent scores a total of 28 points, over the six matches. Each defector scores only 26 points.

Despite the fact that the tit-for-tat agents never won a match and the defectors never lost a match, the tit-for-tat strategy still came out ahead, because the final score is not determined by the number of match wins, but the total points score. Simply put, the tit-for-tat agents gained more points tying with each other than they lost to the defectors.

The more tit-for-tat agents that there are in the described game, the more advantageous it is to use the tit-for-tat strategy.

Implications

The success of the strategy, which is largely cooperative, took many by surprise. In successive competitions various teams produced complex strategies which attempted to "cheat" in a variety of cunning ways, but Tit for Tat eventually prevailed in every competition.

Some theorists believe this result may give insight into how groups of animals (and particularly human societies) have come to live in largely (or entirely) cooperative societies, rather than the individualistic "red in tooth and claw" way that might be expected from individual engaged in a Hobbesian state of nature. This, and particularly its application to human society and politics, is the subject of Robert Axelrod's book *The Evolution of Cooperation.*

Problems

While Axelrod has empirically shown that the strategy is optimal in some cases, two agents playing tit for tat remain vulnerable. A one-time, single-bit error in either player's interpretation of events can lead to an unending "death spiral". In this symmetric situation, each side perceives itself as preferring to cooperate, if only the other side would. But each is forced by the strategy into repeatedly punishing an opponent who continues to attack despite being punished in every game cycle.

Both sides come to think of themselves as innocent and acting in self-defence, and their opponent as either evil or too stupid to learn to cooperate.

This situation frequently arises in real world conflicts, ranging from schoolboy fights to civil and regional wars. Tit for two tats could be used to avoid this problem.

"Tit for Tat with forgiveness" is sometimes superior. When the opponent defects, the player will occasionally cooperate on the next move anyway. This allows for recovery from getting trapped in a cycle of defections. The exact probability that a player will respond with cooperation depends on the line-up of opponents.

The reason for these issues is that tit for tat is not a subgame perfect equilibrium. If one agent defects and the opponent cooperates, then both agents will end up alternating cooperate and defect, yielding a lower payoff than if both agents were to continually cooperate. While this subgame is not directly reachable by two agents playing tit for tat strategies, a strategy must be a Nash equilibrium in all subgames to be subgame perfect. Further, this subgame may be reached if any noise is allowed in the agents' signaling. A subgame perfect variant of tit for tat known as "contrite tit for tat" may be created by employing a basic reputation mechanism.

Tit for two tats

Tit for Two Tats is similar to Tit for Tat in that it is nice, retaliating, forgiving and non-envious, the only difference between the two being how nice the strategy is.

In a tit for tat strategy once an opponent defects, the tit for tat player immediately responds by defecting on the next move. This has the unfortunate consequence of causing two retaliatory strategies to continuously defect against one another resulting in a poor outcome for both players. A tit for two tats player will let the first defection go unchallenged as a means to avoid the "death spiral" of the previous example. If the opponent defects twice in a row, the tit for two tats player will respond by defecting.

This strategy was put forward by Robert Axelrod during his second round of computer simulations at RAND. After analyzing the results of the first experiment he determined that had a participant entered the tit for two tats strategy it would have emerged with a higher cumulative score than any other program. As a result he himself entered it with high expectations in the second tournament. Unfortunately due to the more aggressive nature of the programs entered in the second round, tit for two tats did significantly worse than tit for tat due to aggressive strategies being able to take advantage of its highly forgiving nature.

Real World Use

Peer-to-peer File Sharing

BitTorrent peers use Tit for Tat strategy to optimize their download speed. More specifically, most BitTorrent peers use a variant of Tit for two Tats which is called *optimistic unchoking* in BitTorrent terminology. BitTorrent peers have a limited number of upload slots to allocate to other peers. Cooperation is achieved when upload bandwidth is exchanged for download bandwidth. Consequently, when a peer's upload bandwidth is saturated, it will use a Tit for Tat strategy. *Optimistic unchoking* corresponds very strongly to always cooperating on the first move in prisoner's dilemma. Periodically, a peer will allocate an upload slot to a randomly chosen peer (*unchoke*). This is called *optimistic unchoking.* This allows to search for more cooperating peers and to give a second chance to previously non-cooperating peers.

Explaining Reciprocal Altruism in Animal Communities

Studies in the prosocial behaviour of animals, have led many ethologists and evolutionary psychologists to apply Tit for Tat strategies to explain why altruism evolves in many animal communities. Evolutionary game theory, derived from the mathematical theories formalised by Von Neumann and Morgenstern (1953), was first devised by Maynard Smith (1972) and explored further in bird behaviour by Robert Hinde. Their application of game theory to the evolution of animal strategies launched an entirely new way of analysing animal behaviour.

Reciprocal altruism works in animal communities where the cost to the benefactor in any transaction of food, mating rights, nesting or territory is less than the gains to the beneficiary. The theory also holds that the act of altruism should be reciprocated if the balance of needs reverse. Mechanisms to identify and punish "cheaters" who fail to reciprocate, in effect a form of Tit for Tat, is an important mechanism to regulate reciprocal altruism.

War

The tit for tat strategy has been detected by analysts in the spontaneous non-violent behaviour, called "live and let live" that arose during the First World War.

Popular Culture

The tit for tat strategy was employed in an episode of *Numbers*, where FBI agents were interrogating and attempting to obtain information from an inmate on death row. The strategy was working, but the FBI would not implement a "tit for two tats".

This approach to interactions can be seen as a parallel to the "eye for an eye" approach from Judeo-Christian tradition, where "giving" an eye (or benefit) is reciprocated just as quickly as "taking" an eye.

Trembling Hand Perfect Equilibrium

Trembling hand perfect equilibrium is a refinement of Nash Equilibrium due to Reinhard Selten. A trembling hand perfect equilibrium is an equilibrium that takes the possibility of off-the-equilibrium play into account by assuming that the players, through a "slip of the hand" or tremble, may choose unintended strategies, albeit with negligible probability.

Definition

First we define a perturbed game. A perturbed game is a copy of a base game, with the restriction that only totally mixed strategies are allowed to be played. A totally mixed strategy is a mixed strategy where every pure strategy is played with non-zero probability. This is the "trembling hands" of the players; they sometimes play a different strategy than the one they intended to play. Then we define a strategy set S (in a base game) as being trembling hand perfect if there is a sequence of perturbed games that converge to the base game in which there is a series of Nash equilibria that converge to S.

Trembling hand Perfect Equilibria of Extensive form Games

There are two possible ways of extending the definition of trembling hand perfection to extensive form games.

- One may interpret the extensive form as being merely a concise description of a normal form game and apply the concepts described above to this normal form game. In the resulting perturbed games, every strategy of the extensive-form game must be played with non-zero probability. This leads to the notion of a normal-form trembling hand perfect equilibrium.

- Alternatively, one may recall that trembles are to be interpreted as modelling mistakes made by the players with some negligible probability when the game is played. Such a mistake would most likely consist of a player making another move than the one intended at some point during play. It would hardly consist of the player choosing another strategy than intended, i.e. a wrong plan for playing the entire game. To capture this, one may define the perturbed game by requiring that every move at every information set is taken with non-zero probability. Limits of equilibria of such perturbed games as the tremble probabilities goes to zero are called extensive-form trembling hand perfect equilibria.

The notions of normal-form and extensive-form trembling hand perfect equilibria are incomparable, i.e., an equilibrium of an extensive-form game may be normal-form trembling hand perfect but not extensive-form trembling hand perfect and vice versa. As an extreme example of this, Jean-François Mertens has given an example of a two-player extensive form game where no extensive-form trembling hand perfect equilibrium is admissible, i.e., the sets of extensive-form and normal-form trembling hand perfect equilibria for this game are disjoint.

An extensive-form trembling hand perfect equilibrium is also a sequential equilibrium. A normal-form trembling hand perfect equilibrium of an extensive form game may be sequential but is not necessarily so. In fact, a normal-form trembling hand perfect equilibrium does not even have to be subgame perfect.

Trigger Strategy

A trigger strategy is a class of strategies employed in a repeated non-cooperative game. A player using a trigger strategy initially cooperates but punishes the opponent if a certain level of defection (i.e., the trigger) is observed. The level of punishment and the sensitivity of the trigger vary with different trigger strategies.

Trigger Strategies

- Tit for Tat (the punishment continues as long as the other player defects).

- Tit for Two Tats (a more forgiving variant of tit for tat).
- Grim trigger (the punishment continues indefinitely after the other player defects just once).

War of Attrition (Game)

In game theory, the war of attrition is a model of aggression in which two contestants compete for a resource of value *V* by persisting while constantly accumulating costs over the time *t* that the contest lasts. The model was originally formulated by John Maynard Smith, a mixed evolutionary stable strategy (ESS) was determined by Bishop & Cannings. Strategically, the game is an auction, in which the prize goes to the player with the highest bid, and each player pays the loser's low bid (making it an all-pay sealed-bid second-price auction).

Examining the Game

The war of attrition cannot be properly solved using the payoff matrix. The players' available resources are the only limit to the maximum value of bids; bids can be any number if available resources are ignored, meaning that for any value of *a*, there is a value *a* that is greater. Attempting to put all possible bids onto the matrix, however, will result in an "×" matrix. One can, however, use a pseudo-matrix form of war of attrition to understand the basic workings of the game, and analyse some of the problems in representing the game in this manner.

The game works as follows: Each player makes a bid; the one who bids the highest wins a resource of value *V*. Each player pays the lowest bid, *a*.

The premise that the players may bid any number is important to analysis of the game. They may even exceed the value of the resource that is contested over. This at first appears to be a non sequitur, as it would be foolish to pay more than the value for a resource. Remember, however that each bidder only pays the *low* bid. Therefore, it would seem to be in each player's best interest to bid the maximum possible amount rather than an amount equal to or less than the value of the resource.

There is a catch, however; if both players bid higher than *V*, the high bidder does not so much win as lose less. This situation is commonly referred to as a Pyrrhic victory. In contrast, if each player bids less than *V*, the player bidding *a* will lose, and the other player will benefit by an amount of *V-a*. If each player bids the same amount for *a* less than

$V/2$, they split the value of V, each gaining $V/2$-a. For a tie such that $a>V/2$, they both lose the difference of $V/2$ and a. Luce and Raffia referred to the latter situation as a "ruinous situation"; the point at which both players suffer, and there is no winner.

The conclusion one can draw from this pseudo-matrix is that there is no value to bid which is beneficial in all cases, so there is no dominant strategy. However, this fact and the above argument do not preclude the existence of Nash Equilibria. Any pair of strategies with the following characteristics is a Nash Equilibrium:

- One player bids zero.
- The other player bids any value equal to V or higher, or mixes among any values V or higher.

With these strategies, one player wins and pays zero, and the other player loses and pays zero. It is easy to verify that neither player can strictly gain by unilaterally deviating.

The evolutionary stable strategy below represents the most probable value of a. The value $p(t)$ for a contest with a resource of value V over time t, is the probability that $t = a$. This strategy does not guarantee the win; rather it is the optimal balance of risk and reward. The outcome of any particular game cannot be predicted as the random factor of the opponent's bid is too unpredictable.

Another popular formulation of the war of attrition is as follows: Two players are involved in a dispute. The value of the object to each player is $v_i > 0$. Time is modelled as a continuous variable which starts at zero and runs indefinitely. Each player chooses when to concede the object to the other player. In the case of a tie, each player receives $v_i/2$ utility. Time is valuable, each player uses one unit of utility per period of time. This formulation is slightly more complex since it allows each player to assign a different value to the object. Its equilibria are not as obvious as the other formulation.

Evolutionary Stable Strategy

The evolutionary stable strategy is a mixed ESS, in which the probability of persisting for a length of time t is:

That no pure persistence time is an ESS can be demonstrated simply by considering a putative ESS bid of x, which will be beaten by a bid of $x+\ddot{a}$.

The ESS in Popular Culture

The evolutionarily stable strategy when playing this game is a probability density of random persistence times which cannot be predicted by the opponent in any particular contest. This result has led to the prediction that threat displays ought not to evolve, and to the conclusion in The Illuminatus! Trilogy that optimal military strategy is to behave in a completely unpredictable, and therefore insane, manner. Neither of these conclusions appear to be truly quantifiably reasonable applications of the model to realistic conditions.

Conclusions

By examining the unusual results of this game, it serves to mathematically prove another piece of old wisdom: "Expect the unexpected". By making the assumption that an opponent will act irrationally, one can paradoxically better predict their actions, as they are limited in this game. They will either act rationally, and take the optimal decision, or they will be irrational, and take the non-optimal solution. If one considers the irrational as a bluff and the rational as backing down from a bluff, it transforms the game into another game theory game, Hawk and Dove.

Zero-sum

In game theory and economic theory, zero-sum describes a situation in which a participant's gain or loss is exactly balanced by the losses or gains of the other participant(s). If the total gains of the participants are added up, and the total losses are subtracted, they will sum to zero. Zero-sum can be thought of more generally as constant sum where the benefits and losses to all players sum to the same value of money (or utility). Cutting a cake is zero-or constant-sum, because taking a larger piece reduces the amount of cake available for others. In contrast, non-zero-sum describes a situation in which the interacting parties' aggregate gains and losses is either less than or more than zero. Zero sum games are also called *strictly competitive*.

Definition

The zero-sum property (if one gains, another loses) means that any result of a zero-sum situation is Pareto optimal (generally, any game where all strategies are Pareto optimal is called a conflict game).

Situations where participants can all gain or suffer together are referred to as non-zero-sum. Thus, a country with an excess of bananas trading with another country for their excess of apples, where both benefit from the transaction, is in a non-zero-sum situation. Other non-zero-sum games are games in which the sum of gains and losses by the players are sometimes more or less than what they began with.

The concept was first developed in game theory and consequently zero-sum situations are often called zero-sum games though this does not imply that the concept, or game theory itself, applies only to what are commonly referred to as games.

Solution

For 2-player finite zero-sum games, the different game theoretic solution concepts of Nash equilibrium, minimax, and maximin all give the same solution. In the solution, players play a mixed strategy.

Example

A game's payoff matrix is a convenient representation. Consider for example the two-player zero-sum game pictured at right.

The order of play proceeds as follows: The first player (red) chooses in secret one of the two actions 1 or 2; the second player (blue), unaware of the first player's choice, chooses in secret one of the three actions A, B or C. Then, the choices are revealed and each player's points total is affected according to the payoff for those choices.

Example: Red chooses action 2 and Blue chooses action B. When the payoff is allocated, Red gains 20 points and Blue loses 20 points.

Now, in this example game both players know the payoff matrix and attempt to maximize the number of their points. What should they do? Red could reason as follows: "With action 2, I could lose up to 20 points and can win only 20, while with action 1 I can lose only 10 but can win up to 30, so action 1 looks a lot better." With similar reasoning, Blue would choose action C. If both players take these actions, Red will win 20 points. But what happens if Blue anticipates Red's reasoning and choice of action 1, and goes for action B, so as to win 10 points? Or if Red in turn anticipates this devious trick and goes for action 2, so as to win 20 points after all?

John von Neumann had the fundamental and surprising insight that probability provides a way out of this conundrum. Instead of deciding on a definite action to take, the two players assign probabilities to their respective actions, and then use a random device which, according to these probabilities, chooses an action for them. Each player computes the probabilities so as to minimise the maximum expected point-loss independent of the opponent's strategy. This leads to a linear programming problem with the optimal strategies for each player. This minimax method can compute provably optimal strategies for all two-player zero-sum games. For the example given above, it turns out that Red should choose action 1 with probability 4/7 and action 2 with probability 3/7, while Blue should assign the probabilities 0, 4/7 and 3/7 to the three actions A, B and C. Red will then win 20/7 points on average per game.

Non-zero-sum

Economics

Many economic situations are not zero-sum, since valuable goods and services can be created, destroyed, or badly allocated, and any of these will create a net gain or loss. Assuming the counterparties are acting rationally, any commercial exchange is a non-zero-sum activity, because each party must consider the goods it is receiving as being at least fractionally more valuable than the goods it is delivering. Economic exchanges must benefit both parties enough above the zero-sum such that each party can overcome its transaction costs.

Psychology

The most common or simple example from the subfield of *Social Psychology* is the concept of "Social Traps." In some cases we can enhance our collective well-being by pursuing our personal interests — or parties can pursue mutually destructive behaviour as they choose their own ends.

Complexity

It has been theorized by Robert Wright in his book Nonzero: The Logic of Human Destiny, that society becomes increasingly non-zero-sum as it becomes more complex, specialized, and interdependent. As former US President Bill Clinton states.

The more complex societies get and the more complex the networks of interdependence within and beyond community and national borders get, the more people are forced in their own interests to find non-zero-sum solutions. That is, win–win solutions instead of win–lose solutions.... Because we find as our interdependence increases that, on the whole, we do better when other people do better as well — so we have to find ways that we can all win, we have to accommodate each other.... Bill Clinton, Wired interview, December 2000.

1st Concept of non-cooperative Equilibrium

Best-response-or "Nash" Equilibrium (Nash, USA)

"When everyone's playing their best move to everyone ELSE'S best move, no-one's going to move."

Like most really powerful ideas, the basic notion of Nash equilibrium is very simple, even obvious. Its mathematical extensions and implications are not, however. The idea of this natural "sticking point" is that no single player can benefit from *unilaterally changing* his or her move — a non-cooperative best-response equilibrium.

Competitive Markets come to rest at Nash equilibrium, and the special structure of competitive markets makes them efficient. But it is important to recognize that MOST Nash-Equilibria are NOT efficient. What do we mean by not efficient? It's just the idea of getting the "whole pie" — that if we're really using the whole pie, then no one can get any more unless someone else takes less. That's the economist's basic idea of allocative efficiency.

A famous game is called "Chicken," named after a famous adolescent hot-rod ceremony from the United States of the 1990s. Say that Boeing and Airbus are both considering entering the jumbo jet market, but that because of increasing returns to scale and relatively low demand, there is only enough room for one of them. The game matrix (called the "normal form" of a game) could look like this. (This example is taken from an article by Paul R. Krugman, "Is Free Trade Passe?" in the *Journal of Economic Perspectives*, Fall 1987.)

Air Bus Boeing	***Build***	***Don't Build***
Build	-10-10	-1 10
Don't Build	10 -1	5 5

Note here that the upper-right and lower-left squares are both Nash Equilibria, sometimes called Non-cooperative Equilibria. It can be easily confirmed that neither player will have an interest in moving if it finds itself in either of these cells; doing so would only make it worse off. As in the hot-rod version of "Chicken," the point is to convince the other player that you are commited to going straight ahead and build "no matter what," so that he will take the don't build option. But note also that both of these Nash equilibria are inefficient: the lower-right option would give both players a total pie of size 10, while no other cell can do this well. Consider another famous example of inefficiency, the so-called "Prisoner's Dilemma." Mugsy and Spike have just been nabbed for a crime. They have promised each other not to rat on the other if caught. The DA offers them the following prison-expectations (in years) if they stay silent or rat on the other:

MUGSY SPIKE	***Silent***	***Rat***
Silent	2 2	010
Rat	10 0	77

What should each of them do? Here each is trying to minimize his time in jail. A little thinking shows that each can always do better AS AN INDIVIDUAL by Ratting on the other. From Spike's point of view, if Mugsy is Silent, he should Rat, because 0 years is better than 2. But if Mugsy Rats he should also rat, because 7 years is better than 10. Whereas if they could both really keep their promise to stay silent, they would only get 2 years each. So the Nash Equilibrium here is inefficient from the criminals' point of view. It's easy to see why many kinds of human organizations (not just criminal) go to great lengths to try to get people to keep promises!

The lower-right cell is not only a Nash Equilibrium, it also has another interesting property with which it should not be confused — it is also a "dominant strategy." In a Prisoner's Dilemma game, non-cooperation with your partner is always your best move. The idea of a dominant strategy is that it is always your best move *regardless of what the other guys do.* Note that this is a *stronger* requirement than the idea of Nash Equilibrium, which only says that you have made your best move *given what the other guys have done.*

2nd Concept of non-cooperative Equilibrium:

Sub-game Perfect Equilibrium (Selten, Germany)

"Think Forward, then Reason Backward"

There is a crucial distinction between the "Fog of Business" game (shown in class) and chess, and that has to do with PERCEPTIONS. I can show that in a game like chess (constant sum, with two players) a perfectly rational player does not have to "worry" about whether or not his or her opponent is irrational. You don't worry about perceptions. The simplest example of this is the "Chain Store" paradox.

The established store ("incumbent") threatens to fight a price war if the newcomer ("entrant") comes in. Analysed as a "timeless" normal-form game (the matrix), there is no reason not to believe this threat. And if the entrant does, he will stay out. There are TWO Nash equilibria in this matrix, lower left and upper right.

But in fact the upper-right is *stronger* than just a static Nash equilibrium. It is what Selten called a "sub-game perfect" equilibrium, because just looking at the last *part* of the game where the incumbent finds himself one the entrant has entered (the "sub-game"), it would obviously be irrational for him to follow through on this threat.

That is because by fighting, he gets 10 points, and by giving in, he gets 30. The sequential or "extended form" of the game makes this more clear. Of course the incumbent would like his threat to be believed, and with less than full information (about motivations, future games, etc.), it may well be. But if both players have the full information below, and it is "common knowledge" that each is fully informed and rational — then such a threat is absurd, and will probably never be made.

incumbent entrant	fight	give in
go in	-10 10	20 30
stay out	0 60	0 60

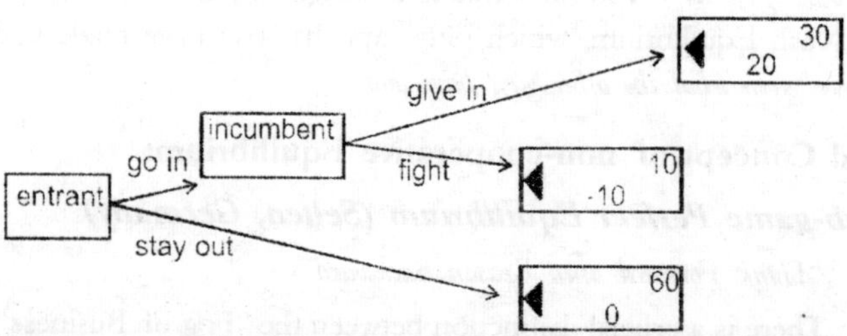

I will now try to give another example of sequential reasoning, with the emphasis on rationality. Say that you are Black, the other player is White, and you are about to make your last of three possible moves in a chess game:

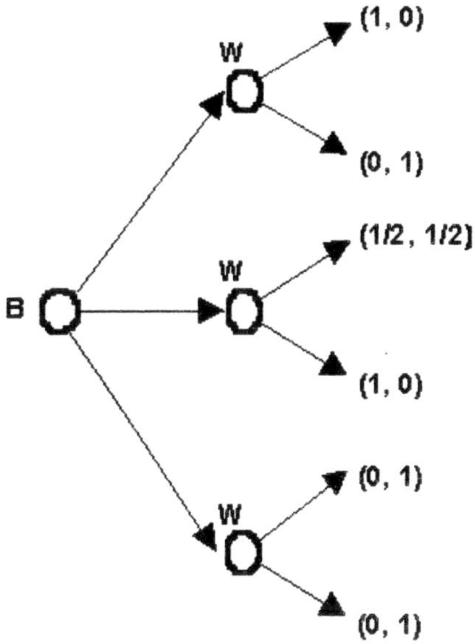

Let the first score in every couple (b, w) be the score of Black, the second be that of white. 1 is a win, 0 is a loss, and ½ denotes a tie. Note (0, 1), (1, 0) and (½, ½) are the only possible outcomes. What should B do? There is one right move for B here, on the assumption of W's rationality. And if W is not rational??? — so much the better for B! Any way you mix up the outcomes, you will fail to find a situation where W's irrationality could possibly hurt B. That's impossible, because in a constant sum, two player game, one player's failure to maximize payoffs must, by the same token, make the payoffs of the other player greater! Note that this result does not deny that W might be able to benefit by lulling B into the FALSE BELIEF W is irrational, when in fact s/he is not. If this belief induces B to relax so much that s/he plays less than optimally, then this would be good for W. The point is, one can never do worse by assuming the opponent is rational, and playing accordingly. This is different when there are more than two players, or, as in the next example, when the sum of the game is not constant.

3rd Concept of non-cooperative Equilibrium:

Best-response, Given Expectations

'*When everyone's playing his or her best move Conditional on Expectations of everyone else's best move, then no-one's going to want to move.*" This idea builds on the forgoing idea of thinking forward and reasoning backward, but now makes it conditional — not on the assumption of perfect rationality on the part of all players — but on one's Perceptions of what the other player is likely to do. One way to think about this is by considering what a famous 19th century German General, Baron Von Cluasewitz, called the "Fog of Battle."

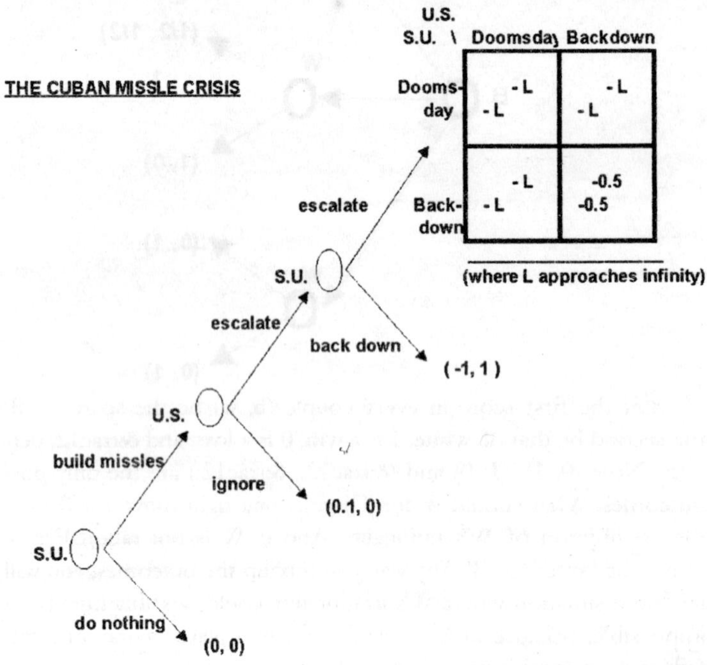

Clausewitz said that the most clear-sighted plans of war must unfold during the actual "fog of battle." UNLIKE the perfect crystal clarity of the chess board, in real battle you are very unsure of what is actually going on, what all the possible moves are, about your opponent's perceptions, his perceptions of your perceptions, his perceptions of your perceptions of his perceptions..... Here we focus just on a couple of levels of this fogginess. Here we can look at the closest the US has ever come to getting into a two-sided nuclear war (that is, one in which both sides had nuclear weapons).

This was the famous Cuban missile crisis of the early 1960s, an episode that is described in the book, "Games for Business and Economics" (Gardner, 1995) with the diagram above.

The crucial point of ambiguity here is that the score is *not* constant-sum. The "–L "score here is a very large negative number, meaning the "end of the world as we know it." Note also that each player's final move has to be made simultaneously; i.e., without knowing what the opponent has done. There are *two* Nash equilibria in this final move, Mutual Doomsday and Mutual Backdown. Doomsday-Backdown combinations are *not* equilibria: one side can change its move here — to Backdown – and improve its payoff. By so-called "backward induction" (thinking forward and then reasoning backward), one can show that the Nash equilibrium of mutual Backdown leads to the Soviets deciding to build the missiles, while the equilibrium of mutual Doomsday leads the Soviets to do nothing; i.e., to not build the missiles.

So different "endings" of the game dictate radically different beginnings, from a strategic point of view. In a game like this, the point is not just to figure out what your opponent is really thinking, but to "psyche out" that opponent, to manipulate her beliefs about what *you* are thinking! Reading the history of the Cuban missile crisis, recently declassified, it becomes clear that the Soviets did not at first believe that the Americans were willing to go "all the way." And so, consistently with this model, they built the missiles. But the Americans *were willing* to play Doomsday – or at least Kennedy made his own Joint Chiefs of Staff believe that. On the evening of his fateful decision, Kennedy told his Joint Chiefs that he hoped they would all be alive tomorrow. With a convincing enough show that the Americans were willing to go Doomsday, the Soviets changed course in midstream, and backed down.

This problem of perceptions, and of managing perceptions, does not just appear in warfare, but in the "war" of business, as well. The great English macro-economist, John Maynard Keynes, described stock market speculation (a game at which he was rather good) as a "newspaper beauty contest". This was a contest of his day in which the goal was not supposed to vote one's own preferences for prettiest faces. The winner was rather he/she who successfully guessed which faces the average contestant found most appealing.

But of course, the average player has a view of what the average player's view is, a view of what the average player's view of the average player's view is, etc., *ad infinitum.* Keynes said that there were a few people in the stock market able to play on the fifth or sixth level of such a series of expectations. But not many could, and no one could play higher than that.

Harsanyi gave us a "fixed point" for analysis, a point at which expectations about other expectations are consistent with one's optimizing strategy. Such consistency is not the same as being correct. The Soviets obviously changed their expectations. Kennedy's "psyche-out" won, but led us to the brink of nuclear disaster. The "players" in this Cuban missile crisis met in Havana in 1992 for a "30th Anniversary." The consensus from both sides was, "Even we didn't imagine how close we really were."

Game Theory

Game theory is a branch of mathematics concerned with the analysis of the behaviour of decision makers (called "players") whose choices affect one another. An important distinction exists between the disciplines of individual and interactive decision making. Individual decision making, whether under certainty or uncertainty, leads to well-defined optimization problems, like maximizing an objective function (e.g., expected utility) subject to certain constraints. While these problems may be difficult to solve in practice, they involve no conceptual issues. Once the objective function is specified, the meaning of "optimal decision" is clear (even when actual behaviour, for one reason or another, is not optimal). In interactive decision making, the meaning of "optimal decision" is unclear, because no player completely controls the final outcome of the interaction. A formal analysis of interactive decision making must address the conceptual issue of defining the problem before providing procedures for solving it. Game theory is concerned with both matters. It defines solutions, known as "solution concepts", to various classes of interactive decision making situations which appear in various areas of application and then investigates their properties and provides procedures for their computation.

The Theory was First Introduced as a Scientific Discipline by Von

Neumann and Morgenstern in their monumental book Theory of Games and Economic Behaviour. It has seen rapid expansion in the last twenty years or so. The largest single area of application of game theory has been economics; many modern textbooks in microeconomics and most of the journals in this discipline present or discuss game theoretical models in one form or another. Other important areas of application include political science (e.g., voting systems, power, international relations), social psychology (e.g., two-person bargaining, social dilemmas, coalition formation), sociology, evolutionary biology, accounting, marketing, computer science, law, and branches of philosophy such as ethics and epistemology. As is the case with many branches of mathematics, the relation between theory and applications has been two-sided: the theory has helped to structure interactive decision making situations in these disciplines, understand their logic, prescribe rational solutions, and occasionally account for empirical phenomena and experimental findings, whereas experimental findings and applications have posed new questions and introduced new challenges that have led to new interpretations of existing concepts and additional theoretical developments. Game theory may be viewed as a sort of umbrella theory for interactive behaviour in the social sciences, where "social" is interpreted very broadly to include human beings as well as other kinds of players (collectives such as corporations and nations, animals, plants, computers, etc.). Only the essential aspects of the interactive situation are discussed and formally analysed rather than the entire situation with its peculiarities, ambiguities and subtleties, and as such can be applied in principle to all interactive situations.

These essential aspects typically include the following: There must be at least two players whose decisions affect each other. The game begins by one or more players making a choice (called "move") among a number of specified alternatives. Following that, a certain situation results determining which player makes the next move and what alternatives are open to her. The choices made by some or all of the players may or may not become known; therefore, when she has to make a choice, the information each player has about the previous choices of all other players must be specified. There is a termination rule determining when the possible plays of the game are completed. Finally, each situation defining an end of a play determines a payoff to each of the bona fide players. The game allows for chance moves by Nature (uncertainty), but if Nature intervenes in the game, it is considered a dummy player in the game deriving no payoff.

Solution concepts are divided in terms of a basic distinction between cooperative games, where agreements, promises, and threats are fully binding and enforceable, to noncooperative games where commitments, even when reached by pre-play communication, are not enforceable. The noncooperative approach focuses on the strategic choices of players—how they play the game and what strategies they choose to achieve their objectives. It is, therefore, intimately concerned with and strongly influenced by the details of the interactive process and the rules governing the game. In contrast, the cooperative approach focuses on the options available to the group of players—what coalitions form and how their members disburse their joint payoff.

The basic solution concept for noncooperative games is the Nash equilibrium. A vector of strategies—one for each player—is a Nash equilibrium if no player has an incentive (in terms of improving his payoff) to deviate from his part of the strategy vector. What makes Nash equilibrium a natural solution concept is the fact that any prediction about the outcome of a noncooperative game is self-defeating if it specifies an outcome that is not a Nash equilibrium. Nash proved the existence (but not uniqueness) of at least one equilibrium for every game with a finite number of strategies for each player. Subsequent research has attempted to eliminate equilibria that rely on noncredibe threats by "refining" the notion of Nash equilibrium, has explored alternative interpretations of Nash equilibria for games played repeatedly by players who are not necessarily "rational" and who need not know the structure of the game, and has started to execute the "Nash program" which calls for reformulating cooperative games as noncooperative ones and then solving for their equilibria. Social psychology has borrowed many of the basic concepts of game theory (e.g., payoff matrix, pure and mixed strategies, equilibrium) in order to construct theories of social interaction and design experiments to test them.

Early experiments were mostly concerned with two-person zerosum games, where the interests of the two players are diametrically opposed, and with two 3 person nonzerosum games such as the Prisoner's Dilemma and Chicken, which include outcomes that are preferred to other outcomes by both players.

Subsequent research has shifted the focus to assess the descriptive power of various solution concepts in the areas of bargaining, social dilemmas, and coalition formation. However, most of the experimental research in the last twenty years or so on interactive behaviour has been conducted outside of psychology within the rapidly growing discipline of experimental economics.

5

Markets for Homogeneous Products

What is a Product?

Product is a complex of tangible and intangible attributes, including packaging, colour, price, manufacturer's prestige, retailer's prestige and manufacturer's and retailer's services which the buyer may accept as offering satisfaction of wants or needs.

Any change in physical feature (design, colour, size, packaging, etc.) however minor it may be, creates an effect of a new product. The seller has an opportunity to use a new set of appeals to reach what may be essentially a new market. The key idea in our definition of a product is that the consumer is buying more than a set of chemical and physical attributes. Fundamentally he is buying want satisfaction. A wise firm sells product benefits rather than just the product.

Manufacturers sell *symbols* as well as products. "People buy things not only for what they can do, but also for what they mean." Goods are psychological symbols of personnel attributes, goals and social patterns.

Product planning embraces all activities which enable producers and middlemen to determine what should constitute a company's line of products. Ideally product planning will ensure that the full complement of a firm's products that are logically related, individually justifiable items, designed to strengthen the company's competitive and profit position. It requires an estimate of the industry's market potential, the company's sales potential, the cost requirements and the profit possibilities of products to determine whether product development is feasible. "Product development"-a more limited term - encompasses the technical activities of product research, engineering and design. Here, we are concerned with product innovation or improvement and are working with production research and engineering departments.

More specifically, the scope of product-planning and product-development activities includes decision making and programming in the following areas:

- Which products should the firm make and which should itbuy?
  - Should the company expand or simplify its line?
  - What new uses are there for each item?
  - Is the quality right for the intended use and market?
  - What brand, package and label should be used for each product?
  - How should the product be styled and designed and in what sizes, colours and materials should it be produced?
  - In what quantities each item be produced and what inventory controls should be established?
  - How should the product be priced?

Approaches For Developing Separate Markets

Monopolislic competition is obviously more attractive to a marketing manager than pure competition. The key to achieving a monopolistic competition situation is to have a total product which a substantial group of customers feel is markedly different from competitive products. If the firm is successful in differentiating its product, it in effect "carves out" a special target market for itself.

There are two basic ways to accomplish this end:

- Product differentiation
- Market segmentation.

When there are direct competitors for the customers in a particular market grid box, however then becomes necessary to stress product differences. This latter approach is called *product differentiation.* Sometimes a firm may use both approaches at the same time. These ideals are explained more fully below:

Market segmentation; seeks to isolate previously unsatisfied target markets and design a unique product for that part *of* market grid. Here the emphasis is on a uniquely different physical product and/or service.

Product Differentiation

Product differentiation seeks to direct customer demand toward the firm's product even though it may be quite similar to competitive products. In other words, it's trying to shift the demand curve to the right.

The approach, which stresses promotion, emphasizes the distinctive points of a particular product. The purpose is to satisfy the many slightly different demands held by customers in one or several market grid boxes. The differences in the various competitive products actually may be minor but nevertheless they may be very important to customers.

Psychological differences may be important in differentiating a product. If a woman truly believes that a cosmetic is more suited to her personality, she may be pleased to see and hear about the distinct qualities of the product. More will be said in the promotion chapters about how promotion actually can "create" new products.

Here it should be noted that promotion of product differentiation, which usually is intended to adapt slightly heterogeneous products to many different market grid boxes, may provide real customer satisfaction.

Different customers, having different needs, may respond to different product appeals-even in the same advertisement. Some women may be concerned with cleanliness, others with beauty and others with glamour; a single advertisement might appeal to all of them in behalf of a particular product.

Product differentiation is seen in many product categories, such as cigarettes, soaps, cosmetics, food and automobiles. On fact, product differentiation is employed for most widely advertised products-those appealing to mass audiences. This approach attempts to adapt a single physical product to the many and varied demands of a sometimes heterogeneous group of potential customer.

Market Segmentation

If the product changes are important enough to narrow the potential market, then the firm uses the market segmentation approach. If major changes are needed to satisfy some part of the market, it may be wise to introduce a new product or modify an old one to satisfy this other market. Product differentiation can not always be used to satisfy this all customers, since partly or wholly new products sometimes are demanded by certain segments of a market grid.

This approach attempts to develop a special total product to satisfy target customers in one or only a few market grid boxes. Here, more drastic changes are made in the total product to appeal to smaller target markets and perhaps achieve a more inelastic demand curve. For a manufacturer, this may actually result in considerable product diversification and expansion of his product line. There might be a special product for each market grid box or even for each individual customer. Theoretically, since most customers are slightly different and have slightly different demands, all products should be custom-made. Taken to the extreme, this would eliminate mass production.

Actually, this policy seldom is carried to its logical conclusion. Few customers desires for different products are so strong that they will pay the higher production costs that completely individualized products entail. Nevertheless a market segmentation policy can expand product lines markedly.

Product Life Cycles

Products, like customers, have life cycles. In fact, the life of a product can be divided into four major periods:

- product introduction.
- market growth.
- market majority sales decline.

A product's marketing mix must undergo changes during these periods. The sales history of the product varies in each of these periods and more importantly, the profit picture changes; nor *do* the two necessarily move together.

Introduction

In the introduction stage, since the product is not sought by customers, promotion is used to "pioneer" acceptance. Potential target customers must be informed about the existence, advantages, and uses of the new product. Even though a firm has successfully carved out a new market for itself, its success may not be apparent. This introductory stage is usually characterized by losses; considerable mono) is expended for promotion and product and place development. Funds are, in effect, being invested with the expectation of future profits.

Market Growth

In this second stage, the innovator begins to enjoy financial success. Competitors start coming into the market. Each of them tries to develop the best and most useful product design. Much product variety may be seen as each firm tries to find the best way to serve this new market. Monopolistic competition with down-sloping demand curves is characteristic of both the product introduction and market growth periods.

During this period, the sales of the total industry are rising fairly rapidly as more and more customers enter the market. The second phase may last from several days to several years, depending on whether the product in hula hoops or television sets. The early innovators usually make substantial profits. The total industry may appear extremely profitable and competitors rush in with copies *of* the most successful products. As far as this product is concerned, this is the time of peak profitability

Market Maturity

In this third stage, many competitors have entered the market. We now move into a more competitive situation with declining profits. Promotion emphasizes the advantages of particular brands, but products differ only slightly because most of the companies have settled on the same way to appeal to the mass market. There is a tendency to copy competing features.

Mass production methods also discourage product variety. This market, still characterized by monopolistic competition, is becoming much more competitive on product, price and promotion. Basic product similarities and mass production mean that firms must resort to product differentiation practices.

At this time, emotional appeals become more common-the only remaining way to add value to the product. Industry profits decline throughout the market maturity period because the cost of promotion rises and competitors begin to cut prices to attract business. Although each firm still has its own demand curve, the curves are becoming, increasingly elastic as the various products become almost homogeneous.

Prices may be cut even as total industry volume rising. This has been the case recently in plastics and transistors, for example.

Sales Decline

As new products come along to replace the old, this fourth and final stage of the life cycle reached. Price competition from dying firms may become more vigorous, but companies that have strong customer franchises may continue to profit almost until the end. These competitors will have down-sloping demand curves because they have successfully differentiated their products. As the new product goes through the introductory stage, the old product may still be able to retain some sales, until finally sales decline so much that the product is withdrawn from the market.

Classification of Products

Just as it's necessary to segment markets for meaningful programming in market, so also it's helpful to separate products into homogeneous classifications. Ýlere we shall divide all products into two groups: CONSUMER GOODS and INDUSTRIAL GOODS a classification that parallels our segmentation of the market.

Consumer Goods and Industrial Goods

There are many kinds of consumer goods. So many, in fact, that is impossible to discuss the marketing process for each of them. Further, some products usually considered consumer goods may also be industrial goods since they are destined for use by intermediate customers. *Consumer goods* are those goods or services destined for the ultimate consumer in such a form that they may be used without further commercial processing.

These contrast with *industrial goods,* which are defined as those goods and services destined for use in producing other goods and services. ' All goods fit into either of these two categories.

The type of customer buying the good determines whether it should be classified as a consumer and industrial good. Although the same physical product may be involved, an entirely different marketing mix may be required, depending upon the type of buyer and intended use. The following products and services can be either consumer or industrial goods, depending upon whether they are destined for a final consumer or some intermediate customer (such as a manufacturer, farmer or government agency): typewriters, typing paper, rugs, decorators" services, lighting fixtures, brooms and plumbing services.

Consumer goods include all products which are "destined for use by ultimate consumers or households and in such form that they can be used without commercial processing. Industrial goods are those which are "destined to be sold primarily for use in producing other goods or rendering services as contrasted with goods destined to be sold primarily to the ultimate consumer.

Need for A Classification System

Fresh meal, cannot salmon and lettuce are all foods, vet all are marketed differently. Hosiery and women's party dresses are clothing items, but the marketing mixes for each are quite dis-similar. Hosiery is available in many different types of outlets and has a much simpler fitting problem. And hosier) has been successfully branded, while few women's dress brands are widely recognized by customers.

There are many other examples of apparently similar products with dissimilar marketing problems. It is clear that the nature of the product has considerable bearing on how the four P's are combined in a marketing mix. To avoid treating every product as a special case, we must try to develop some sensible, if tentative, generalizations about how products are related to marketing mixes. Let us see if we can develop such *a* product classification system.

Some Possible Classification Systems

One system of classification might be by the type of outlet through which the products are marketed. All products usually found in grocery stores could be treated alike, for example. So could those found in drugstores, clothing stores, sporting goods stores, hardware stores and so on.

Under such a system, how would we treat a product such as toothpaste? Toothpaste is now being sold in drugstores, food stores, variety stores, department stores, college book stores and many other places. At one time stores specialized in certain products, but there is a definite trend for several types of store. This is called "scrambled merchandising."

Another possibility would be to categorize a product as a necessity or as a luxury. The difficulty with this system is that it would depend on the rater's attitudes. A "necessity" to one person might be a "luxury" to another. Moreover, while broad categories such as food are obviously necessities, relatively few individual food items are.

Classifying by the degree of demand elasticity is another possibility. But the elasticity of demand for general categories such as food does not hold true for all the products within the category.

Within the meat category alone (which might be considered to have a fairly inelastic demand) the demand for special meat products, such as hamburger or porterhouse steak, are much more elastic. The reason is that there are many substitute ways of satisfying the general demand for meat.

A Useful Classification System

We need a classification system based on *the way people buy products.* The purpose of the marketing process is the satisfaction of consumers. It follows that, to develop and market products effectively, we must know how they feel about these products and especially their basis of choice. It follows that, then, that any classification system should be based upon customer behaviour. Our system works that way, separating goods into four categories.

1) Convenience goods,
2) Shopping goods,
3) Speciality goods,
4) Unsought goods.

Convenience goods are those which customers wish to purchase immediately and with a minimum effort. Put another way, convenience goods are those goods for which the probable gain from making price and quality comparisons is thought to be *small* relative to the value of customers." time and effort.

Shopping goods as the name implies, are those goods for which customers actually do shop. That is, they compare price and quality of various brands. They may read about performance, search newspaper advertisements and even go to several stores. In short, they feel that the gain from making these comparisons is worth their time and effort.

Speciality *goods* are those which customers characteristically insist upon and for which they are willing to make a special effort.

Unsought goods are those which potential customers do not yet want or know they can buy. They do not search out these goods. Furthermore, they would be unlikely to buy them they saw them.

Shopping Behaviour Determines Classification

It should be noted that some kind *of shopping* behaviour characterizes convenience and shopping goods. These goods can be seen as being at either end of a continuum of customer "shop-ping effort". The amount of search and comparison increases steadily as one moves from shoe strings (a convenience good) to suits and dining room furniture (shopping goods).

Speciality and unsought goods are not on the same continuum of shopping effort. They are special cases. No shopping at all is done for unsought goods. In the case of speciality goods, customers would be willing to travel extensively for a particular product but not to shop for the most satisfactory product.

The customer has already made a decision about a particular pro-duct, probably a specific brand and will look as far as necessary to find it. This does not mean that she will have to look very far, however. Knowing the strength of customers' preferences and willingness to search, many retailers may carry such a product, knowing that otherwise they will lose the business.

It is very important to see that customers' attitudes are crucial in this classification system *not* the methods of distribution. Distribution should (low naturally from how customers think about the products or services.

Marketing Significance of Product Classification

The two-way product classification is a useful framework for programming marketing operations because each major class of products ultimately goes to a different market and requires different marketing methods.

In the field of product planning, for example branding, packaging, colour and fashion are generally for more significant for a consumer product than for an industrial goods.

Convenience Goods

Convenience goods, again, are those goods for which the probable gain from making price and quality comparisons is through to be *small* relative to the value of the customer's time and effort. Usually considered as convenience goods are items such as cigarettes, soap, drugs, newspapers, magazines, che-wing gum candy and most grocery products.

These products are frequently and readily purchased, require little service or selling, are not very expensive and may even be bought by habit. Typically, the customer is not willing to put very much time or effort into the purchase or convenience goods. The classic cigarette slogan "I'd walk a mile for a Camel", tried to imply that Camels were not a convenience goods, but it is doubtful that many consumers think of their own cigarette brand in this light.

Care must be exercised in classifying goods as convenience goods too quickly. The attitudes (perhaps based on income and wealth as well as other factors) of target customers are important.

Note that the product classification may be related to elasticity of demand. If customers do not give much thought to price when purchasing convenience goods, probably the demand for these products will be relatively inelastic.

Three Types of Convenience Goods

Convenience goods can be subclassified into three types, based primarily on how customers think about and buy such products:

1) Staples,

2) Impulse goods,

3) Emergency goods.

Staples. Staples, such as food and drug items used regularly in every household, are usually bought without much thought beyond the initial decision to buy such products. Staples are usually purchased frequently. Branding becomes important, since brand recognition or preference helps the customer reduce her shopping effort. Furthermore, if her store changes prices only infrequently on these items, she does not need to reconsider which item to purchase, but can stay with familiar ones.

Staples items are offered for sale in many convenient places because of customers' reluctance to search very far. They are found in food stores, drugstores, hardware stores and vending machines, for example. Some customers value convenience so highly that they prefer to have such goods delivered to their home. Some think of milk, ice and newspapers as items which ought to be delivered to them. This extra service often increases the price but, because of the convenience, customers are willing to pay slightly more.

Impulse goods. Contrasted to staples, impulse goods are those which customers typically do not seek. They are included in the category of convenience goods (rather than unsought goods) mainly because they are items which the customer wishes to purchase on sight and may have purchased the same way many times before. For example, ifa housewife were to pass a street corner vendor, decide eating ice cream would be a good idea and purchase an ice cream bar, this bar probably would be an impulse good.

However (and this is the important distinction) if the same housewife were to purchase a box of ice cream bars while shopping with the invention of using them for a family dessert, then the bars would be regarded as staples.

She was looking for desserts, among other things. The distinction is a subtle but important one. If the customer docs not purchase an impulse good immediately, the need may disappear and no purchase will be made whereas she probably will buy some dessert. If the housewife passed a man selling balloons and considers buying one for her small child but finds she has not the proper change, it is most unlikely that she will go back later looking for a balloon.

Other probable impulse goods include fountain service, roasted chestnuts or peanuts, candy and novelties, some women's hats and blouses and costume jewellery. As the income and buying power of consumers grow, the number of impulse items seems to be expanding. But it should not be assumed that all impulse goods are purchased for emotional reasons. To be sure, impulse goods may satisfy emotional motives, but they may also satisfy economic motives. A housewife might buy a new floor mop which promises to make her housework easier even though she had not even been thinking about one.

Just because a product seems to be purchased as an impulse good does not mean that the customer was not already aware of the product category and perhaps even of the brand. There might even be strong brand preference on some items which are purchased on impulse for example Coca-Cola and some brands of candy bars.

An impulse purchase might satisfy a strongly felt need in the same way that the need had been satisfied many times before. This would still be an impulse purchase, however, because the particular purchase in question was not planned and the need might not be satisfied (at least with the particular product involved) if it had not been seen.

This means place will be extremely important for impulse goods. Department stores often place such goods on the first floor near main doors, while supermarkets and drugstores put them near the checkout counter.

Emergency goods. Emergency goods are purchased less frequently, only when the need is urgent. Then the customer wants the product available in the most convenient place. Price, perhaps even quality, is of small concern especially if the need is immediate enough. The demand for such goods may be extremely inelastic. Ambulance services, umbrellas or raincoats during a rainstorm and tire chains during a driving snowstorm are examples of emergency goods.

Shopping Goods

Shopping goods are those for which the probable gain from making price and quality comparisons is thought to be *large* relative to the time and effort needed to shop properly for these goods. When a substantial group of customers find it worth-while to shop around for a particular product, then we arc dealing with a shopping good.

Shopping Goods can be divided into two classifications depending on what customers are seeking:

- Homogeneous
- Heterogeneous.

Homogeneous Shopping Goods

Homogeneous products (those which consumers view as essentially similar) begins to bear fruit here. It will be recalled that when consumers view the various products offered in a category as essentially the same, each competitor has an almost perfectly elastic demand curve. In such a case, a slight price cut would substantially increase sales volume (if competitors did not match this cut), and thus we might expect price competition among the various competitors in the market.

We do, in fact, find this condition in many markets. Many consumers, for example, find certain sized and types of refrigerators, television sets, washing machines and even automobiles to be essentially similar and are primarily concerned about shopping for the best price.

Manufacturers seek to emphasize their differences and retailers try to promote their "better service". But if the customers do not believe these differences are real, they will emphasize the one variable which they feel is or can be different price.

Heterogeneous Shopping Goods

We are dealing here with the products which the customer sees as nonstandardized and wants to inspect for quality and suitability. Furniture, draperies, dishes and clothing are good examples of this type of shopping good. Style is important and price is secondary. Sometimes consumers will go to three or four stores to be sure they have done a good job of shopping, even if the item is not high priced.

Price is not totally ignored. But for nonstandardized merchandise, there are fewer bases for price comparison. When the customer has found the right product, she/he may not be too concerned with price, provided it is within a reasonable range. That is, the demand for the product may be quite inelastic. The more close substitutes there are, of course, the more elastic becomes the demand. But it does not approach the extreme elasticity found with homogeneous shopping goods.

Branding may be less important for heterogeneous goods. The more a consumer wishes to make her/his own comparisons of price and quality, the less reliance she/he places on a brand. Brands are usually found on these goods, but often little effort is made to publicize them. Women's dresses have labels, but the style and quality is usually of more importance especially when the label cannot be displayed by the wearer.

The buyer of these goods often not only wants but expects some kind of help in buying, the kind depending upon the social class of the purchaser. Often, she/he wants expensive service, such as alterations on clothing or installation on appliances, because of the size and importance of purchase. A short shirt picked up on the run (a convenience good) need not be nearly as satisfactory with respect to size and fit as a suit (shopping good), which has a higher price and has required considerable shopping.

Speciality Goods

Speciality goods are those consumer goods on which a significant group of buyer characteristically insist and for which they are willing to make a special effort. The special effort the customer expends is not to compare the product with others, but merely to locate it. Searching in shopping goods sense does not take place.

Speciality goods are usually specific branded items rather than product categories that is, they are specific products which have passed the brand preference stage and reached the brand insistence stage. Product differentiation and market segmentation efforts seek to create speciality goods. A unique product in the introductory or market growth stage, even though not branded, might also be a speciality good. A new drug compound, even though available from several manufacturers, might be a speciality good for some target customers. Generally, however, a specific brand is involved.

It is sometimes assumed that speciality goods are limited to relatively expensive items, probably durable, which are normally purchased infrequently. There seems to be no valid reason for making these restrictive assumptions, however. Any successfully branded item which develops a strong consumer franchise may achieve speciality goods status. Consumers have been observed asking for a drug product by its brand name and when offered a substitute, actually leaving the store in anger.

Same well-advertised food a drug products seem to have carved out a market for themselves. If they achieve the brand insistence stage, we call them speciality goods. As might be expected, the demand for speciality goods will be relatively inelastic, at least within reasonable price ranges, since target customers are willing to insist upon the product.

Unsought Goods

Unsought goods are those which potential customers do not yet want or know they can buy and therefore do not search for at all.

Furthermore, if these target customers happen to come upon the product, they probably would not buy unless additional promotion were directed toward them.

In talking about unsought goods, it becomes extremely important to bring in the market grid concept again and state specifically what target markets are being considered. Mobile homes, for example, would probably be a shopping good for those who are logically in the market: construction workers, servicemen, students and elderly couples. At certain times, such families are definitely seeking a mobile home and for them (at that time) the product would be a shopping good. Most mobile home dealers treat the product as a shopping good, selling against other mobile homes rather than against tract home builders.

But if the target market is defined as all those families who might be interested in purchasing homes, then mobile homes probably are unsought goods. Again the classification depends upon the attitudes of the relevant target market.

Industrial Goods

While a consumer goods classification system is useful for developing effective marketing mixes, an industrial goods classification is even more valuable. In the family, even allowing for the growing importance of husbands and children, the wife is the prime buyer; she buys all types of goods.

But is an industrial plant, there are a number of buying influences, depending mostly on the product but partly on the company involved. While most purchases are made by a purchasing agent, the major influence may be exerted by the office manager, plant foreman or the executive group.

General Characteristics of Industrial Goods

Most industrial goods have the following general characteristics:

- Their demand is derived from the demand for final consumer goods,
- Industrial demand may be inelastic while one company's demand may be elastic,
- Buyer interest in price depends on the nature of the product,
- Buying is basically concerned with economic factors,

- The buyer's attitude seems to be affected by the tax treatment accorded the product

Whether the expenditure for the product is charged off as a capital or an expense item.

Industrial Goods Classifications

Industrial goods buyers do relatively little shopping as compared with consumer goods buyers. The accepted practice is for the seller to come to the buyer. This means that a product classification system based primarily on shopping behaviour is not appropriate.

The industrial goods classification we will use is determined by how buyers look at products. Our categories are:

- Installations,
- Accessory equipment,
- Raw materials,
- Component parts and materials,
- Supplies,
- Services.

Installations

Installations are large and expensive items which do not become a part of the final product, but instead are used up over many years. All installations are *capital items.* They represent major expenditures for the company and are depreciated over a period ranging from 2 or 20 or more years.

There are two major classification of installations: *buildings and land rights* and *major equipment.* Buildings and land rights include factories, warehouses, barns, retail stores, office buildings, wheat fields, mining deposits, timber rights, etc.

Major equipment includes large items of machinery, such as diesel engines, boilers, tractors, combines, paper-making machines, electrical generators, printing presses, furnaces, kilns, rolling mills and large conveyor systems.

Major equipment can be subdivided into two types:

1) Custom-made,
2) Standard.

Custom-made equipment is made especially for a particular company and installed on the basis of special needs and detailed drawings or specifications.

Standard installations include products like tractors, general purpose diesel engines, lathes and printing presses, which are regular production items.

For our proposes, buildings and custom-made equipment are treated alike, since both require special negotiations for each individual product. Standardized major equipment, being more homogeneous, can be treated more routinely. All installations, however, are important enough to require high-level and even top management, consideration.

Accessory Equipment

Accessory equipment (like installations) does not become a part of the final product. These products are usually less expensive and shorter lived than installations, but still are *capital items.*

Actually, accessory equipment is very similar to the smaller standard installations. This category includes tools and equipment which facilitate production or office activities, examples include portable drills, sanding machines, electric lift trucks and small lathes.

Raw Materials

Raw materials are those products which have undergone no more processing than is required for convenience, protection or economy in storage, transportation or handling. In cont rast with our first two categories, they become part of the physical product.

Raw materials are *expense items* and are regarded in an entirely different light from the capital items we have been considering. Their purchase has a major impact on the current profit and loss situation, but less impact on the long-run situation. Even so, where raw materials represent a large part of the firm's costs, top executives may enter into the negotiation, especially of annual contracts. Subsequently, routine purchase orders are sent through against suck contracts. Obviously these products would come directly from farms, forests, seas or mines. Since many different products come under this raw materials category it is useful to break them into two broad categories:

1) Farm products,

2) Natural products. These may be subdivided as follows:

1. Farm Products :

Crops

- Fibers: cotton, flax, etc.
- Fruits and vegetables,
- Grains: wheat, rye, barley, oats, etc.
- Miscellaneous crops: tobacco, sugar cane, etc.

Domestic Animals and Products

- Livestock: cattle, hogs, sheep, etc.
- Poultry,
- Products obtained from animals: wool, milk, etc.

2. Natural Products

Animal Life

a) Fish and game,

b) Fur-bearing animals,

Forest Products

- Lumber,
- Miscellaneous: rubber, rosin, maple syrup, etc.

a Mineral Product,

1. Nonferrous metals: copper, lead, zinc, etc.
2. Iron ore,
3. Petroleum,
4. Coal and other fuels.

It is obvious from a review of this listing that many products are included which final consumers can use directly. Many fruits and vegetables, poultry, eggs, milk and meat products are purchased fresh by customers. These products have not undergone further processing since, for practical purposes, they are finished products. Although they may require special handling because of their perishability, they can properly be thought of as consumer goods and probably convenience goods at that. Fresh fish and game, some forest products (such as fire-wood), and mineral products (such as coal) also can be used directly as consumer goods.

Component Parts and Materials

Component parts and materials (like raw materials) become a part of the finished product. Both are treated as *expense items* and have somewhat similar characteristics. These, however, undergo more processing than is required for raw materials.

Component parts include those items which are:

- Finished and ready for assembly,
- Almost finished

Requiring only minor additional processing (such as grinding or polishing) before being assembled into the final product. Examples include automobile batteries, spark plugs, small motors, tires, forgings or castings, all of which are incorporated directly into a finished product. Also included in this category are tools or other items such as automobile jacks, which are sold with the product but not physically attached to it.

Component materials include already processed materials like wire, paper, textiles or cement, which will be further processed or shaped before becoming pail of the final product.

Supplies

Supplies (like raw materials and component parts and mate-rials) are continually used up in a company's operation. Because of this, they are *expense items.* Unlike the previous two categories of products, however, *supplies do not become a part of the physical product.* Thus, while they are necessary, most supplies are not nearly as vital as the products in the firs four classifications.

Supplies may be divided into three categories:

1. Maintenance,
2. Repair,
3. Operating supplies.

From this, supplies are commonly called M.R.O. items.

Maintenance items include such things are paint, nails, light bulbs, sweeping compounds, brooms and windows-cleaning equipment. *Repair items* are nuts and bolts or parts which are needed to repair existing installations or accessory equipment. *Operating supplies* include items such as lubricating oils and greases, grinding compounds, coal, typing paper, ink, pencils and paper clips.

Services

Services frequently are necessary or desirable to plan, facilitate or support operations. Engineering or management consulting services might improve the plant layout or the organization of the company. Design services may be useful for store, ware-house, plant or product design. Outside maintenance services may be desired for window cleaning, painting or general housekeeping services; these services are commonly offered to small retailers. Other services, such as in-plant lunch services and music systems to improve employee morale and production may be purchased from private contractors.

All these services are considered *expense items.* The cost of buying them outside would be compared with the cost of providing the services by company personnel. If special skills are involved and the services are purchased only irregularly, then an outsider may be in a strong selling position. As our economy becomes more and more complex, specialists in various activities are developing; this trend will probably continue. The demand for these services may be fairly inelastic if the supplier has a unique product.

Bibliography

Anindya Bakrie & Morendy Octora.: *Schooling, Experience, and Earnings*, New York, Singapore National University, Columbia University Press 2002.

Baran, Paul A.: *The Political Economy of Growth*, New York, Modern Reader Paperbacks, 1975.

Bardsley, N., Cubitt: *Assessing Experimental Economics*, Princeton, Princeton University Press, 2009.

Basu, Kaushik. *Analytical Development Economics, The Less Developed Economy Revisited*, Cambridge, Mass.; MIT Press, 1997.

Bazilevskii, Y. Y.: *The Theory of Mathematical Machines*, Pergamon Press, Macmillan Co., New York, 1963.

Benería, Lourdes. *Gender, Development, and Globalization, Economics as if All People Mattered*, New York and London, Routledge, 2003.

Borcherding, K., : *Contemporary Issues in Decision Making*, Amsterdam, North-Holland, 1990.

Burke, Frank M., *Valuation and Valuation Planning for Closely Held Businesses*, Englewood Cliffs, NJ, Prentice Hall, 1981.

Caplin, A. and Schotter, A.: *The Foundations of Positive and Normative Economics*, New York, Oxford University Press, 2008.

Caviglioni O. : *Mapwise: Accelerated Learning Through Visible Thinking*, Network Educational Press, 2000.

Cohen, Lizabeth, *Making a New Deal, Industrial Workers in Chicago, 1919-1939* Cambridge University Press, 1991.

Commons, J. R., *Institutional Economics-Its Place in Political Economy*, The University of Wisconsin Press, Madison, Wisconsin, 1934.

Cootner, Paul : *The Random Character of Stock Market Prices*, MIT Press, 1964.

Copeland, Tom, Tim Koller, and Jack Murrin, *Valuation: Measuring and Managing the Value of Companies*, New York, Wiley, 1994.

Damasio, AR.: *Descarte's Error: Emotion, Reason and the Human Brain*, New York, 1994.

Daniel Kahneman, Amos Tversky.: *Choice, Values, Frames*, The Cambridge University Press, 2000.

Desmond, Glenn, and John A, Marcell, *Handbook of Small Business Valuation Formulas and Rules of Thumb*, Valuation Press, 1993.

Dimson, Elroy: *Stock Market Anomalies*, Cambridge University Press, 1988.

Fraser, Steven, *Labor Will Rule, Sidney Hillman and the Rise of American Labor*, Reprint ed. Ithaca, N.Y.: Cornell University Press, 1993.

Fruhan, W. E.: *Financial Strategy, Studies in the Creation, Transfer and Destruction of Shareholder Value*. Homewood, 1979.

Goleman D.: *Emotional Intelligence*, New York: Bantam, 1995.

Gowdy, J., *Coevolution Economics: The Economy, Society and the Environment*, Kluwer, Boston, 1994.

Granger, Clive W. J.: *Empirical Modeling in Economics, Specification and Evaluation*, London, Cambridge University Press, 1999.

Guala, F.: *The Methodology of Experimental Economics*, New York, Cambridge University Press, 2005.

Guarti, Luigi, *The Valuation of Firms*, Blackwell Publishing, 1994.

Gul, F. and Pesendorfer, W.: *The Foundations of Positive and Normative Economics*, New York, Oxford University Press 2008.

Harrigan, K. R.: *Strategies for Declining Businesses*. Lexington, MA: Heath, 1980

Hausman, D. M.: *The Inexact and Separate Science of Economics*, Cambridge, Cambridge University Press, 1992.

Hayek, F. A. *Individualism and Economic Order*, The University of Chicago Press, Chicago, 1948.

Hunt, E. K. *History of Economic Thought, A Critical Perspective*, New York, HarperCollins, 1992.

Janis, I. L., & Mann, L.: *Decision Making, A Psychological Analysis of Conflict, Choice and Commitment*. New York, Free Press, 1977.

Kasper, Larry J.: *Business Valuations, Advanced Topics*, Westport, CT, Quorum Books, 1997.

Knapp, C. L.: *Commercial Damages, A Guide to Remedies in Business Litigation*, Matthew Bender, 1993.

Lindblom, C. E.: *A Strategy of Decision: Policy Evaluation as a Social Process*, New York, The Free Press, 1970.

Link, Albert N.: *Evaluating Economic Damages, A Handbook for Attorneys*, Westport, CT, Quorum Books, 1992.

Lipsitz, George. *Rainbow at Midnight, Labor and Culture in the 1940s*, Urbana, Ill.: University of Illinois Press, 1994.

Loomes, G.: *Current Issues in Microeconomics*, New York: St. Martin's Press, 1989.

Magnussen, L., *Evolutionary and Neo-Schumpeterian Approaches to Economics*, Kluwer, Boston, 1994.

March, J. G.: *A Behavioural Theory of the Firm*, Englewood-Cliffs, Prentice Hall, 1963.

Marris, R. L., and Wood, A.: *The Corporate Economy*, London: Macmillan, 1971.

Martin, Gerald D.: *Determining Economic Damages*, Santa Ana, CA: James Publishing, 1995.

Meyer, M. W.: *Theory of Organizational Structure*, Indianapolis, 1977.

Mooney, J. D., and Reiley, A. C.: *Onward Industry*, New York, 1931.

Nelson, Judy A.: *Feminism, Objectivity and Economics*, London and New York, Routledge, 1996.

Peirson, G., Bird, R., Brown, R., & Howard, P.: *Business Finance*, Roseville, 1990

Pennings, J. M.: *Decision Making, An Organizational Behaviour Approach*, New York, Markus Wiener Publishing, 1983.

Pfeffer, J., and Salancik, G. R.: *The External Control of Organizations, A Resource Dependence Perspective*, New York, 1978.

Plous, S.: *The Psychology of Judgement and Decision Making*, New York, McGraw-Hill, 1993

Rappaport, A.: *Creating Shareholder Value, The New Standard for Business Performance*, New York, Free Press, 1986.

Ross, D.: *Economic Theory and Cognitive Science*, Cambridge, Mass., MIT Press, 2006.

Roth, A. E.: *The Handbook of Experimental Economics*, Princeton, Princeton University Press, 1995.

Santos, A.C.: *The Social Epistemology of Experimental Economics*, London, Routledge 2009.

Schumpeter, J. A., *The Theory of Economic Development*, Harvard University Press,Cambridge, Massachusetts, 1934.

Scott, W. R.: *Organizations: Rational, Natural, and Open Systems*, Englewood Cliffs, 1981.

Selznick, P.: *Leadership in Administration, A Sociological Interpretation*, New York, Harper & Row, 1957.

Smith, Gordon V., and Russell Parr, *Valuation of Intellectual Property and Intangible Assets,* New York: Wiley, 1994.

Smith, V. L.: *Papers in Experimental Economics*, Cambridge, Cambridge University Press, 1991.

Taylor, F. W.: *The Principles of Scientific Management*, New York, 1917.

Throsby, David, *Economics and Culture*, Cambridge University Press, 2001.

Tietenberg, Tom, *Environmental Economics and Policy,* New York, HarperCollins, 1994

Tinbergen, Jan.: *On the Theory of Economic Policy*, Amsterdam, North-Holland 1952.

Towse, Ruth ed.: *A Handbook of Cultural Economics*, Edward Elgar, 2003.

Trugman, Gary R., *Guide to Conducting a Valuation of a Closely Held Business*, New York, American Institute of Certified Public Accountants, 1993.

Ullman, D. G.: *Making Robust Decisions,* Trafford, 2006.

Warwick, D. P.: *A Theory of Public Bureaucracy*, Cambridge, MA: Harvard University Press, 1975.

Weber, M.: *The Theory of Social and Economic Organizations*, New York, Oxford University Press, 1947.

Weibull, J. W.: *Advances in Understanding Strategic Behaviour*, New York, Palgrave, 2004.

West, Thomas L.: and Jeffrey D. Jones: *Handbook of Business Valuation*, New York: Wiley, 1992.

Woodward, J.: *The Oxford Handbook of Philosophy of Economics*, New York, Oxford University Press, 2009.

Yegge, Wilbur M., *A Basic Guide for Valuing a Company*, New York, Wiley, 1996.

Zipp, Alan S., *Business Valuation Methods* New York, American Institute of Certified Public Accountants, 1990.

Index

D

E

F

G

H

I

L

M

O

P

□□□